Recollecting Hunger: An Anthology

Cultural Memories of the Great Famine
in Irish and British Fiction, 1847–1920

Recollecting Hunger: An Anthology

Cultural Memories of the Great Famine in Irish and British Fiction, 1847–1920

Marguérite Corporaal
Christopher Cusack
Lindsay Janssen

IRISH ACADEMIC PRESS
DUBLIN • PORTLAND, OR

First published in 2012 by Irish Academic Press

2 Brookside
Dundrum Road,
Dublin 14, Ireland

920 NE 58th Avenue, Suite 300
Portland, Oregon,
97213-3786 USA

www.iap.ie

British Library Cataloguing in Publication Data
An entry can be found on request

Recollecting hunger : cultural memories of the great famine
in Irish and British fiction, 1847-1920.
1. Ireland—History—Famine, 1845-1852—Fiction.
2. Short stories, English. 3. Short stories, English—
Irish authors.
I. Corporaal, Marguerite. II. Cusack, Christopher.
III. Janssen, Lindsay.
823.8'08035299162-dc23

ISBN 978 0 7165 3128 9 (cloth)
ISBN 978 0 7165 3129 6 (paper)

Library of Congress Cataloging-in-Publication Data
An entry can be found on request

Typeset by FiSH Books, Enfield, Middx.
Printed and bound by CPI Group (UK) Ltd, Croydon, CR0 4YY

Table of Contents

CONTENTS

Acknowledgements

This anthology is part of the research project *Relocated Remembrance: The Great Famine in Irish (Diaspora) Fiction, 1847–1921*, financed by a Starting Grant from the European Research Council.[1] We would like to thank the ERC for their support.

We are also grateful to the National Library of Ireland for permission to reproduce the images on the title pages of sections 2, 5 and 7 of this anthology.

Marguérite Corporaal, Christopher Cusack
and Lindsay Janssen
September 2011

---

1   See http://famineliterature.com for further information about the project.

Recollecting Hunger: An Introduction

Marguérite Corporaal, Christopher Cusack and Lindsay Janssen

> Oh Past! thou fragment of the Tale of Time!
> Where lived the Spirit which is ages dead[1]

These lines from the anonymous poem 'The Feast of Famine, An Irish Banquet' (1870) address the dominant presence of history in the conceptions of Irish identities. As Emilie Pine has recently argued, 'Irish culture is obsessed with the past', that is, haunted by the thorny controversies and painful episodes of bygone days, and as such can only be understood in a 'framework of remembrance and trauma'.[2] Her claim of an Irish imagination haunted by the ghosts of the past is illustrated by 'The Feast of Famine'. The poem shows how a group of absentee landlords 'in a London square', about to enjoy a sumptuous banquet 'of viands all costly and rare', are confronted with a spectral throng of starvation victims who come to claim redress for the wrongs 'of centuries gone' when the ghost of Famine 'stalked ... upon Irish earth'.[3]

In his seminal work on cultural memory, Jan Assmann introduces the term 'figures of memory' to describe 'fateful

---

1 *The Feast of Famine; An Irish Banquet with Other Poems* (London: Chapman & Hall, 1870), p. 32.
2 E. Pine, *The Politics of Irish Memory: Performing Remembrance in Contemporary Irish Culture* (Basingstoke: Palgrave Macmillan, 2011), p. 3.
3 *Feast of Famine*, pp. 9–11.

events of the past whose memory is maintained through cultural formation', in artefacts and social practices.[4] Among the many fateful events that marked Ireland's colonial history is the Great Famine (1845–1851), a bleak period of wide-scale starvation, cruel evictions of tenant farmers, a mass exodus of mostly young Irish men and women and the financial decline of the Ascendancy class. The remembrance of these traumatic years has been performed not only in their immediate aftermath when a 'calm and just apportionment of blame and merit'[5] was often deemed problematic. The publication of Marita Conlon-McKenna's *Children of the Famine Trilogy* in the early 2000s and the commissioning of Famine memorials – such as John Behan's 'Coffin Ship' (1997) in Murrisk, Co. Mayo – to mark the Great Hunger's 150th anniversary are proof of the lasting impact of the period in current memory. The wide-scale commemoration of the Famine in Ireland and Irish diaspora countries such as Canada and the United States during the 1990s and the recent creation of sites with 'symbolic investment',[6] such as monuments, moreover, gave a significant boost to Famine scholarship in the fields of sociology, history and art.

From the mid-1990s prominent scholars in Irish studies have started to direct their attention to the presence of Famine recollection in literature, contesting Terry Eagleton's widely repeated claim that Famine remembrance is notoriously absent from the Irish literary canon, since according to Eagleton there are only 'a handful of novels and a body of poems' dealing with

---

4   J. Assmann, 'Collective Memory and Cultural Identity', *New German Critique*, 65 (1995), p. 129.

5   A.M. Sullivan, *New Ireland: Political Sketches and Personal Reminiscences of Thirty Years of Irish Public Life* (Glasgow: Cameron & Ferguson, 1877), p. 58.

6   A. Rigney, 'Divided Pasts: A Premature Memorial and the Dynamics of Collective Remembrance', *Memory Studies*, 1, 1 (2008), p. 93.

the event.[7] Christopher Morash edited a pioneering anthology of Famine poetry, *The Hungry Voice*, and elsewhere discusses the representation of the Great Hunger in fiction by such authors as William Carleton and Anthony Trollope.[8] Margaret Kelleher's *The Feminization of Famine* examines feminine imagery in Famine literature by authors such as Margaret Brew and Annie Keary,[9] and Melissa Fegan's *Literature and the Irish Famine 1845–1919* lists and briefly discusses an important range of texts which are suffused with Famine memory.[10] These studies made significant strides in charting the hitherto overlooked role of Famine memory in key works of Irish literature. However, there is still a large unexplored corpus of lesser-known fiction which recalls the Great Hunger and which spans several post-Famine generations.

The present anthology constitutes the first attempt to bring together a body of both more familiar and lesser-known fiction remembering the Great Famine written between 1847, when the first Famine fiction was published, and 1922, the year the Irish Free State was established. It is our belief that these texts – many of which have never been published in modern editions and can only be accessed in copyright libraries – deserve more critical attention than most have received so far. We place these novels and short stories in the limelight for several reasons. First of all, many of these texts offer alternative perspectives to the large number of historical narratives which recollect the Great Hunger. The memories they (re)present were often omitted from historical accounts because they are

---

7   T. Eagleton, *Heathcliff and the Great Hunger: Studies in Irish Culture* (London: Verso, 1995), p. 13.

8   C. Morash, *The Hungry Voice: The Poetry of the Irish Famine* (Dublin: Irish Academic Press, 1989; rev. edn 2009); and C. Morash, *Writing the Irish Famine* (Oxford: Clarendon Press, 1995).

9   M. Kelleher, *The Feminization of Famine: Expressions of the Inexpressible?* (Cork: Cork University Press, 1997).

10 M. Fegan, *Literature and the Irish Famine 1845–1919* (Oxford: Clarendon Press, 2002).

those of socially powerless groups, such as evicted tenant farmers, defeated rebels or bereaved mothers. As scholars in memory studies have observed, prose fiction as a genre accommodates different, often marginal and subaltern, narratives and memories[11] and is characterized by a 'multiperspectival expansion' in general,[12] which in the case of the texts incorporated here manifests itself in a wide range of narrative focalizers that cannot only be distinguished between texts but also within texts. Margaret Brew's three-decker *The Chronicles of Castle Cloyne*, for example, recalls the Famine through the perspective of both a native Irish lower-class woman and the ruined landlord Hyacinth Dillon. At the same time, the novels and stories in this anthology also engage consciously with the religious, political and cultural discourses of their time. That this is the case becomes clear from our annotations, which provide quotations from and links to both literary and non-literary contemporary writings, thus inviting readers to a New Historicist approach to the novels and stories. In a few cases, particularly in Emily Lawless's 'Famine Roads and Memories' and *Poor Paddy's Cabin*, texts also adopt the narrative mode of genres such as travel literature, history and political treatise, thus blending what may at first glance seem non-fictional elements with literary forms.

A second reason why these stories and novels deserve more scholarly attention is the fact that they were written in an age in which Irish nationalism flourished and during which the legacy of *An Gorta Mór*, 'the Great Hunger', was central to the

---

11   See A. Rigney, 'Portable Monuments: Literature, Cultural Memory, and the Case of Jeanie Deans', *Poetics Today*, 25, 2 (2004): 'This affinity between literature and the history "of the inside" might seem to suggest that novelists are somehow more sensitive than others to the sufferings of the downtrodden and to the importance of the marginal' (p. 375).
12   B. Neumann, 'The Literary Representation of Memory', in A. Erll and A. Nünning (eds), *Cultural Memory Studies: An International and Interdisciplinary Handbook* (Berlin and New York: De Gruyter, 2008), p. 339.

development of an Irish (postcolonial) identity: between the event's immediate aftermath and the establishment of the Irish Free State in 1922. Katharine Hodgkin and Susannah Radstone emphasize memory's function as a tool 'with which to contest "official" versions of the past', and their remark is particularly applicable to imperial contexts.[13] As Barbara Misztal states, '[c]ontesting memories was also an important strategy in the process of discursive resistance in colonial societies',[14] mainly because in the process of imperialism, as Oona Frawley contends, an 'official' colonial historical narrative overwrites 'an indigenous culture's version of its own history'.[15] The alternative, often subaltern recollections that one finds in such works as Richard Baptist O'Brien's *Ailey Moore* and Reginald Tierney's (Thomas O'Neill Russell's pen name) *The Struggles of Dick Massey* challenge the often official imperial versions of the Famine as, for instance, divine punishment or Providence. Furthermore, some of the texts included employ the recollections and even the setting of the Famine as a backdrop against which to discuss current national issues. For instance, W.C. Upton's *Uncle Pat's Cabin* and Emily Lawless's *Hurrish* perform the memories of the Famine in order to address current politics with regard to landowners and tenantry as well as the violence employed in the crusade of radical nationalism.

Thirdly, the often unexamined corpus of Famine fiction enables a study of the transformations of cultural memory over time. Recollection is a continuous process of change, an

---

13   K. Hodgkin and S. Radstone, 'Introduction: Contested Pasts', in K. Hodgkin and S. Radstone (eds), *Memory, History, Nation: Contested Pasts* (New Brunswick, NJ: Transaction, 2006), p. 5.

14   B.A. Misztal, 'Memory and History', in O. Frawley (ed.), *Memory Ireland. Volume I: History and Modernity* (Syracuse, NY: Syracuse University Press, 2011), p. 7.

15   O. Frawley, 'Toward a Theory of Cultural Memory in an Irish Postcolonial Context', in Frawley (ed.), *Memory Ireland. Volume I: History and Modernity*, p. 31.

infinite dynamic between remembering and forgetting. As Mieke Bal writes, 'the past is continuously modified and redescribed even as it continues to shape the future',[16] and is therefore marked by transgenerational developments, often depending on what Marianne Hirsch calls 'postmemory'.[17] The fact that literature, as a so-called portable monument, can 'be recycled among various groups of readers living in different parts of the globe and at different historical moments'[18] not only implies that literature can affect the cultural recollection of different communities and generations, but also that the memories carried by works of literature interact with other modes of recollection and may therefore change.[19] The (extracts of) texts published in this anthology cover different time frames. Because in each section the texts are placed in chronological order, they display the as yet uncharted evolvements in the cultural memory of the Famine over time.

The excerpted texts are divided over seven sections which each centre on a specific cluster of mnemonic images. As James Wertsch, among others,[20] has rightly argued, the act of remembrance involves a narrative structuring of memory. This 'narrative organization' takes the shape of 'schematic narrative templates',[21] which involve specific plotlines, recurring tropes and stock characters. An investigation of Famine fiction reveals

16   M. Bal, 'Introduction', in M. Bal et al. (eds), *Acts of Memory: Cultural Recall in the Present* (Hanover, NH: University Press of New England, 1999), p. vii.
17   M. Hirsch, *Family Frames: Photography, Narrative and Postmemory* (Cambridge, MA: Harvard University Press, 1997).
18   Rigney, 'Portable Monuments', p. 383.
19   In this sense, following Michael Rothberg, memory can be called 'multidirectional'. See *Multidirectional Memory: Remembering the Holocaust in the Age of Decolonization* (Stanford, CA: Stanford University Press, 2009).
20   The notion that memory is organized by narrative templates is becoming increasingly accepted in various disciplines. See, for instance, E. Zerubavel, *Time Maps: Collective Memory and the Social Shape of the Past* (Chicago, IL: University of Chicago Press, 2003), and D. LaCapra, *Writing History, Writing Trauma* (Baltimore, MD: Johns Hopkins University Press, 2001).
21   J.V. Wertsch, *Voices of Collective Remembering* (New York: Cambridge University Press, 2002), p. 57.

that the narrativization of Famine recollection also frequently involves such templates and that it is marked by emplotment, characterization and symbolism that can all be brought back to seven dominant mnemonic clusters. These thematic clusters, concerned with starvation, landscape, religion, landlords and tenants, nationalism, femininity and migration, will be discussed below. The presentation of our material in seven sections that are related to these clusters not only makes it possible for readers to study texts concerned with specific topics of their interest. It will additionally facilitate the study of transformations in Famine memory over time which this anthology seeks to promote as well as encourage an investigation of which literary aspects are carriers of cultural memory.

The Spectre of Starvation

Historians generally assume that the Great Famine killed approximately one million people.[22] As such, the Great Hunger classifies as a traumatic historical episode, and it dramatically altered Ireland's demography and rooted out the cultural traditions of the Gaelic-speaking rural classes. The texts incorporated in the first section all address the horrors of starvation, disease and communal mourning, and illustrate the transgenerational nature of a collective trauma over a long period.

Literature appears to have a significant function in trauma processing. As Cathy Caruth claims, '[s]peech helps integrating the experience of trauma',[23] and, as James Wertsch argues,

---

22 See C. Ó Gráda, *Ireland Before and After the Famine: Explorations in Economic History* (Manchester: Manchester University Press, 1993), pp. 138–44.
23 C. Caruth, 'Recapturing the Past: Introduction', in C. Caruth (ed.), *Trauma: Explorations in Memory* (Baltimore, MD: Johns Hopkins University Press, 1995), p. 154.

unresolved trauma resists integration into narrative.[24] The stories and novels in section one display very different ways of coping with the trauma of Famine. In some, the spectacle of starvation is incorporated in the main plot and described in painstaking detail, while in other texts the gruesome picture of hunger is pushed to the margins of the narrative, as what Christopher Morash calls 'a series of tangents':[25] loose images in the text that are not fully integrated, and placed at a safe distance from the reader. Early texts such as Mrs Hoare's story 'The Black Potatoes' and Susannah Meredith's 'Ellen Harrington' clearly elucidate that the trauma of the Famine years is still too fresh to be confronted too openly. In Mrs Hoare's tale the pain of loss is often unspeakable, and the omniscient narrator glosses over the anguish of the suffering mother Mary Mahoney.

Moreover, as the excerpts show, both in 'The Black Potatoes' and 'Ellen Harrington' scenes of starvation are enframed in enclosed settings, such as cabins or hovels, from which the reader or focalizing characters can step back. While in these early stories hunger becomes a horror that is literally contained in space and therefore more controllable, a later novel like Patrick Sheehan's *Glenanaar* zooms in on the bodily effects of starvation in its description of Nodlag. *The Hunger* by Andrew Merry (Mildred Darby) takes starvation scenes into the political arena by making them part of the discussion between an absentee landlord and his more socially engaged nephew.

The stories and novels evoke similar mnemonic images and issues, such as the inedibility of Indian meal, the keening rituals of the local inhabitants and the excessive number of corpses which makes it impossible to observe proper burial rites. Another recurrent motif is that of spectrality. Often, emaciated

24   J.V. Wertsch, *Voices of Collective Remembering*, p. 47.
25   C. Morash, *Writing the Irish Famine*, p. 187.

Famine victims are compared to walking spectres who have also been transformed mentally, becoming ghosts of their former selves. This is, for instance, the case in Rosa Mulholland's story 'The Hungry Death', which is included in section five.

Ghosts and living skeletons in Famine literature also have more symbolical functions, representing dead generations who claim retribution for the atrocities perpetrated against them, and therefore haunt the present; or as metaphors for the need to remember the painful past. As Emilie Pine has recently observed, '[t]he ghost represents the unbiddable, irrepressable, and uncontainable nature of memory', and is a 'manifestation of the excessive grip of the past on the imagination of culture in the present'.[26] In 'Slieve Foy's' story 'Attie and His Father', the grandmother's dream of a gigantic, almost sublime skeleton that embodies hunger and forebodes her own death is an unerasable trope that will continue to trouble her mind.

Golden Hills and Blackened Fields

While texts such as Emily Lawless's 'Famine Roads and Famine Memories' and William Carleton's *The Black Prophet* inform us that nature gave several warnings of the great calamity, the Famine still came as a devastating shock. This sense of a sudden calamity is evoked in Famine fiction by descriptions of an overnight dark mist hovering over and destroying the crops, followed by images of blackened fields and the stench of rot – figures recurrent through the decades which suggest that the performance of memory often resides in the remembrance and reappopriation of previously used tropes.[27]

---

26   Pine, *Politics of Irish Memory*, p. 16.
27   In *Writing the Irish Famine* Christopher Morash argues that authors who had no direct experiences with Famine Ireland resorted to collective memories and 'semiotic systems of representation' (p. 54).

As Oona Frawley observes, the Famine signified 'the literal failure of the pastoral',[28] in that a pastoral version of the Irish landscape functioned as an identity marker. In Famine fiction a strong link is established between the inhabitants and the landscape, which appears to naturalistically reflect the inner turmoils of the Irish and figures as a symbolical space. The emptiness and desolate spirit of the Irish landscape hint at the death of its inhabitants. In *The Struggles of Dick Massey* Tierney describes newly created pastures as wastes of grass, and in *The Black Prophet* the scenery resonates with the disappearance of the people: a 'brooding stillness, lay over all nature; cheerfulness had disappeared'.[29]

In his seminal work of that title, Pierre Nora introduces the term *lieux de mémoire* to describe physical and symbolical spaces where 'memory crystallizes and secretes itself'.[30] In fiction which recalls the Famine, landscape serves as a *lieu de mémoire* which provides access to remnants of the past and bears witness to history. This is especially the case in Lawless's work, and in 'Famine Roads', the unfinished Famine roads – metaphors for the abruptly and prematurely ended Irish lives – haunt the landscape. Like the ruins of cottages also described by Lawless, such roads serve as traces of memory of who or what has been lost rather than what has survived.

In Famine fiction, the representation of the landscape often takes on a pastoral and even picturesque tone. These pastoral and picturesque representations then come to function as both an escapist 'breathing spell from the fever and anguish of being',[31]

---

28   O. Frawley, *Irish Pastoral: Nostalgia and Twentieth-Century Irish Literature* (Dublin: Irish Academic Press, 2005), p. 45.
29   W. Carleton, *The Black Prophet: A Tale Of Irish Famine* (London: Simms & M'Intyre, 1847), p. 17.
30   P. Nora, 'Between Memory and History: Les Lieux de Mémoire', *Representations*, 26 (1989), p. 7.
31   R. Poggioli, 'Pastorals of Innocence and Happiness', in B. Loughrey (ed.), *The Pastoral Mode* (Basingstoke: Macmillan, 1984), p. 104.

and a critical contrast to the disruptive influences of English colonization, industrialization and modernization.[32] Thus, the artistic principles of the pastoral and picturesque not only figure as a return to nature, but can also be used to voice strong social critique.[33] For example, the excerpts from *The Struggles of Dick Massey* included in this section present the (Anglo-Irish) city as highly corruptive and full of temptation and vice. Russell – in a manner common in Irish literature in the aftermath of the Famine[34] – then juxtaposes these urban dystopias with utopian representations of the Irish landscape, thus highlighting the disruptive influences of English colonization and modernization on the Irish traditional landscape and way of life.

Priests and Proselytizers

The wide-scale outbreak of the potato blight and the subsequent mass starvation were often interpreted in providential terms. Many contemporary commenters claimed that the Famine was a divine scourge to discipline Ireland, a God-given opportunity to enforce a policy that 'would transform Irish behaviour' and thus make Ireland susceptible to modernization along British lines.[35] Yet harsher critics read the Famine as divine intervention aimed at rooting out Catholicism in

---

32   O. Frawley, *Irish Pastoral*, pp. 4–5, 59. For a discussion of the Irish pastoral as an identity marker for Irish diaspora famine fiction, see M.C.M. Corporaal, 'From Golden Hills to Sycamore Trees: Pastoral Homelands and Ethnic Identity in Irish Immigrant Fiction, 1860–85', *Irish Studies Review*, 18, 3 (2010), pp. 331–46.

33   C. Fairweather, 'Inclusive and Exclusive Pastoral: Towards an Anatomy of Pastoral Modes', *Studies in Philology*, 97, 3 (2000), p. 278.

34   Seamus Deane in *Strange Country: Modernity and Nationhood in Irish Writing Since 1790* (Oxford: Clarendon Press, 1997) points out that in the aftermath of the Famine, a common tendency among the Irish both at home and in diaspora was to gloss over the Famine and its impact on Irish life and cultural identity and to look back to pre-Famine and pre-colonial history and landscape and to infuse these images with Irish folklore and mythology (p. 51).

35   P. Gray, 'Ideology and the Famine', in C. Póirtéir (ed.), *The Great Irish Famine* (Dublin: Mercier Press, 1995), pp. 92–3.

Ireland. Revd Hugh McNeile, in his infamous *The Famine a Rod of God* (1847), declared that '[p]lagues, pestilences, famines, wars are used by God as national punishments for sin'.[36]

Many of the novels and stories that recollect the Famine, such as Richard Baptist O'Brien's *Ailey Moore*, address the religious rhetoric that surrounded the dire event. Moreover, considering the intensive religious controversies about the Great Hunger, many of its literary recollections are written from a particular sectarian perspective, each laying claim to 'true' Irishness and often lambasting other religious positions. For instance, William Francis Barry's *The Wizard's Knot* approaches the Famine from a strictly Catholic brand of Celtic nationalism, while Margaret Percival's *The Irish Dove* and the anonymous *Poor Paddy's Cabin* are fiercely anti-Catholic in their depiction of the conditions of the famishing peasantry.

As Jeffrey Alexander observes, in 'creating a compelling trauma narrative, it is critical to establish the identity of the perpetrator, the "antagonist"'.[37] In Famine fiction, this antagonism is often translated to a scenario or mnemonic 'emplotment'[38] of sectarian conflict in which two recurrent characters feature: the proselytizer and the priest. In Catholic Famine fiction, the souperist, who attempts to convert famished Catholics by offering them food if they forswear their faith, is presented as the villain, whose efforts to harvest souls with the promise of relief are usually fruitless. In *Ailey Moore*, but also in Emily Bowles's *Irish Diamonds*, the Catholic characters stay true to their religion and thus set an example to a Catholic readership. In Protestant novels, such as *Poor Paddy's*

---

36 H. McNeile, *The Famine a Rod of God: Its Provoking Cause – Its Merciful Design* (London: Burnside & Seeley, 1847), p. 8.

37 J.C. Alexander, 'Toward a Theory of Cultural Trauma', in J.C. Alexander et al., *Cultural Trauma and Collective Identity* (Berkeley, CA: University of California Press, 2004), p. 15.

38 E. Zerubavel, *Time Maps*, p. 15.

Cabin, priests are ineffective in offering relief and sacrifice their parishioners in order to retain their tyrannous power over the Irish. By contrast, Catholic fiction depicts the priesthood as the embodiment of charity, morality and piety.

This portrayal of a devoted, moralizing clergy, which can be found in *Irish Diamonds,* appears to be influenced by the post-Famine Devotional Revolution. This reform campaign, started in the 1850s by Archbishop Paul Cullen, sought to use the identity crisis caused by the Famine's eradication of traditional culture[39] to formalize the faith of the Irish peasants by emphasizing clerical discipline, mass attendance, confession, and devotional practices such as the rosary and vespers.[40] The fact that in some novels of the 1850s and 1860s Famine remembrance is coloured by current religious concerns furthermore underlines that recollection 'is an active and constantly shifting relationship to the past, in which the past is changed retrospectively'[41] by ongoing processes of 'cultural negotiation'.[42]

Landlords and Tenants

One of the recurrent schematic plots in fiction that recalls the Famine is sectarian conflict between the Ascendancy and the impoverished peasants. Partly due to restrictions preventing Catholics from acquiring land,[43] the relationship between landlords and tenants had been strenuous before the Famine, and several militant secret societies, such as the Whiteboys and

---

39   P. Ward, *Exile, Emigration and Irish Writing* (Dublin: Irish Academic Press, 2002), p. 145.

40   See E. Larkin, 'The Devotional Revolution in Ireland, 1850–75', *American Historical Review,* 77, 3 (1972), pp. 625–52.

41   A. Rigney, 'Plenitude, Scarcity and the Circulation of Cultural Memory', *Journal of European Studies,* 35, 1 (2005), p. 17.

42   M. Sturken, 'Memory, Consumerism and Media: Reflections on the Emergence of the Field', *Memory Studies,* 1, 1 (2008), p. 74.

43   M. Cronin, *A History of Ireland* (Basingstoke: Palgrave Macmillan, 2001), p. 82.

Ribbonmen, were established.[44] The potato blight and the subsequent inability of many tenants to pay the rent led to evictions on a massive scale.[45] Eviction scenes feature prominently in the fiction which remembers the Great Hunger, and novels such as *Frank O'Donnell* by Allen H. Clington (David Power Conyngham) focus on the suffering of the poor cottiers who have to face the brutal measures of archetypal evil landlords with speaking names such as Lord Clearall.

One of the largest problems of Irish rural society was absenteeism, for it usually meant that landlords spent little time and money on agricultural improvements.[46] Many felt that absentee landlords were partially to blame for Ireland's dire condition during the Famine years.[47] The character of the absentee landlord figures in various novels, including Charles Lever's *The Martins of Cro' Martin* and Lalla McDowell's *The Earl of Effingham*. When landlords did not reside on their Irish estates, they left their management to so-called middlemen. In various fictional works the middleman is an almost diabolical creature, striving to belong to the upper Anglo-Irish echelons of society and willing to get there at any cost. A representative example is Hester Sigerson's agent Billy Finnigan in *A Ruined Race*, who removes the starving protagonists from their cottage without a moment's compassion.

---

44   T. Garvin, 'Defenders, Ribbonmen and Others: Underground Political Networks in Pre-Famine Ireland', *Past and Present*, 96 (1982), pp. 140, 154.

45   M.E. Daly, *Social and Economic History of Ireland since 1800* (Dublin: Educational Company of Ireland, 1981), pp. 39, 47.

46   Mary Daly explains in *Social and Economic History of Ireland since 1800* that '[t]he most valid criticism which can be made of Irish landlords concerns their spending on improvements. On average they spent a mere 5% of their income on improvements, considerably less than their English counterparts' (p. 40).

47   As 'an Irish Landlord' stated in *Ireland: Her Landlords, Her People, and Their Homes* (Dublin: George Herbert, 1860), 'it is certain that while the masses of the Irish people are dependent on a certain class for support and protection; while they do not possess the means of acquiring independence themselves, but must look to their landlords for employment and subsistence, the absence of that class from the country, and from the proper sphere of their duties, is a great and serious evil' (p. xii).

While the representation of a stereotypical uncaring Ascendancy class and its conflicts with a pitiable tenant class may seem central to Famine fiction, in fact the corpus of novels and stories conveys variegated perspectives, and with this, a mnemonic heterogeneity. For one thing, some texts, such as Anthony Trollope's *Castle Richmond*, show how the fortunes of the landed classes were also affected by the consequences of the blight, and even became debt-ridden by governmental measures such as the Encumbered Estates Act of 1848–49.[48] Furthermore, some novels, such as William Carleton's *The Squanders of Castle Squander*, *The Earl of Effingham*, and William Barry's *The Wizard's Knot*, provide a multifaceted picture of landlord–tenant relationships, depicting members of the Ascendancy who are genuinely concerned about the fate of their suffering tenantry. Interestingly, these compassionate characters are often upper-class heroines who passionately plead for an improvement of tenant conditions. The fact that their empathy contrasts starkly with the views expressed by their peers makes the novels dialogic and even multidirectional in their presentation of Famine memory, thus exposing the 'public sphere as a malleable discursive space in which groups do not simply articulate established positions but actually come into being through their dialogical interactions with others'.[49]

Young Ireland and Colonial Rebellion

The Great Famine took place in an era of nationalist struggle, during which Daniel O'Connell, the 'Liberator', unsuccessfully

---

48   As *The Spectator* of 5 August 1848 wrote, Parliament had passed a bill that made it possible to 'sell encumbered lands without the concurrence of all persons interested' (p. 743), thus facilitating the passing of heavily endebted property from landlords to new owners.

49   Rothberg, *Multidirectional Memory*, p. 5.

sought to repeal the Union[50] and the Young Ireland movement launched a fruitless rebellion against British imperial rule.[51] Nationalist sentiments were prompted by the many casualties of starvation, for many Irish considered the administrative response to the disaster inadequate, especially after Lord John Russell succeeded Sir Robert Peel as Prime Minister in 1846. Russell's adherence to the doctrine of Political Economy, which combined Malthusian economics with Adam Smith's laissez-faire principles and religious rhetoric, meant that many relief efforts were discontinued and landlords were made responsible for the afflicted tenants on their estates.[52]

The close intersections between Irish nationalism and the Famine also surface in the fiction included in section five. Louise Field's *Denis* refers back to Daniel O'Connell's political campaigns, and novels such as Annie Keary's *Castle Daly* and W.G.Wills's *The Love that Kills* are peopled with historical characters like William Smith O'Brien and Thomas Francis Meagher. Justin McCarthy's *Mononia* is a nostalgic reflection on the Young Ireland movement of 1848, describing how the Young Irelanders were driven to rebellion by witnessing the government's disastrously lacking response to the Famine. In Walsh's *The Next Time*, one nationalist character concludes that 'all this destruction and misery and ruin and death might have been avoided, if we had had a native government'.[53]

---

50   See P.M. Geoghegan, *King Dan: The Rise of Daniel O'Connell 1775–1829* (Dublin: Gill & Macmillan, 2008).

51   See R. Sloan, *William Smith O'Brien and the Young Ireland Rebellion of 1848* (Dublin: Four Courts Press, 2000).

52   As John O'Rourke writes in *The History of the Great Irish Famine of 1847* (Dublin: M'Glashan & Gill, 1875), Russell showed 'great ignorance or forgetfulness' (p. 249) in assuming that the landed clas were able to bear these responsibilities for relief single-handedly.

53   L.J. Walsh, *The Next Time: A Story of 'Forty-Eight* (Dublin: M.H. Gill, 1919), p. 230.

Many of these texts were written by authors who can be regarded as a 'postmemory' generation, that is, offspring of Famine survivors whose lives were 'dominated by narratives' of a past that 'preceded their birth'.[54] As Daniel Levy remarks, in processes of cultural recollection 'present political concerns and dominant (nation state) interests are projected onto the past'.[55] These writers' revisitation of the Famine past indeed seems to be directed by the nationalist concerns of their own age. Their works invoke the Famine to legitimize the Irish struggle against British colonial rule, using the traumatic past as a canvas on which to project the anti-colonial discourses of their own era. Patrick Sheehan's *Glenanaar* and William Francis Barry's *The Wizard's Knot*, for example, appear to have been heavily influenced by the cultural climate in which they were written: they display the impact of Celtic revivalism, looking back to a (partly imagined) Gaelic past to reinvent the island's culture which had been changed deeply by centuries of imperial oppression.

While these novels conjure up a shared, fateful past to transform it into a source of identity for a generation struggling against colonial power,[56] there are also novels set during later episodes of Irish history, implying that there are significant connections between the Famine and other events of national importance. W.C. Upton's *Uncle Pat's Cabin* and Emily Lawless's *Hurrish*, for instance, suggest parallels between the Famine and the Land Wars of the 1870s and 1880s, which once again saw intense conflicts between landlords and tenants and the threat

---

54   Hirsch, *Family Frames*, p. 22.

55   D. Levy, 'Changing Temporalities and the Internationalization of Memory Cultures', in Y. Gutman et al. (eds), *Memory and the Future: Transnational Politics, Ethics and Society* (Basingstoke: Palgrave Macmillan, 2010), p. 15.

56   Barbara Misztal argues that a 'shared sense of the past' often 'becomes a meaning-making repository which helps define aspirations for the future'. See 'Memory and History', p. 16.

of another famine.[57] As such, these two novels demonstrate the transgenerational significance of the Famine past.

Maidens, Mothers and Old Crones

As Birgit Neumann asserts, '[n]arratology... has proven to be of great value in the exploration of the representation of memory' in literature,[58] for plot and focalization display how processes of recollection and forgetting interact and which perspective on the past is privileged. In the schematic narrative formats employed in fiction to give shape to memories, recurring characters also play a significant role.

According to Margaret Kelleher, the strong presence of women in Famine literature can be attributed to Ireland's colonial condition: Ireland was symbolically embodied by female figures in response to a 'hypermasculine' regime of imperial oppression.[59] One of the major roles that women play in Famine fiction is that of the suffering mother who is made to go through the ordeal of seeing her children die of starvation. This image can, for instance, be found in Mrs Hoare's story 'The Black Potatoes' in section one. Among the texts included in section six, we find other representations of maternity. Oonagh McDermott in Margaret Brew's *The Chronicles of Castle Cloyne* adopts her cousin's toddler when she collapses with disease, and subsequently manifests the 'heroic, self-sacrificing attributes' which Margaret Kelleher notes in maternal figures in Famine fiction.[60] The substitute mother who takes up the care of a Famine orphan can also be

---

57   See B. O'Hara, *Davitt: Irish Patriot and Father of the Land League* (Temple, PA: Tudor Gate Press, 2009).
58   Neumann, 'Literary Representation of Memory', p. 333.
59   Kelleher, *Feminization of Famine*, p. 187.
60   Ibid., p. 74.

found in the character of Mrs Gwynne in *Forlorn; but not Forsaken* by 'Ireland', although her concern with little Biddy means training her to become a servant and educating her in Protestant doctrine. Here Mrs Gwynne's position as part of the Anglo-Irish landed class clearly adds a colonial context to her charitable enterprise.

Ascendancy women feature frequently in Famine fiction, often as providers of Famine relief. Examples of these high-born philanthropic female characters are very common presences in fiction dealing with the Famine; thus, they also feature in many of the texts included in other sections of this anthology. A good illustration can be found in Anthony Trollope's *Castle Richmond*, in section four, which illustrates how young girls from the gentry help out in a flour shop run by the relief committee. In several texts excerpted in section four, such as Thomas O'Neill Russell's *The Struggles of Dick Massey* and Charles Lever's *The Martins of Cro' Martin*, Anglo-Irish maidens play a pivotal role in mediating between the conflicted classes of Protestant landlords and Catholic tenants by showing concern for the latter without betraying their own caste. Moreover, the young Ascendancy daughters in these texts display a cultural hybridity which transcends social contention, while they also negotiate their gender roles. Often, these women simultaneously comply with the ideal of the empathic Angel of the House who safeguards the moral well-being of her family, while overstepping gender boundaries by challenging the authority of a paternal figure who represents colonial power.[61]

---

61 As the article 'Employment for Women', published in *The Dublin Review*, 52 (1862–63) states, a woman should instil her family with moral principles, and thus guarantee the moral well-being of the public sphere in which her relatives engage: '[t]he very soul and secret of a nation's strength is its sound morality' (p. 17). For further reading, see M.C.M. Corporaal, 'Memories of the Great Famine and Ethnic Identity in Novels by Victorian Irish Women Writers', *English Studies*, 90, 2 (2009), pp. 142–56.

Powerful female figures in Famine fiction are as often from the Catholic, Gaelic-speaking class. A telling example is Brigid Lavelle in Rosa Mulholland's 'The Hungry Death', who forms a stark contrast with the traditional female figure of the *aisling* tradition who is 'in need of protection and comfort' from British imperialism and the disasters that have hit the nation.[62] Brigid provides rather than seeks assistance, saving the lives of many who nearly perish with hunger. Describing her as majestic, the characterization of Brigid moreover alludes to the mythical Cathleen Ni Houlihan figure, with the difference that she gives her life for her former lover and his new mistress rather than demanding offers from him.

Often, the conflicts between landlords and tenants are translated in a seduction plot centring on a landlord who rapes a young peasant girl or leads her astray. Louise Field's *Denis and Julia* and Edmund O'Ryan's *In re Garland* present such a plotline, but *In re Garland* at the same time subverts this narrative template by showing how the cruel landlord in the end has to rely on the charity of his illegitimate daughter in order to survive the blows of Famine. As such, this novel gives expression to a changing social order in post-Famine Ireland.

Emigration and Exile

Between 1845 and 1855 an estimated 2.1 million Irish, mostly poor Catholic labourers and tenant farmers, left for Britain, the Americas and Australia, in an attempt to escape the effects of the Famine.[63] While the statue of Annie Moore and her brothers in Cobh – the port of departure for most Irish

---

62   C.L. Innes, *Woman and Nation in Irish Literature and Society, 1880–1935* (Athens, GA: University of Georgia Press, 1993), pp. 16–17.

63   See J.S. Donnelly, *The Great Irish Potato Famine* (Stroud: Sutton, 2003), p. 179.

emigrants – is one of the most significant *lieux de mémoire* crystallizing the recollections of the massive Irish exodus, Irish and British fiction which recollects the Famine years equally addresses the traumatic memories of departure and exile. As Caroline Brettell argues, migration is a 'rite of passage' which 'involves departure, the liminal status of being away, and the reintegration of return'.[64] All three stages are represented in the texts incorporated here, which feature emigrant characters, both outbound and returning, who face the difficulties of settling on foreign soil, and who, in, for instance, Margaret Brew's *The Chronicles of Castle Cloyne*, return to an equally foreign, utterly changed post-Famine Ireland.

As these texts were written mostly by authors who had no direct experience with emigrating themselves, but had to rely on the mediated, 'prosthetic' memories[65] of those who had relocated to far-off territories, the novels shed an interesting light on how the isolation and alienation concomitant with emigration and the new homelands of Irish émigrés were imagined in the mother country.

A central topos in Famine literature depicting transatlantic emigration is the coffin ship.[66] Steerage conditions on board the ships taking the Irish to the US and Canada were notoriously dire; on average, up to 30 per cent of all passengers perished at sea due to the insalubrious atmosphere below-decks, which often resulted in epidemic disease,[67] as Thomas O'Neill Russell's *The Struggles of Dick Massey* also illustrates.

---

64   C. Brettell, *Anthropology and Migration: Essays on Transnationalism, Ethnicity, and Identity* (Walnut Creek, CA: AltaMira Press, 2003), p. 18.

65   The term is derived from A. Landsberg's *Prosthetic Memory: The Transformation of American Remembrance in the Age of Mass Culture* (New York: Columbia University Press, 2004), p. 2.

66   For an extensive discussion of this topos see M.C.M. Corporaal and C.T. Cusack, 'Rites of Passage: The Coffin Ship as Site of Immigrants' Identity Formation in Irish and Irish-American Fiction, 1855–1885', *Atlantic Studies*, 8, 3 (2011), pp. 343–59.

67   K.A. Miller, *Emigrants and Exiles: Ireland and the Irish Exodus to North America* (Oxford: Oxford University Press, 1985), p. 292.

Not all texts focus on transatlantic emigration. Miss Mason's *Kate Gearey*, for example, relates the experience of an Irish girl who moves to London to make a living as a domestic servant. The novel highlights the differences between rural Ireland and metropolitan England, and it tries to dispel the notion that emigration will always lead to improved circumstances. Texts depicting immigrant life in America similarly evoke a transatlantic urban climate which corrupts the religious and sexual morality of the Irish newcomers. While Charles Kickham's *Sally Cavanagh* suggests that the New World opens up opportunities for acquiring wealth, the novel remains unconvinced about the benefits of emigration, for two immigrant females come to bad ends: Rose Mulvany loses her virtue, whilst her sister Mary perishes during the crossing to New York. As the novels in this section imply, Irish immigrants should focus on the retention of the Irish identity, and, specifically, Catholicism. Thus they should espouse an essential, continuous Irish identity which is to be strengthened by the establishment of Irish immigrant 'imagined communities'[68] in diaspora, forming heterotopic spaces used to resist assimilation in host societies.[69]

---

68   See B. Anderson, *Imagined Communities: Reflections on the Origin and Spread of Nationalism* (London: Verso, 1987), p. 15.

69   For the concept of heterotopia see M. Foucault, 'Of Other Spaces', *Diacritics*, 16 (1986), pp. 22–7.

Section 1

The Spectre of Starvation

Mrs Hoare (c.1818–72)

In a letter dated February 1852, British novelist Mary Russell Mitford informs her friend Miss Jephson: 'Mrs Hoare has sent me a little book of her own writing, called "Shamrock Leaves", a painful book, since it deals in details of the years of famine, and tells its story with much apparent truth.'[1] As Mitford implies, the collection of stories that she received contains some of the earliest examples of fiction recollecting the Great Hunger. Its author, Mary Ann Hoare, née Pratt, was born in Monkstown, Co. Cork, around 1818, and witnessed the horrors of the Famine in Ireland first-hand, during her early years of marriage to solicitor William Barry Hoare.[2]

The stories in *Shamrock Leaves* originally appeared 'in various periodicals,'[3] and are generally considered to express 'much sympathy for the lowly'.[4] The tales are concerned with the living conditions of Ireland's rural population, but not exclusively with the Famine. Nevertheless, in her preface Hoare makes a direct connection between her volume and the fateful Famine years, trusting that 'the British Public will not utterly despise these few wild "Shamrock Leaves", gathered with a loving hand from the famine-stricken fields of my native country'.[5] Though little is known about the period of original composition, the notes to some stories indicate that they were written during the Famine: 'The Black Potatoes' dates from 1846 and 'A Sketch of Famine' was 'written in 1847'.[6]

Hoare addresses a British readership in her foreword, and her stories are often consciously directed at an English audience unfamiliar with peasant life in Ireland. As an author who contributed to English periodicals such as *Household Words*, Hoare sought to familiarize the English reading public with Irish culture and the Irish national character. At the same time she tried to root out negative stereotyping of her countrymen and countrywomen

---

1   Quoted in A.G.K. L'Estrange (ed.), *The Friendships of Mary Russell Mitford* (London: Hurst & Blackett, 1882), p. 357.
2   T. O'Toole, *Dictionary of Munster Women Writers, 1800–2000* (Cork: Cork University Press, 2005), p. 97.
3   Mrs Hoare, *Shamrock Leaves; or Tales and Sketches of Ireland* (Dublin: J. M'Glashan, 1851), p. vi.
4   S.J.M. Brown, *Ireland in Fiction* (Dublin: Maunsel & Company, 1919), p. 138.
5   Hoare, *Shamrock Leaves*, p. vi.
6   Ibid., p. 205.

by suggesting that 'the "Irish" of the present day are, upon the whole, pretty much like other well-bred, well-educated members of the civilised world'.[7] In *Shamrock Leaves*, Hoare also attempts to bridge the gap between the world of her English readers and her native country; she often positions the reader as a tourist who needs further guidance on Irish life and customs, and tries to evoke her audience's sympathy for the suffering of the population.

This appeal to the readers' emotions is particularly present in the four Famine stories in *Shamrock Leaves*. 'The Living and the Dead' describes how the Famine has changed Ireland from a merry rural community into a bleak country where victims of starvation are interred uncoffined. 'A Sketch of Famine' shows how the tradition of keening is eradicated by the numerous deaths among the population, but also hints that the liberality 'of our English brethren' has prevented more extensive misery.[8] 'Little Mary' describes the fate of a family perishing from hunger and disease. 'The Black Potatoes' also zooms in on the sufferings of a family stricken by want. The story focuses on the sufferings of a helpless mother forced to see her children die of starvation and sickness, thus presenting us with an example of the conventional maternal figure with 'heroic, self-sacrificing attributes' commonly found in Famine fiction.[9]

From 'The Black Potatoes', in *Shamrock Leaves; or Tales and Sketches of Ireland*

Dublin: J. M'Glashan, 1851, pp. 32–49.

In former years it was a pleasant thing to take a summer ramble through the shamrock-covered fields, and among the wild mountain districts, of the green isle. To be sure, the features of the scenery were not so bold and

---

7   Mrs Hoare, 'An Irish Peculiarity', *Household Words*, 3 (1851), p. 364.
8   Hoare, *Shamrock Leaves*, p. 207.
9   M. Kelleher, *The Feminization of Famine: Expressions of the Inexpressible?* (Cork: Cork University Press, 1997), p. 74.

striking as those of the Scottish Highlands, nor did the country present that aspect of rich and high cultivation that distinguishes the rural districts of 'Merrie England' from those of all the world beside: yet many and abounding were the points of interest that caught the tourist's attention, including the humours of the light-hearted Irishman, as well as the romantic beauties of his land.

Among the more homely and characteristic charms of the latter, the stranger never failed to notice wide districts covered with the rich green leaves and star-shaped purple-and-white flowers of the potatoes, which, in the months of August and September, were wont to render the island one fragrant garden, and held out the prospect of winter plenty to the poor dwellers in the roadside cabins, whose most valuable possession was frequently the large iron pot, in which they boiled their sole and simple food.[10]

But what a change has the present year brought![11] Nothing in autumn was to be seen save black withered stalks, exhaling a strong offensive odour. I have been lately sojourning in a remote district of Munster, and there I have seen a ghastly famine-stricken figure, feebly wielding a spade, which, after hours of toil, would not dig out a sufficiency for one meal, of such roots as an English pig would turn away from in disgust. I have entered the cabins where working men were seated at their dinner, consisting of potatoes, a great proportion of which were about the bigness of marbles, the larger ones not much exceeding the size of a walnut. Happy the labourer who could obtain in addition a small quantity of thick milk; for to many of the poor it is an unwonted luxury. Before the time arrived for digging the miserable crop, Relief Funds, supported partly by a government grant, and partly by liberal subscriptions from the landlords,

---

10   The story evokes a pastoral landscape, which forms a stark contrast with the image of blight-stricken fields in the next paragraph. As Oona Frawley argues, the pastoral idealization of the Irish landscape in much literature from the colonial era should be read as a way to resist the cultural appropriation of Ireland by England and to commemorate 'the physical landcape' that expresses pre-colonial Irishness. The Famine was problematic in that it constituted 'the literal failure of the pastoral' that underpinned the formation of an ethnic identity. See *Irish Pastoral* (Dublin: Irish Academic Press, 2005), pp. 2, 45.

11   As the original note indicates, this is the year 1846.

were established through the country.[12] The committees appointed were enabled to sell yellow Indian meal at one shilling for fourteen pounds: and great was the delight with which the poor women, whose husbands and sons were working on the roads for eightpence a day, would walk a distance of six, eight, and sometimes ten miles, to purchase the meal and carry it home on their backs. About the end of August this seasonable supply was obliged to be stopped, and the poor were thrown on the resources afforded by their miserable gardens.

Then I have seen the labourer, his once stout limbs reduced by the presence of famine to the semblance of a skeleton's bones, standing in the furrows of an apparently empty field, languidly trying to strike his spade into the brown parched earth, and turn out the unripe blasted roots, which for many a long autumn day were to form his and his family's sole sustenance. His wretched ill-clad wife, standing beside him, with a dish, to receive the black unwholesome food, looked first on the ground, and then, glancing upwards with such a look of patient death-stricken anguish as Englishmen seldom see, said, 'Well! God Almighty look down upon us! What will become of us at all, at all?'[13]...

Instead of dwelling longer on an abstract view of the subject, let me relate a little narrative which may serve, in some slight measure, to illustrate the sufferings of the poor; and I trust, on their behalf, to awaken the efficient sympathy of our kind English and Scotch fellow-subjects.

In a mountainous part of the south-west of Ireland lived Tade Mahoney, his wife, and six children. He was a labourer employed on the

---

12 These public works were introduced by Peel's government as a way to 'provide employment and thus to furnish the money that the destitute needed to buy food'. See J.S. Donnelly, *The Great Irish Potato Famine* (Stroud: Sutton, 2003), pp. 53–4. However, public works such as the drainage of landed estates, the development of piers and, most notoriously, the building of roads, were hardly effective in regenerating the Irish economy. As *The Cork Examiner* reported on 2 April 1847, labourers were often dismissed when projects could no longer be subsidized: 'the poor labourers have been in great numbers discharged from the Works here, and no provision made for themselves or their wretched families. They are thus literally left to starve.' Moreover, many of the employed perished with exhaustion and hunger during labour. *The Cork Examiner* of 6 January 1847 reports of a man 'feebly affecting labour' until 'he falls prostrate on the unbroken pile of stones before him', collapsing with hunger and '*The Road-sickness*'.

13 This appeal to God appears to echo the providentialist discourse that was often present in contemporary discussions of the blight. For example, in the anonymous poem *The Farmer of Inniscreen: A Tale of the Irish Famine in Verse* (London: Jarrold & Sons, 1863), the potato blight is represented as 'a curse from Heaven' because 'the land had sinned, / And had not been forgiven' (p. 4).

ground of a middle-man, who rented a farm on the estate of a rich absentee landlord. Tade was an honest, industrious, poor fellow, who, at the age of twenty, had married a blooming girl of sixteen, possessing the considerable fortune of a feather bed, a dresser, two goats, and a lamb.

He had a brother who was usually described by the neighbours as 'a wild young devil that wouldn't be sed nor led by the priest himself'; and to whom even his best friends could not deny the possession of that 'truant disposition' which better befits the Prince of Denmark's favourite on the stage, than the son of a poor Irish labourer in real life.[14] Yet the lad, whose name was James, possessed a fund of native untaught energy that seemed to promise no common results; and when, at the age of nineteen, on the death of his father, he sold his share of the patrimonial goods and chattels and set sail for America, to seek his fortune, the old village schoolmaster shook his head and said, 'Well, there goes the 'cutest lad and brightest scholar that ever thumbed a Voster in my siminary. If his heels don't carry him off from the work that his hands know well how to do, and his head to plan, the never a fear but he'll be coming back to us a gintleman one of these days.'

After some time a letter arrived from him, to say that he had got into excellent employment in New York, and hoped soon to send for his brother. But after this no more was heard of him, and his friends, after making many fruitless inquiries, came to the conclusion that he must be dead. . . .

[T]he summer of 1846 came, and with it a blight on the food of the poor. Never was Egyptian plague more swift and noiseless, and deadly in its effects than the fearful 'potato cholera'.[15] One by one their scanty articles of furniture, and then their goats and sheep were sold by the Mahoneys, to procure food for their starving children; and this resource would soon have failed, had not public works been established in the beginning of August. Until the funds of the relief committees were exhausted, most of

---

14   The quote, Horatio's reply to Hamlet's question why he has returned from Wittenberg, is from William Shakespeare's *Hamlet*, I.ii.

15   The analogy between plague-stricken Egypt and Famine Ireland was commonly drawn. For instance, in C.A. Rawlins's *The Famine in Ireland, a Poem* (London: Joseph Masters, 1847) Famine Ireland is compared to '[a] stricken Egypt by JEHOVAH's hand' (p. 8). Similarly, in a sermon preached at Margaret Chapel during the Vigil of the Annunciation in 1847, Revd E.B. Pusey describes the Famine as one of the 'plagues of Egypt' come upon British shores. *Chastiments Neglected, Forerunners of Greater*, 3rd edn (Oxford: John Henry & Parker, 1859), p. 15.

the men in the country were employed on the roads at eightpence a day; poor wages, indeed, yet hailed by the perishing people as a blessed boon.

One wet day, towards the end of last August, Tade Mahoney returned to his cabin about six o'clock, faint and weary, after a day's work, which he thought himself only too fortunate to have obtained. He had tasted nothing since the previous evening, save a small piece of Indian meal cake, and a draught of water; and yet he did not feel hungry. His head was dizzy, his hands hot, and burning pains darted through his frame. He entered the cabin, and throwing his hat on the floor, sank heavily on a wooden stool placed near the small turf fire. His eldest daughter, a fair, blue-eyed child of ten years old, ran up to him, and, putting her little hand in his, said, joyfully: –

'Ah, daddy, we're to have a fine supper tonight, for mammy went to I – for the male! And she brought home a bagful of it on her back; and see what a potful of it there's down for us all. She left Johnny and me to stir it, while she'd be out to look for a dhrop of milk.'

The father tried to smile, as he replied, in a tone of sorrow, 'I'm proud to hear it, Mary; 'tis long since ye had yer 'nough to ate, *ma colleen bawn.*'[16]

Just then Jude entered with an empty wooden can in her hand.

'Well, Tade', she said, 'I thought to have a dhrop of milk for yer supper, so I wint to Mrs McCarthy to ax it; and I towld her I'd pay her in fresh eggs when the hens would lay to-morrow: but she said she had none for me, and so we must ate the boiled male dry – thanks be to God for giving us that same! But, Tade, *a chree,*[17] what ails you? You look very white, and there's a thrimblin' over you.'

''Tis only a sudden hate and pain in my heart I got, Jude; plaze God 'twill be nothing. I'll go to bed, and I'll be well wanst I'm asleep.'

'And daddy, won't you ate any supper?' said little Mary and Johnny together, while his wife, laying one hand on his, and pressing his forehead with the other, looked anxiously in his face.

'I couldn't ate any thing, childher', he said, 'if I was paid for it; and sure there'll be the more left for yees all to-morrow. Give me a dhrink of wather, Jude', and, rising with difficulty, he went towards a bundle of straw, which, scattered on the damp floor, formed, with an old rug, and the tattered

---

16   My pretty young girl.
17   Darling.

remnant of a blanket, the only sleeping place for the whole family. The children felt frightened, they knew not why; yet the healthy appetite of their age prevailed, and they made a hearty supper on the Indian meal stirabout. Very little, however, did their poor mother swallow; her heart, as she expressed it, 'rose to her mouth', when she thought that perhaps her husband was struck with 'the sickness', as the poor people emphatically designate typhus fever, the plague that in wet and scarce seasons is wont to desolate the country. With a heavy heart she took a little straw, and placed it for the children as far as she could from the spot where their father lay, and then tried in vain to cover them with a few torn rags, in addition to their own miserable clothing. She lay down near her husband, whose burning skin, heavy breathing, and restless tossing to and fro, showed too plainly that her fears were well-founded. In the morning his illness had greatly increased; he called incessantly for water, and soon became quite delirious. ...

Heart-rending were the lamentations of poor Jude, when, on the tenth day of his illness, she saw him, who was indeed the 'delight of her eyes', stretched before her cold and lifeless as the clay on which he rested. Her neighbours flocked in, and, regardless of danger from infection, crowded the house for two days while the body was 'waked'. Part of that time the widow was seated on the ground, rocking herself to and fro, in the stupor of grief; and, when occasionally she was roused to a full consciousness of her loss, she would pour forth a torrent of that eloquent heart-felt lamentation, which is seldom heard out of Ireland – calling on her husband to return to her and to his 'fair-haired jewels', and almost cheating herself into the belief that he could indeed hear and answer her entreaty.[18]...

Soon after sunrise they prepared to set out on their mournful journey; for nothing was left for them but *to travel*, that is, to wander about the country, calling at every house they passed, and subsisting on the charity which is never withheld from the beggar, by those who are themselves but a few degrees better off. Jude had told the farmer for whom her husband

---

18   While the scene presents us with an example of the tradition of the *caoineadh*, or keening, the Famine, with its high mortality rates and the concomitant disappearance of Gaelic culture, deeply affected this 'tradition of grieving the dead'. As becomes clear from the scene, the *caoineadh* was 'pre-eminently a woman's genre'. See K. Whelan, 'The Cultural Effects of the Famine', in J. Cleary and C. Connolly (eds), *The Cambridge Companion to Modern Irish Culture* (Cambridge: Cambridge University Press, 2005), p. 141.

had worked, that she would surrender her house and now worthless garden; and this day he was to take possession. With a bursting heart the poor woman set out, carrying her youngest child a year old on her back, and leading the next little creature of three by the hand; the others walking on. She carried nothing with her save an empty bag, which Johnny bore across his shoulder, and in which they meant to deposit any donation of meal, bread, or black potatoes, which they might receive.

They had not gone far when they were met by two men, whom Jude recognised as distant cousins of her husband, and who were themselves poor labourers living in the county of Kerry, about thirty miles from the village of I – .

'God save you, Jude', said the elder of the two, ''twas only yesterday we heard of your trouble, or else we'd have come to poor Thady's berrin'; and thinking that, now your provider is gone from you, and the times so bitther ye'd have nothing to do but to take to the road with the *grawls*,[19] we settled with our women that, if it's plasing to you, we'll ache take one of the young [t]hings from you, and give it the run of the cabin along with our own, till such time, plase God, as you'll be up in the world again.'

The widow's eyes filled with tears; gratitude to the kind-hearted speaker mingled with reluctance to part from her little ones, yet she knew that in her situation it would be madness to hesitate; so she answered: 'God for ever bless you, Denis and Jerry, for thinking of me and mine in our desolation; and sure, though it tears the sore heart within me to part with them that I bore and suckled at my breast, 'tis all for the best, and may be I'll be able some time or other to travel into your parts, and get a sight of the crathurs that ye're taking now for the love of God.'

'Then 'tis you that will be kindly welcome', said the man, rubbing the back of the hand across his eyes, ''tis little we have to give, because 'tis little we have for ourselves, but little or much, your *lanuveens*[20] shall share the bit and sup with our own. Which of them will come with us, Judy?', he continued in a more cheerful tone. The mother hesitated, but at length it was decided that the youngest boy and girl should be taken, as being the least able to bear the hardships of a wandering life; and, with mingled tears and blessings, Jude gave them into the hands of their relatives, to whom

---

19   Children.
20   Young children.

feeling hearts had taught more true tenderness than dwells under many a smooth aspect and jewelled robe. She watched them on their homeward path, till a turning in the road hid them from her view, and then with the other children she resumed her weary journey.

It would be tedious and harrowing to the feelings to accompany this poor family through their wanderings for the next month. Sometimes they got a night's shelter and a piece of bread in the house of a farmer; often they had to sleep under an open shed, or behind a haystack; and their fasts were frequently prolonged for twenty-four hours. Yet Jude preferred undergoing those privations to seeking admission into the overcrowded pestilential precincts of the workhouse, where she would be separated from her children. They travelled, as the poor little ones' failing strength would admit, over a distance of many miles. One evening, at sunset, they stopped at a cabin, a little removed from the high road, to ask for a night's lodging. They had travelled all day without food, save a few fragments of hard oaten cake, given them the night before by a farmer's wife: they were now therefore faint with hunger, and the poor children's blistered feet refused to carry them farther. The youngest boy, of six years old, a fair-haired child with regular features and soft intelligent eyes, showed symptoms all day of heavy sickness. He did not complain, but, whenever they sat down for a brief rest, his head was nestled in his mother's bosom, his little hot hand stole round her neck, and his white lips (once so rosy) asked plaintively for 'water, mammy! more water!' She carried him in her arms, or on her back, as long as she could; for their path lay over a desolate mountain, where for many a mile, no human habitation was to be seen; but for the last hour the little fellow insisted on trying to walk, saying, 'You're wake, mammy, and 'tis worse to me to be tiring you than to walk myself.'

But now his emaciated limbs failed, and, when they were within a few steps of the cabin, he sank on the ground.

'God Almighty help my child, and look down on him', said the poor mother, raising him in her feeble arms; and, entering the cabin with the customary salutation, 'God save all here', she asked a woman who was seated inside the door, to give a night's lodging to her '*lanuv brotha*'.[21]

---

21 Sick child.

'You shall have that same', replied the woman. 'but 'tis little else I have to give. Look here', and she took from the shelf a wooden can containing about a pint of coarse flour. 'My husband', she continued, 'is working on the Caherah road since yesterday week without getting a penny wages:[22] he went there to day without breaking his fast, except with a drink of water and a small taste of cold cabbage; and now that's all I have to cook for him and five of us besides, for this night and the whole of to-morrow.'

Famine, with his stern graving tools, had indeed carved deep lines in the haggard countenances of the two women; and the miserable children of the wanderer, when mingled with those of the dweller in the cabin, presented a lamentable picture of premature decay. The husband soon came in, and the meal, if such it could be called, was prepared for him. He just tasted it, and then calling his wife and children, insisted on their sharing the morsel; he even offered some to the poor travellers, and the three elder children ate a scrap each; but the widow thanked him and refused to touch it. Her heart was full, and her eyes were fixed on the heaving chest and clammy forehead of her dying child; for it was evident that the sorrows of the little wanderer were nearly ended. She watched him through the night while he lay insensible; towards morning he gave a few convulsive sobs, and then, with one long sigh, the gentle spirit was released.

I will not try to paint the mother's anguish; nor what she felt when, on that day week, another child was taken from her – her dark eyed smiling little Ellen. In the midst of her sorrow she knew they were at peace.[23] ...

At length the widow's wanderings brought her back to her former abode. The cabin had not been since inhabited, and beneath its desolate roof she and her two remaining children prepared one night to take up their lodging. They had a few turnips and a bit of barley bread to eat, and they had collected a bundle of fern and heath to sleep upon. They were all ill and feeble, but Jude had, as she expressed it, 'a weight of sickness on her heart', that she felt would soon terminate her earthly sorrows.

---

22 This refers to the digging of roads as part of public work schemes. As Emily Lawless later observed in *Ireland* (1885), this was a futile undertaking, as work was carried out in places 'where no road was ever wanted or could possibly be used' (London: T. Fisher Unwin), p. 399.

23 Here we see the common representation of the bereaved mother that we also find in John Keegan's 'The Dying Mother's Lament' (1846): 'To see my ghastly babies – my babes so meek and fair – / To see them huddled in that ditch, like wild beasts in their lair' *Legends and Poems* (Dublin: Sealy, Bryers & Walker, 1907), p. 507.

Johnny closed the door, they lay down on the ground, and were trying to sleep, when a loud knocking outside aroused them.

'Who's there?' asked Jude, starting up.

'Is it here', said a voice, 'that Tade Mahoney lives!'

'God help me, 'tis here he did live, but he's gone to his rest these six weeks.'

An exclamation of surprise and sorrow was the answer, followed by a request for admission. Jude hesitated, but at length opened the door. There was no light in the cabin, but she lighted a splinter of bogwood which happened to have remained on the ground, and the uncertain flame shone on the person of her visitor. He was a tall good-looking man, well dressed, more in the fashion of a town than in that of the country; and there was an expression in his countenance of amazement, almost horror, as he looked on the cabin and its inhabitants.

'Can you', said he, 'tell me any thing of Tade Mahoney's family?'

'I'm his wife', replied the poor woman, 'and these are his childher. I buried two more of them since the light of my eyes was taken from me, and there are two living with his cousins.'

The man seemed deeply moved; he trembled as he asked in a faltering voice –

'Don't you know me, Judy? I'm James, your husband's brother, and little I thought to find you this way on my return. My poor Thady! Many's the time I longed for a warm shake of your hand, and a welcome home from your pleasant voice.'

He could say no more, but, turning towards Mary and Johnny, he clasped them both in his arms.

After some time he continued: –

'Now, Judy, you must not be this way any more; I'm well to do in the world, for, when I left New York, I got a fine farm far up the country. There I married an English girl, whose family are settled near me, and a good wife she makes. I often wrote to Thady, but never got an answer.'

'We never heard from you', said Judy, 'and so we thought you were dead.'

'Letters often miscarry in these remote places', answered James, 'and I suppose it happened that way. At all events, I came over now, intending to take you all out with me; and rely on it, Judy, I'll do as much for you and the children as if my poor brother was alive.'

The widow burst into tears – 'God for ever bless you, James', she said, 'and sure 't was He sent you here to us, when I didn't know where to get another bit to keep life in my perishing orphans. For myself it doesn't matter; the hand of death is on me, and soon I'll be where hunger and thirst and nakedness won't part me from them that were more to me than life itself. My blessing be ever on you and about you, and keep you and yours from harm and loss. I know you'll be a father to them two darlings, and to the other two weeny ones that I'll never see more in this world.'

James could no longer restrain his emotions: he sobbed like a child, and pressing the wasted hand of his sister-in-law, he could only say –

'May God protect and bless them, Judy – I'll do for them as if they were my own. My wife has a tender heart, and I'll answer for her she'll be a mother to them.'

In a fortnight after the scene I have described, the widow breathed her last in a comfortable lodging in Cork, whither her brother-in-law had removed her. In the meantime he went into Kerry, and rewarded the kind-hearted Denis and Jerry for the care of the little orphans, who were brought to receive their mother's blessings. In accordance with her wish, he arranged to pay their protectors liberally for their board and lodging until they should be old enough to cross the Atlantic. After a little time he succeeded in calming the wild grief of Mary and Johnny, and reconciling them to go with him. He now only waits the approach of spring, to engage a passage for himself and them in a packet bound for America.

Mrs Meredith (1823–1901)

Susanna Meredith (née Lloyd, 1823–1901) is primarily known for the social work she carried out in London. Upon her migration from Co. Cork to London, Meredith began to visit female convicts in Brixton, engaged in the public debate about the condition of the capital's prisons, and eventually founded a small mission house for women who were discharged from prison, in order to set up employment schemes[1] for those 'struggling back to honesty and virtuous living'.[2]

However, few will be familiar with the fact that Meredith, as a newly married woman and later as a young widow in the Ireland of the 1840s and 1850s, was greatly concerned with the social welfare of the Irish poor. Perhaps stimulated by the example of her father, the governor of County Cork Gaol,[3] who during the Famine 'organized … a co-operative company to keep down the price of bread, and a soup kitchen for … relief, and started also an asylum for the pauper blind', Meredith sought to teach deprived peasant girls how to make crochet lace, so they could earn a living in those calamitous times.[4] Meredith saw making lace as a fine art specific to the Celtic race, and a trade that would offer Ireland further possibilities for development.[5]

Meredith's collection *The Lacemakers* (1865), consisting of reflections on the lace trade in Ireland and published after her immigration to England, contains one story specifically addressing the memory of the Irish Famine. 'Ellen Harrington' is set in June 1848 in a village on the west coast of Ireland. The HM *Breeze* has come to supply food to the hunger-stricken population. The fragment reproduced below shows how the lieutenant in charge of the steamer, Mr Hartley, comes to visit the charitable reverend Mr Longwood and his wife. After the scene the story further focuses on Ellen Harrington, the orphaned daughter of Mrs

1   M.A. Lloyd, *Susanna Meredith: A Record of a Vigorous Life* (London: Hodder & Stoughton, 1903), pp. 27, 37.
2   S. Meredith, *The Sixth Work; or, The Charity of Moral Effort* (London: Jackson, Walford & Hodder, 1866), p. v.
3   C. Hartley and S. Leckey (eds), *A Historical Dictionary of British Women* (London: Routledge, 2003), p. 315.
4   Lloyd, *Susanna Meredith*, p. 14.
5   Ibid., p. 15.

Longwood's brother who had been taken in by the couple. She is once again left to fend for herself when the Longwoods, having contracted disease during their charity work, die of fever. Ellen manages to make a living for herself by setting up a relief school where she and the children she teaches make crochet lace to be sold on the English market. The story ends with the suggestion that working in the lace trade can help girls to earn passage to countries such as Canada, America and Australia where they have better futures ahead of them than in Ireland.

From 'Ellen Harrington', in *The Lacemakers*

(London: Jackson, Walford & Hodder, 1865), pp. 59–65.

It transpired, in conversation, that Mr Longwood was recovering from the epidemic fever, and that his wife was lying down in it, and that their only nurse was the little girl that had opened the door. With much kindness and pity, and already feeling quite a friendship for the uncomplaining sufferer, who so simply told such a sad tale, Mr Hartley took his leave.

When he was going down the avenue, a young man rode past him, and he observed that he dismounted near the house, released his rough horse from bridle and saddle, and let him run loose in the grass, while he himself familiarly entered the dwelling.

Hartley, on reaching the high road, turned in the direction of a village that he perceived at a little distance; and was not many minutes walking along, when he heard a voice calling after him:

'I say, Captain, don't walk so fast. Let me be talking to you.'

On looking back, he saw the same individual that had gone into the Parsonage, a few minutes before, so he stood and waited until he came up.

'Tom Neligan, *M.D.*, at your service, sir', said the pursuer, lifting his hat, bowing, and waving his hand towards himself. Hartley returned the salutation and fell into line to walk with the stranger, and submit to the 'talking to' for which he had been called back. It ran on in the following manner: – 'So you've brought the food at last! The moment that I heard how you let the people lay hands on it, I made after you to blow you up. Why, it would be as well to let them die for the want of it, as to allow them to burst from the eating of it, as I expect the half of them will now do! Didn't you know we have no boilers? And how is the meal to be cooked? And who is to do it? Why didn't you bring the bread ready-made? A set of fine boys, all of you! If it was ye that were wanting it, what good stuff would be baked for ye; and the dinners laid on plates, and everything to your hand! But you won't set us up with such attendance!'[6]

Hartley could hear the accusing tone of this style of address no longer: –

'Sir', said he, 'you are strangely ignorant of the nature of my duties. Your complaints should be addressed to the Commissariat Department.'

And, turning on his heel, he was about to part company abruptly with his singular companion, when the doctor exclaimed,

'Holloa, I offended you, did I? Well, I'm sorry for it, but you must not quarrel with a man who wants a new friend to help him to save some of the old ones.'

And, putting out his hand, he made a very humble apology, and smiled so pleasantly, that Hartley, though offended by the imputation of mis-management, did not refuse to accept the proffered *amende*.[7] He also now observed, that the man was as queer in his appearance as in his speech, was dressed in a very nondescript fashion, and was encumbered with three or four game-bags and a fishing-basket, all of which hung about him, as if he were a stand for their especial accommodation; the only possible conclusion was that he was deranged, and must be humoured accordingly. But his conduct in the village which they were just entering, gave proof, that,

---

6   In Ireland there was controversy over the fact that corn was shipped to English markets while the Irish were perishing. Jane Francesca Elgee's 'The Stricken Land', published under the pen-name 'Speranza' in *The Nation* of 23 January 1847, voices a protest against the 'Stately ships' that transport the corn reaped on Irish soil to England: 'that bear our food away, amid the stranger's scoffing'. In 1845 and 1846 Prime Minister Sir Robert Peel tried to relieve the Famine crisis by importing cheap 'Indian corn and meal … through the agency of Baring Bros. & Co.' from the United States. J.S. Donnelly, *The Great Irish Potato Famine* (Stroud: Sutton Publishing, 2003), p. 49. The practically inedible food mentioned in this passage appears to be Indian meal. Before it could be consumed, it had to be boiled for a long time. See C. Kinealy, *This Great Calamity: The Irish Famine 1845–52* (Dublin: Gill & Macmillan, 1994), p. 57. Since many famishing peasants did not know how to prepare the coarse, lumpy maize, they experienced severe bowel complaints. As Asenath Nicholson writes, the meal was mockingly called 'Peel's brimstone'. Many 'were actually afraid to take it in many cases, the *government* meal in particular', fearing that the '"Inglish intinded to kill them" with the "tarin and scrapin"'. *Annals of the Famine in Ireland* (New York: E. French, 1851), pp. 30, 32.

7   French: apology. Note that Dr Neligan is repeatedly associated with French terms, perhaps to underline Hartley's view of the doctor's strange appearance.

whatever his mania was, there was method in it; and that it did much in its own way to relieve the miserable destitution which every step revealed.

'Look at that side of the village, captain', said he, 'every house there is shut up, nearly all the people that belonged to it lie buried in that ditch, where you see the earth red; and not a day passes that two or three more don't join them.

'Come into my Dispensary, – but sure it is "kitchen" it ought to be called, and kitchen-stuff is the physic I ought to have in it – I'm afraid the boiler won't be up until we are all past wanting it.'

Groups began to gather round the gentlemen, and the hearer discovered, that though but two days had elapsed since the doctor's last visit, many of his patients had found their rest in the long sleep that knows no waking; he mourned for them somewhat in this style: –

'Don't tell me, the Doolans are all gone, and the Roddys – eight strong men, in all, let alone women and children! Driscoll, you're all right again. Here, take this drink of broth.'

'Yes, yer honour, I'm on my legs, thank God! Still I'm sorry to be the one to be going to turn the sod over Leary and Looney, that are lying on their backs yonder.'

'You! man, you're not able.'

'An' sure I'm saisoned for it, doctor, glory be to God!' (crossing himself reverently), 'any way, none of thim that are not, ought to go anear that ditch.'

'Dead, or alive; you're all dangerous company, my poor fellow. This gentleman and I will dig you a fresh hole. Captain, this will be a real charity; not a soul here is strong enough to use a spade properly, and they can't bury the bodies deep enough. Will you bear a hand?'

'I'll do better, if you wait a little, for I'll send you men, and get a trench of some depth dug for you; but where is the churchyard?'

'Four miles off, and there's neither money, nor strength, nor time to get at it. To convince you of the necessity for this rude and hasty burial, just come in here.'[8]

---

8   The high mortality rate during the Famine made it impossible to provide proper burial rites to each victim. See, for instance, Lord Dufferin and G.G. Boyle's *Narrative of a Journey from Oxford to Skibbereen during the Year of the Irish Famine* (Oxford: John Henry Parker, 1847): 'by these graves, no service had been performed, no friends had stood, no priest had spoken words of hope, and of future consolation in a glorious eternity! The bodies had been daily thrown in, many without a coffin, one over another' (p. 13).

They entered one of the best looking cabins, and, as soon as they got accustomed to the gloomy light, they saw in one corner of the wretched apartment, a man lying on his back, almost naked, and evidently dying; a woman was sitting upright near him, rigid in despair; two children were dead at her side, and one, in the delirium of fever, lay tossing and moaning on her lap.[9] The doctor produced a bottle from his basket, and administered a cordial to the mother, the only creature able to swallow in this almost tomb. The poor woman rose, laid aside the baby, and staggered over to her husband's side; at that moment he drew his last, long breath, and the miserable wife fell across his body, also giving up her weary life.

Such a sight drove Hartley into the open air, and it was many minutes before he rejoined the doctor, who had no time to give way to his feelings, and who was now found in the midst of a wretched crowd; to whom he administered mingled doses of orders, rebukes, pity, and cordials; while their thanks, prayers, blessings, and complaints, produced a medley of sounds, in which the various tones of the sufferers with the voice of their benefactor made the chords of a beautiful melody, whose key-note of kindness was easily found. With this in his ears Hartley turned to Neligan, anxiously hastening to discover how he could contribute to his assistance; and now, indeed, he listened to his *clinique*[10] with growing respect, as they continued to walk through roads that seemed to lead, at every step, to some fresh and more distressing case of misery.

'Captain, no pharmacopoeia can furnish me with formula to suit the various symptoms of this radical disease. We want ready-made diet, or bring us cooks and kitchen-ranges! The very whiskey, that used to assist the work of digestion in their half savage stomachs, is also absent; and without stimulant it is of no use to give them nourishment; with the help of it, they used to turn potatoes into humanity quickly enough; but now all the soup and stirabout they swallow, is as much outside them as ever, without "the drop" that used to excite their functions, and preserve their tissues.'

---

9   The witnessing of human suffering inside a cabin was a common scene in much travel writing on Famine Ireland. For instance, in Nicholson's *Annals of the Famine in Ireland* (1851) we can read about the author's difficulty coping with the horrible conditions inside the cabins: 'We went from cabin to cabin till I begged the curate to show me no more' (p. 102). In 'The Indigent Sublime: Specters of Irish Hunger', David Lloyd draws interesting analogies between these encounters of travel writers with the starving poor and the Sublime. *Representations*, 92 (2005), p. 52.

10   French; a clinical lecture given at the bedside.

Hartley took the doctor on board with him; and the boat that brought him back to the shore contained a contribution to his Dispensary of the grog for that day of every man on board the *Breeze*.

'Deeds like these', said Neligan, 'shall be rewarded when the great Inquest sits on our poor souls.'

Patrick Sheehan (1852–1913)

Canon Patrick Augustine Sheehan (1852–1913) was a well-respected priest, a prolific author, and an indefatigable political activist. Born in Mallow, Co. Cork, he was educated at the seminary in Maynooth, Co. Kildare. After being ordained as a priest in 1875 he took up a post in the diocese of Plymouth in England. In 1877 he returned to Ireland, where in 1895, he was installed as parish priest of Doneraile, a position he held until his death in 1913.[1]

Sheehan achieved yet greater fame with his literary output: 'during his own lifetime, sales of his novels ... exceeded a hundred thousand copies'.[2] As a novelist, Sheehan is considered an exponent of the Irish Literary Revival; his fictional Ireland is a rural society that harks back to an idealized traditional culture, re-imagining the Irish past for nationalist purposes. Catholicism is central to Sheehan's novels, and many of his narratives feature priests in important roles.

The narrator of *Glenanaar*'s frame narrative is also a priest, who recounts his friendship with the Irish-American Terence Casey, the grandson of informer Patrick Daly who emigrated to the United States after discovering his grandfather's heinous crime. Having made his fortune abroad, Casey has returned to the village of Glenanaar to marry his childhood sweetheart. As Heuser states, *Glenanaar* 'is actual history, based upon authentic records':[3] Sheehan did archival research into the novel's central event, the 1829 'Doneraile Conspiracy' trials, which saw a number of Corkmen accused of organizing a rebellion. In *Glenanaar*, the ramifications of the case are traced across three generations. The novel describes not only the trial itself – at which the defence was mounted by famous politician Daniel O'Connell (1775–1847) – but also focuses on the child and grandchild of Daly, who falsely accused a number of his acquaintance for financial gain. Daly's wife abandons their baby daughter, who is then taken in by the Connors. They name her Nodlag (Christmas) and raise her as their own. When Nodlag discovers her true background,

---

1   R. Hogan et al. (eds), *Dictionary of Irish Literature, Revised and Expanded Edition* (London: Aldwyck Press, 1996), pp. 1105–7.
2   M.P. Linehan, *Canon Sheehan of Doneraile: Priest, Novelist, Man of Letters* (Dublin: Talbot Press, 1952), p. 53.
3   H.J. Heuser, *Canon Sheehan of Doneraile* (New York: Longmans, Green & Co., 1917), p. 191.

she abandons her suitor Red Casey because she cannot deal with her hereditary shame. Yet she returns at the height of the Great Famine, emaciated and at death's doorstep. In the passage below, as Christopher Morash points out, she is 'represented in a manner familiar from earlier Famine texts',[4] but here the victim does not die. Nodlag is nursed back to health and she and Casey eventually marry, producing one son, Terence, whose conversations with the narrator-priest bring the narrative full circle.

From *Glenanaar: A Story of Irish Life*

(London: Longmans, Green & Co., 1905), pp. 197–204.

Looking back on that appalling period in our history, the great wonder is, not that so many perished in the famine, but that so many lived, and lived in comfort, in the years previous to that dread visitation. When old men point out today places where whole villages then existed, each with its little army of tradesmen, fullers, spinners, masons, stonecutters, carpenters, etc., we, whose economic conditions are not yet up to the normal standard of living, ask ourselves in amazement, 'how did the people then live?' The land is as rich today as ever; the population has dwindled down to one-half of what it was then. If today the struggle for existence is still keen, what must it not have been then? And yet, the remnants of the ancient peasantry assure us, and they themselves are the best proof of the assertion, that the men of those bygone days, nurtured exclusively on potatoes and milk, were a far more powerful race than their descendants; could endure greater hardship, and accomplish greater work.[5] But when the potato was the sole sustenance of the people, we can imagine what a horror, slowly creeping on their minds, finally seized them with utter panic, when, in the autumn of '47, and again in the autumn of

---

4   C. Morash, *Writing the Irish Famine* (Oxford: Clarendon Press, 1995), p. 145.

5   The novel here challenges the frequently cited view that the Irish peasants' exclusive reliance on the potato was a backward custom which had indirectly led to the wide-scale famine. For example, in *On Famine and Fever As Cause and Effect in Ireland* (Dublin: J. Fannin & Co., 1846) D.J. Corrigan calls the potato 'a curse to our country' (p. 22) which has affected the labourers' wages and caused wide-scale starvation.

'48, that strange odour filled the atmosphere, and told of the deadly blight.[6] Even today that word has an ominous significance. Men seem to grow pale at the thought of it. The farmer or labourer sniffs the air on one of those sweet autumnal evenings, and goes into his cottage a depressed man. A newspaper report from the far west of the country, that the 'blight' has appeared, makes men still shudder. What must it have been in these far days, when no other food was to be had; when the granaries of the great prairies were yet unlocked, and a whole people might perish before the hands of the charitable could reach them.

And they did perish; perished by hundreds, by thousands, by tens of thousands, by hundreds of thousands; perished in the houses, in the fields, by the roadside, in the ditches; perished from hunger, from cold, but most of all from the famine-fever. It is an appalling picture, that which springs up to memory. Gaunt spectres move here and there, looking at one another out of hollow eyes of despair and gloom. Ghosts walk the land.[7] Great giant figures, reduced to skeletons by hunger, shake in their clothes, which hang loose around their attenuated frames. Mothers try to still their children's cries of hunger by bringing their cold, blue lips to milkless breasts. Here and there by the wayside a corpse stares at the passers-by, as it lies against the hedge where it had sought shelter. The pallor of its face is darkened by lines of green around the mouth, the dry juice of grass and nettles.[8] All day long the carts are moving to the graveyards with their

---

6   In his depiction of the Famine, Sheehan echoes earlier descriptions of the catastrophe. For instance, in Richard Baptist O'Brien's *Ailey Moore; A Tale of the Times* (London: Charles Charles Dolman, 1856) the blight-affected fields are described as rotting weeds sending forth 'the odour of the charnel-house' (p. 261).

7   This representation of the starving as walking spectres is very common in Famine writings. Living skeletons and ghosts exemplify the 'living dead', the ghastly, starving bodies of the Famine-stricken, but also feature figuratively, as the spirits of the deceased victims who claim retribution. Spectrality as the embodiment of a buried past which requires vengeance is addressed in Jane Francesca Elgee's poem 'The Stricken Land' (1847). Later republished as 'The Famine Year' (*Poems by Speranza*. Glasgow: Cameron & Ferguson, 1871), it warns the English who refused help to the starving Irish that the 'whitening bones' of the Famine casualties 'against ye will rise as witnesses, / From the cabins and the ditches, in their charred, uncoffin' masses' as a 'ghastly, spectral army' (p. 12) on Judgement Day. Likewise, in 'Song of the Irish-American Regiments', from *The Poems of Richard Dalton Williams* (Dublin: T.D. Sullivan, 1883), Richard D'Alton Williams describes a 'ghastly spectre throng' of Famine victims who call the new generation to 'Vengeance', exhorting them to 'right their wrong' (p. 50).

8   Dandelion was frequently dug up and eaten by Famine victims in order to still their extreme hunger. In Rudolf Virchow's *On Famine Fever; and Some of the Other Cognate Forms of Typhus* (London: Williams & Norgate, 1868), one can read that '[t]he distress became so great that in many places the inhabitants could only find turnip – parings, dandelions' (p. 10).

ghastly, staring, uncoffined loads. In the towns it is even worse. The shops are shuttered. Great fires blaze at the corners of streets to purify the air. From time to time the doctors send up into the polluted air paper kites with a piece of meat attached. The meat comes down putrid. At the government depots, here and there, starving creatures dip their hands into the boiling maize, or Indian meal[9] (hence and forevermore in Ireland the synonym of starvation and poverty), and swallow with avidity the burning food. A priest is called from his bed at every watch of the night. As he opens his hall-door, two or three corpses fall into his arms. Poor creatures! Here was their last refuge! Here and there along the streets, while the soft rain comes down to wash more corruption into the festering streets, a priest kneels in the mud over a prostrate figure. He is administering the last rites, whilst a courageous bystander holds an umbrella above his head to guard the Sacred Species. No graves, but pits, as after the carnage of a great battle, are dug in the cemeteries; and the burial service is read over twenty corpses at a time. ...

As he[10] looked out over the cold, bleak landscape, he saw the closely-shawled figure of a woman coming up the road with slow, painful steps; and then, after a moment's pause, turning into the little boreen[11] that led from the smithy to the road. Here, evidently, her strength failed, for, putting out one hand, as if she were blind, she groped for the ditch, and then fell against it heavily. Redmond rushed into the cottage, and cried to his mother:

'Run out, mother! There's another of thim poor crachures in the ditch!'

'The Lord betune us and all harrum', cried the mother. 'Will it ever ind?'

She took up a porringer of milk (into which she poured a little hot water), and a piece of home-made loaf, and went out. Making her way with some dread and caution, she came within a few feet of where the

---

9   Lord John Russell, who succeeded Sir Robert Peel as Prime Minister in 1846, discontinued the Indian meal relief scheme. Providing corn flour did not comply with his laissez-faire policy or 'Political Economy', which held that non-intervention was the right response and that the effects of the Famine would make Ireland more amenable to social, economic and agricultural reform. See C. Kinealy, *This Great Calamity: The Irish Famine 1845–52* (Dublin: Gill & Macmillan, 2006), p. 72.

10   Redmond Casey.

11   A narrow rural road.

fainting woman was lying; and afraid of the fever to approach nearer, she placed the food on a large stone, such as is always found near a smithy, and shouted:

'Here, poor 'uman, here is milk and bread for you! Thry and rouse up, alanna,[12] and God 'ill give you the strinth.' ...

Just at the moment, however, that she lifted face and hands to heaven in the agony of a final supplication, the young smith caught a glimpse of eyes that were unchanged amidst the general and terrible transformation of famine, and of one stray lock of auburn hair that had freed itself from the hooded shawl; and with one wild leap he tore through the smithy door, along the boreen, and in a moment had the fainting girl in his arms. He raised her weakened and emaciated form as if it were a child's, and bringing it into the house, he laid it on his mother's bed, and shouted in a suppressed whisper:

'Mother, quick, quick! A little milk at wanst. An' a dhrop of sperrits in it!'

The mother, amazed at his temerity, was too panic-stricken to remonstrate. She only moaned and lamented over the fire:

'Oh, Lord, Lord! he has lost his five sinses, an brought the faver and aguey into the house! Oh, Red, Red, what's come over you at all, at all?'

'Mother', he cried in a hoarse whisper, bending down his face to hers, 'if Nodlag dies, I'll never forgive you, living or dead!'

'Nodlag! Yerra, glory be to God! your sinses are wandering, boy. Nodlag! what Nodlag?'

But Redmond saw no time was to be lost in asking or answering questions. He put a small tin vessel of milk hastily on the fire, and went over to the cupboard to get the bottle of whiskey. As he did, he took a swift, secret look at the poor girl. To all appearance she was dead. Her shawl had been flung aside, and her features were now quite visible. But, oh! What a dread change! Beneath the cheek-bones, her face had sunk in in dreadful hollows, and her neck was thin and withered. There was a blue line across her lips. Her forehead (though her temples were sunken), and the thick masses of auburn hair that crowned it, alone retained their graciousness.[13]

---

12   Beautiful.

13   In much Famine fiction a young woman's hair is the only physical attribute which retains its former beauty and by which she can be recognized by relatives or friends despite her sunken frame. For instance, in Margaret Brew's *The Chronicles of Castle Cloyne; or Pictures of the Munster People*, vol. 2, Oonagh only recognizes a starving, diseased girl as her cousin Susie because of her 'rich golden hair that even sickness or neglect could not deprive of its silky gloss' (p. 280).

The young smith poured some spirits into the black, hollow palm of his hand, and rubbed the blue lips lightly with his fingers. This he repeated several times, only interrupting the process to go over and dip his grimy finger into the vessel containing the milk, to test its warmth. After some time he had the satisfaction of seeing a slight colour come back to the marble face. He then took up the vessel of milk, and said to the weeping and distressed mother:

'Mother, for the love of God, keep quiet! This is no time for keening. Here, lift Nodlag's head, and lemme see if I can get a drop of milk into her mouth!'

The mother, with some fear, yet with many an endearing Irish expression, raised the head of the poor girl, whilst Redmond tried to force a little milk between her lips. For some time the attempt was ineffectual, and life seemed to be flickering under the broad wings of death, as a candle-flame flickers blue and thin in a strong wind. But at last she swallowed a teaspoon of the milk, then another, and another, until at length her eyes opened, and fell first upon the face of the young smith. She continued to gaze at him earnestly for a few seconds, then she whispered, 'Red!' and lay back wearily, yet refreshed, on the pillow. Though it was like the opening of the gates of Paradise to Red Casey, he went out and wept like a child.

Andrew Merry (Mildred Darby) (1867–1932)

In 1889, Anglo-Irish author Mildred Darby (1867–1932), née Dill, married Jonathan Darby, becoming mistress of Leap Castle in Co. Offaly. Little is known about her life. Darby is nowadays mostly remembered for her writings on the occult; she claimed that Leap Castle was the haunt of a ghastly apparition she termed 'the Elemental', 'the thing', or simply 'It'.[1]

Writing pseudonymously as Andrew Merry, she published novels such as *An April Fool* (1898), *The Green Country* (1902) and *Anthropoid Apes* (1908), as well as short stories such as 'Kilman Castle: The House of Horror' (1908), which is based on the supernatural phenomena she believed to have witnessed at Leap Castle.[2] After the publication of *The Hunger* (1910), her husband Jonathan, who disapproved of his wife's literary career, forced Darby to cease publishing her work.[3] On 30 July 1922, during the Irish Civil War, the ancestral castle was set alight by the IRA, and in the conflagration a good deal of Darby's unpublished writings were lost.[4]

Although Darby was a Protestant and had been raised in England, Andrew Tierney argues that she should be considered a Celtic Revivalist; she endorsed the nationalist resistance to Ireland's colonization and in *The Green Country* 'expressed a deep sympathy for the mystic rituals of Catholicism'.[5] The most sustained demonstration of her deep interest in Irish history and customs is *The Hunger*, Darby's account of the Famine. Although Darby did not experience the Famine herself, she extensively researched the local impact of the Famine and emphatically asserts that her narrative is based on eyewitness accounts: 'every incident is fact, not fiction'.[6] Darby was aware of the lasting impact of the Famine not only upon those who witnessed the event, but also on the following

---

1   A. Tierney, 'The Gothic and the Gaelic: Exploring the Place of Castles in Ireland's Celtic Revival', *International Journal of Historical Archaeology*, 8, 3 (September 2004), pp. 195–6.

2   M. Byrne, 'Mrs Mildred Darby', *The Contribution of Offaly Writers to Irish Literature*, Offaly Historical and Archaeological Society, February 2007, http://www.offalyhistory.com/articles/252/1/ The-Contribution-of-Offaly-Writers-to-Irish-Literature/Page1.html.

3   Tierney, 'Gothic and the Gaelic', p. 197.

4   N. Guerin, 'Darbys of Leap', *Irish Midlands Ancestry*, 2007, http://www.irishmidlandsancestry.com/content/family_history/families/darbys.htm.

5   Tierney, 'Gothic and the Gaelic', p. 194. According to Tierney, '[t]he extant evidence strongly suggests that Darby suffered from acute colonial guilt.'

6   A. Merry, *The Hunger: Being Realities of the Famine Years in Ireland, 1845–48* (London: Andrew Melrose, 1910), p. 2.

generations. As she states in the preface to *The Hunger*, the pain and anger towards the British colonizer live on 'not only in the hearts of the actual victims of the famine, but quite as strongly in the breasts of their descendants'.[7]

Like some other novels from this period, *The Hunger* constitutes what might almost be called a systematic catalogue of the horrors of the Famine. It focuses on the absentee landlord Lord Torrabegh, who returns to his estate in Ireland during the Famine and experiences a conflict between his eagerness to return to England to escape the suffering and the moral imperative to run his estate and assist in providing relief. This struggle is also played out between Torrabegh and his nephew Reginald, who devotes himself entirely to his charitable efforts, as the passage below makes clear. Though written by a Protestant, the novel is largely non-sectarian in its sympathies: Protestants, Quakers and Catholics all play important roles in providing relief to the famishing community.

From *The Hunger: Being Realities of the Famine Years in Ireland, 1845–48*

(London: Andrew Melrose, 1910), pp. 129–37.

When a man has been absent from a neighbourhood for over thirty years, he does not find it easy to pick up the threads of his old life; when his exile has been self-chosen, the resumption of past interests is yet more difficult.[8]

In addition to all this, the time the self-exiled man had chosen to revisit Ireland was exceedingly inauspicious. No matter how self-centred a man

---

7   Ibid., p. 7.
8   Lord Torrabegh is a clear example of the so-called absentee landlord who chooses to reside in England, rather than on his Irish estate. As we can read in the anonymous *What Have the Whigs Done for Ireland? Or the English Whigs and the Irish Famine* (Dublin: Edward J. Milliken, 1851): 'The nobleman was generally a recognised and confirmed absentee; and as many of the gentry as could, followed his example, and those who from necessity or inclination remained at home, looked on themselves rather as the occupiers of a hostile country than the citizens of a well-governed state' (p. 10).

might be, it was difficult not to feel the effects of the culmination of misery, which had resulted in the dread and dire famine raging over the whole Island. From the other side of St George's Channel[9] it had seemed ridiculous that part of the British Isles should be threatened by actual want of any food. Scarcity of food there might perhaps be – such an unheard-of thing elsewhere had indeed been known more than once in Ireland, the land where the impossible was generally what occurred. But that all the food on the market should be consumed, and the people die in hundreds from sheer starvation, while a bountiful harvest was actually being reaped and stored, exceeded the wildest imagining of any ordinary brain. Mad Irishmen, it was true, had arisen in Parliament and in other public places to prophesy some such absurdity the year before – but their words were disregarded by the vast majority of sensible men, and treated much as Jonah's prophesying must have been treated by the man in the street in Nineveh of old.[10] Yet every warning note they had struck, was already more than justified – they had spoken of privation amounting to famine being probable in *many* districts if the potato crop was not a good one.[11] Now a few short weeks after the Blight had for the second time smitten the land, the *whole* Island was in the throes of a famine, the extent of which, the universality of which was simply appalling. What wonder that the lord of many famine-stricken acres should feel depressed?

'One thing I am determined upon, Gavin. Another week I will not remain in the Island! If my nephew likes to make a cross between a Scripture Reader and a Soup Distributor of himself, he may. However, I fail to see any reason for my remaining. I shall go back to London this week. There are at most but a handful amongst all the people round I ever wish to see again, so my farewells will not be a tax. You might write a few letters

---

9   The Irish Sea between Great Britain and Ireland.

10   The Biblical prophet Jonah was commanded by God to preach to the citizens of Nineveh and order them to mend their ways. Darby's use of this parallel is erroneous, because no sooner had Jonah finished his preaching than the citizens of Nineveh repented, upon which God decided to spare the city: 'And the people of Nineveh believed God. They called for a fast and put on sackcloth, from the greatest of them to the least of them.' Jonah 3:5.

11   Ironically, the Irish themselves were often held responsible for not being better able to prepare for a return of the blight. Charles Driscoll, for example, argues in a sermon given in 1847 that the Irish are 'nationally uncalculating and light-hearted' and display much 'improvidence' even in these times of Famine. *The Duty of Showing Mercy to the Afflicted* (London: Hatchard & Sons, 1847), p. 21. Writers such as Sir Lucius O'Brien refuted the idea that the Irish could have prevented the large-scale starvation, claiming that 'no prudence' on the farmers' part, 'no foresight could have averted such a calamity'. *Ireland; The Late Famine and the Poor Laws* (London: Hatchard and Son, 1848), p. 2.

for me and ask one or two of my friends to dine here – let me see – yes, the day after to-morrow, Gavin! Tell them it is to say good-bye to me. For Reggie or no Reggie I have made up my mind to go to England at the end of the week.' . . .

Reginald Armstrong came into the room as the Agent left it. The only remark his uncle made to him was that he looked tired, and no wonder, the old man added testily, when he forgot to come home for his proper meals at the right time!

'Not tired exactly, uncle', the young man replied. 'A bit used up. One thing is true, though, I *am* hungry. At least I can eat my luncheon with every feeling of satisfaction. I am so sorry I am late again, uncle, but the delay has given me a better appetite, I am the hungrier for it! At least one hardly likes to use the word hungry for so very mild a feeling – when real Hunger hits one in the face on every side! As I have seen it this morning we – you and I – have never known real Hunger.' . . .

'The doctors have a busy time before them, and so have the grave-diggers', said Lord Torrabegh grimly. 'But everyone else is stagnating in this country. Why will you not come back to England with me, Reggie, and leave this plague-smitten Island until it is swept clean by death?'

'You would not ask me, uncle, if you saw what I have seen to-day. If you really knew what a lot there is for everyone to do here you would not ask me to leave. I only wish I had gone in for a profession – had begun to qualify as a doctor! Oh! I do so admire McClusky, he is such a grand fellow, it shames me to see how he works both day and night. In addition to his ordinary dispensary work he may at any time be called – generally at night – to go to help the village wise-women.'

'Spare me the details, Reggie. I declare you talk like an old woman at a mothers' meeting.'

The young man flushed under his uncle's bantering glance.

'I beg your pardon, uncle, for mentioning the subject if it disgusts you. When McClusky told me it struck me as so – so pitiful, and I thought it might interest you, for it is rather a curious fact, now is it not?'

'What else did you do with yourself this morning?' his uncle asked, ignoring the question.

'Miss Goodbody came across a most frightful case yesterday evening quite late', said the young fellow. 'She was passing by an out-of-the-way cabin where two old brothers lived – nice old fellows she knew in a way –

just to say good-day to, as she passed, and to whom she had often nodded. One is what they call a "widowman" in these parts, his wife and children all dead long ago, the other an old bachelor who had never time to be bothered with a wife, so he had told Barbara. Well, it struck her, as she had not seen or heard anything of these old men for a couple or three weeks, that she had better turn aside when passing by, to visit their cabin. They live down a boreen[12] a hundred yards or so off the high road. She found the cabin door shut, saw no smoke coming out of the chimney, and no one answered her repeated knocking. When at last she lifted the latch and went in, a fearful sight met her eyes. Both of the old men were lying stretched out on the bare earthen floor of the cabin – too enfeebled by starvation to get up or move a hand to help themselves. They must have died if they had been unaided before this morning, but Barbara Goodbody like an – '

'An "angel of light"? Of course she did wonders for them. There, there, eat your own food and don't season it with too many horrors of this starvation sort. I understand you took a message from the little Quakeress[13] to the doctor with a medical relief ticket for him to go and see them?'

'Yes, and then I rode on to tell Father Spain about the poor old fellows. They are both Roman Catholics, and Miss Goodbody promised them she would get the priest for them. I could not see Father John, but I met the little curate, Father Toby; that was just as good, for he said he would see to the matter immediately. Then I went back to Fergus McClusky and helped him by making up a lot of ointment for him.'

'Ointment?' exclaimed Lord Torrabegh. 'What will you do next? Ointment for – for – nasty contagious complaints? On my word, Reggie, I trust you stopped short at rubbing it on? I wish you would not rush into the dangers you do. Before you know where you are you will be catching some horrible disease; worse, bringing one back for *me* to catch! I hear smallpox is lately added to the long list of prevalent disorders, and although your parent – quite illegally by the way – had you inoculated

---

12 A narrow rural road.

13 The Quakers, also known as the Society of Friends, were crucial in providing relief to the starving community, especially after the British government curtailed its measures to combat starvation after 1846. The Quakers did not use their relief schemes for proselytization purposes, unlike many other (Protestant) charitable organizations. See Miriam Moffitt's *Soupers & Jumpers: The Protestant Missions in Connemara 1848–1937* (Dublin: Nonsuch Press, 2008). For a contemporary account of such relief efforts, see *Transactions of the Central Relief Committee of the Society of Friends During the Famine in 1846 and 1847* (Dublin: Hodges & Smith, 1852).

when you were a child – it does not follow you won't fall a victim to the plague.'[14]

Reginald laughed at his uncle's horrified face.

'Don't alarm yourself, my dear uncle. I did not apply my manufacture. The ointment I made was some mild and soothing unguent Fergus prescribed for the children, so many have been lately breaking out all over their bodies with appalling looking sores. Nothing catching, dear uncle; don't seem so upset. Painful enough for the unfortunate infants, all the same. Some of them had not a square inch of sound skin over their bodies. I declare it was a heartrending sight to see the mothers, gaunt and drawn in the face themselves, bringing in these unfortunate infants, wrapped up in coarse rags which must have given excruciating pain to their inflamed bodies.'

'We must double our subscription to the dispensary, eh?' Lord Torrabegh was moved in spite of his disgust.

'Yes, do, uncle. McClusky has to buy all the medicines and lint and bandages himself. I wish you could see how tenderly he dressed these babes with the ointment and soft rags – gentle and tender to the veriest beggar child, as if he were treating the infant of some great man.'

'I am very glad I did not see him all the same, thank you, Reggie', his uncle shuddered. 'But I will tell Gavin to double our subscription at once. Are you sure the – the – eruptions you describe so – realistically are not contagious, my dear lad? What would I do if I had you without a sound piece of skin – eh?'

'Not a bit catching, but probably due to bad food and want of food.' Reginald unconsciously spoke in imitation of McClusky's brusque manner. 'The doctor thinks this form of systematic disturbance – big boils and angry sores breaking out are the symptoms – is entirely due to the use of the Indian meal. The children's stomachs cannot stand it. For the matter of that, it has been in a great measure the reason for all the dysentery going, McClusky declares! However, what can these people do but give their children the cheapest food they can get?'

---

14 During the Famine, more victims died as a result of infectious diseases than of starvation as such. Malnutrition compromises the immune system, paving the way for epidemic diseases including dysentery, relapsing fever and tuberculosis. See J. Mokyr and C. Ó Gráda, 'What Do People Die of During Famines: The Great Famine in Comparative Perspective', *European Review of Economic History*, 6 (2002), pp. 339–63.

'Slieve Foy'

It is unknown who was behind the pseudonym 'Slieve Foy'. Slieve Foy, or Sliabh Feá in Irish, is the highest peak of the mountain ridge known collectively as Carlingford Mountain, Co. Louth. According to local legend, the mountain is in fact the sleeping giant Fionn mac Cumhail (Finn McCool). The reason why the author behind Slieve Foy chose this name is shrouded in mystery; certainly, none of the stories in the collection *Stories of Irish Life, Past and Present* provide any clues.

Apart from this collection, Slieve Foy published at least two more works: *An Unnatural Mother* (1911) and *Mrs McIvor's 'Paying Guests' and Other People* (1920). Some of the stories in *Stories of Irish Life* first appeared in the Dublin-based journals *Weekly Freeman* and *Irish Emerald*.[1] 'Attie and His Father', here reproduced in part, is set in Co. Kerry in 1847 and tells the story of the destitute John Sullivan and his family. Sullivan's poverty forces him to take his children and mother to the poorhouse while he sets out for Dublin to find employment. When he returns to the workhouse he finds his son Attie dying of fever. Like many other Famine texts by authors who did not (consciously) experience the Famine, 'Attie and His Father' draws upon a store of stock themes and recurring images, including the scene given below, which is a harrowing version of the typical deathbed scene often found in Famine fiction.

From 'Attie and His Father', in *Stories of Irish Life, Past and Present*

(London: Lynwood & Co., 1912), pp. 45–7, 52–5.

When, at length, the grandmother lay down on her poor bed, it was with a feeling akin to what she might have experienced had she

---

1 S.J.M. Brown, *Ireland in Fiction* (Dublin: Maunsel & Company, 1919), p. 14.

descended alive into an open grave, and heard the clink of spades that were soon to cover her with clay.

Her unutterable depression brought on a deep sleep, in which she dreamed that she stood in a wide sandy plain, between two rows of skeleton trees.[2] The whole scene lay in a weird light, that showed an encircling range of coal-black hills, on which multitudes of men, women, and children, walked about in their death-clothes. To her horror, she saw coming towards her, down between the naked trees, a hideous skeleton, of gigantic size, clothed in black, and wearing a badge, on which the word 'hunger' was written in large white letters.[3] She fell prone, and awaited her doom, every moment expecting to feel the monster's foot on her neck. She tried to move her lips in prayer that she might die, but could not move them. Oh, the agony of that interminable suspense! Then a voice, but of thrilling sweetness, sounded in her ears. So full were its accents of tenderness, that she felt it must be the voice of Christ the Lord. She was told to rise and fear not.

Penetrated to the depths of her soul with a feeling of unspeakable happiness, she quickly obeyed. All was changed. In her dream, the ghastly light was succeeded by one that was full of life and joy. Large, lovely stars were visible, in a blue and rose-coloured sky; the trees were in leaf, while crowds of primroses and violets did homage at their feet. A meadow stretched where the sand had been; beautifully rounded green hills were covered with numerous flocks of sheep and lambs, whose fleeces were white as the white clouds that float in the summer sunshine. Raising her eyes, she saw one of the bright stars open, then Attie's mother, resplendent in glory, came forth, and beckoned her to come.

The grandmother awoke, and a smile passed over her face.

'God pardon me', she said, 'fur bein' so cast down wid me sorra.' She fell asleep, and did not dream again that night.

---

2   The foreboding dream often features in Famine fiction. Compare, for instance, Brigid Lavelle's dream of being judged by a black-winged angel in Rosa Mulholland's story 'The Hungry Death', included in this collection.

3   This particular image is reminiscent of newspaper cartoons published after the Famine. See, for instance, J.D. Reigh's drawing 'Ireland Wrestles with Famine While Mr Balfour Plays Golf' from *United Ireland*, 23 August 1890. The picture, published during the Land Wars, shows Erin, personified as a woman, wrestling with a maliciously grinning skeleton on whose shroud the words 'BLIGHT' and 'FAMINE' are printed.

In the morning, before John Sullivan left to procure a horse and cart, his mother, who could not walk without assistance, asked him to help her outside, that she might take a farewell look at the old places, so he left her seated on a chair in front of the house.

It was a beautiful dawn, and the land was flushed with golden light. Around, shone the green flames of furze and fern. In the distance the great azure sky bent down to lave her forehead in the deep blue sea that lay like a broad band between the horizon and the valley that stretched to the foot of the mountain, on whose side the grandmother had dwelt so long. Every spot of the landscape was endeared by some association of her youthful days, and memory kept flying over the past, now here, now there, but still returned without a token from the bygone years. The last sight – if we know it to be the last – of anything we are bound to by tender recollections, is intensely sad. Mrs Sullivan was sustained in this bitter hour by the remembrance of the wonderful dream, or rather vision, of the previous night. She believed her end was near, and looked forward to the inevitable hour with unbounded trust. The Valley of Death is only dark to those who contemplate it without hope, and the greatest sorrows are best borne by those who view them in the light that falls from the Cross.

. . .

When John reached the poorhouse,[4] he was informed that his dear old mother had gone to her rest ten days after her admission to the infirmary.

The children – what of them?

The girls were well; but the little boy had caught scarlet fever, and was not likely to recover. The father's face blanched; he trembled, and grew cold. After all agonising delay, he was allowed to go to the sick ward.

---

4   During the Famine the poorhouses were unable to accommodate the many destitute who had been evicted from their homes. As Asenath Nicholson wrote in *Annals of the Irish Famine in 1847, 1848 and 1849* (New York: E. French, 1851): 'Before the famine they were many of them quite interesting objects for a stranger to visit, generally kept clean, not crowded, and the food sufficient. But when famine advanced, when funds decreased, when the doors were besieged by imploring applicants, who wanted a place to die, that they might be buried in a coffin, they were little else than charnel houses, while the living, shivering skeletons that squatted upon the floors … added a horror if not terror to the sight' (p. 166).

There lay Attie, beautiful as an angel, his cheeks aglow, his broad blue eyes wide open, his gold curls on the pillow. Soon the child's arms were round his father's neck, and fond kisses were imprinted on his own little burning mouth.[5]

'Thank God, thank God, my darlin' looks so well', exclaimed John in the fullness of his heart.

'See what I've brought to sonny', he continued, producing the whistle.

The child smiled, seized the toy and raised it to his lips, but could emit no sound. This was disappointing. Several attempts were made – always the same result.

'It's dumb, faser', said Attie in a low, husky voice, as he examined the whistle to find what was wrong in the workmanship.

There was still the whip. Surely, it would not fail to give satisfaction. John held onto his hand to give Attie an opportunity of testing the excellence of this present.

'Don't strike hard, sonnie', he said, in an undertone.

On receiving a faint lash, he drew his hand hastily back, exclaiming: 'Thunder an' 'ouns but that's tarrible.'

Attie was radiant. This little by-play between father and child was enacted so quietly, that only the patient in the next bed could tell what was going on.

In a little while the whip dropped from Attie's hand, and he fell back exhausted. The excitement of seeing his father over, his dangerous condition became at once apparent.

John instinctively looked about, as if for a place of refuge.

He had the feeling of a hunted animal when it first hears the cry of the pursuing hounds. The feeling was but momentary. With yearning love, he passed the night in attending to his sick child. The most skilful nurse could not have excelled this hard-handed man in deftness and lightness of ministration.

---

5   This idealized depiction of the dying child victim of hunger and disease is common in Famine fiction. Compare, for example, Mrs Hoare's 'Little Mary' from *Shamrock Leaves; or Tales and Sketches of Ireland* (Dublin: J. M'Glashan, 1851) in which a toddler who dies of sickness and starvation is described as 'quite still, with her little hands crossed on her lap, and her head drooping on her chest' (p. 92). See also *A Tale of the Irish Famine in 1846 and 1847, Founded on Fact* (Reigate: William Allingham, 1847) by 'Ireland', in which the starving child Mona is 'a golden haired … fair angel-like child' (p. 25) who passes away quietly.

Morning brought no hope to the heart of the watcher. A great change had taken place, the fever had subsided, but daylight fell on waxen eyelids, and death-like calm of cheek and brow.

The nurse came, as she had done often during the night. She looked upon the dying child, moistened his lips, smoothed his golden hair, and turned aside to hide her springing tears. The distracted father wrung his hands, and hung over the little sufferer, pouring out words of love and despair.

'Me whee, tindher pet, can I do nothing to aise ye? Pulse o' me heart, life will be black when yir taken away.' Then, when he heard that ominous sound in the throat, the import of which we all know so well, he flung up his arms in frantic supplication, crying out, 'Oh, God! oh, God! will he die?' and fell senseless on the floor. ...

Yes, Attie was dead. There was no dressing of the bed, no assembling of relations to speak of the departed, as one too bright and good to live – an unconscious, but common, sarcasm on those spared to make the pilgrimage of life. The body was washed, the limbs composed, the hands folded on the breast, and the gold curls arranged on the brow. The beautiful, dead child looked the embodiment of a holy prayer.

Five or six old women stood round the bed, and a soft light stole into their careworn faces as they contemplated the lovely remains. Evidently, their thoughts were lifted to that life in which there were no poor. A ray of sunshine, happening to stream in, so irradiated Attie's head and face that one of the women said suddenly: 'I'll go an' see, wud his father be able to come, the sight iv the blessed chile will do his heart good.'

John was brought. With a wild, haggard look he approached the spot where his darling lay.

'Hid yi ivir see a sight like that since yi wur born?' asked one of the poor creatures in a low voice, as she caught hold of the father's arm. 'Don't yi see by that smile, that he saw Heaven open to him before his sowl wus out o' the body? Would ye grudge him to the Lord, that has left yi sich a token o' yer chile's bliss?'

'I don't grudge him to the Lord, Nancy. Praise be to Him fur ivir an ivir. He gev' an' He has tuk away; but it's hard to part wid him that wus the light o' me life, an' I feel as if me heart wus broke.'

'An' na blame to yi', at all, at all', said one of the sympathisers. 'Iv coorse, its hard on ye, ye poor crathur.'

Sullivan knelt down, and buried his face in the pallet at Attie's feet; and his frame heaved, with the great sobs that expressed his grief.

The door of the ward was thrown open, by a man who carried a small, rude coffin, which he placed in an unoccupied bed, where one of the old women considerately covered it, until the father could be got away.

Golden Hills and Blackened Fields

AN EASTERLY WIND BLIGHTING THE IRISH PIKE CROP.

'AN EASTERLY WIND BLIGHTING THE IRISH PIKE CROP.'
By P. Gavarni, *Puppet Show*, 14 October 1848, p. 57.

William Carleton (1794–1869)

William Carleton was born on 24 February 1794 in Clogher, Co. Tyrone, as the youngest of fourteen children in an Irish-speaking Catholic tenant family. As the family moved frequently, Carleton was educated at a variety of hedge schools, and at a grammar school in Donagh, Co. Monaghan. Initially intending to enter the priesthood, he abandoned this plan when he was 19, and eventually converted to Protestantism. He held a variety of odd jobs, working as a tutor, a taxidermist, and a clerk, and contributed to the *Christian Examiner*, an anti-Catholic newspaper. His fame was secured with the publication of *Traits and Stories of the Irish Peasantry* (1830–33), a two-volume collection of stories and vignettes about lower-class Irish life. Carleton's social and political opinions vacillated: though initially the pet of Irish Evangelicals because of his publications in the *Christian Examiner* and his anti-Catholic collection *Traits and Stories*, he alienated many of his Protestant supporters by publishing *Valentine M'Clutchy* (1845), whose villains are 'a group of loutish Orangemen'.[1]

Because of his background, he had an intimate knowledge of the Irish peasantry as it was before the Famine nearly obliterated its traditional way of life, and according to critics, in his depictions of this particular class, he is 'unrivalled'.[2] In a long essay in the *Edinburgh Review* entitled 'Traits of the Irish Peasantry' (1852), for instance, Patrick Murray states that '[i]t is among the peasantry that Mr Carleton is truly at home.'[3] Nowadays, however, many of Carleton's portrayals of the Irish – usually in a comic register – seem somewhat crude; indeed, as John Sutherland also points out, 'Carleton popularised the Paddy stereotype.'[4] Carleton died in Co. Dublin in 1869.[5]

Carleton experienced the Famine from close-by, and wrote extensively about the event, most notably in his novels *The Squanders of Castle Squander*

---

1 C. Morash, *Writing the Irish Famine* (Oxford: Clarendon Press, 1995), p. 156.
2 P. Murray, 'Traits of the Irish Peasantry', *Edinburgh Review*, 69, 196 (October 1852), p. 386.
3 Ibid.
4 J. Sutherland, *The Longman Companion to Victorian Fiction* (London: Longman, 1988), p. 106.
5 This biographical sketch is based on J. Kelly, 'Carleton, William (1794–1869)', *Oxford Dictionary of National Biography*, Oxford University Press, 2004, online edn, 2007, http://www.oxforddnb.com/view/article/4679; and Sutherland, *Longman Companion to Victorian Fiction*, pp. 106–7.

(1852) and the story 'Owen M'Carthy; or the Landlord and Tenant', published in *Alley Sheridan and Other Stories* (1857), in which farmer Owen 'by toil and exertion' first manages to make a decent living but is beaten down by the blight and 'the united visitations of disease and scarcity'.[6] Carleton's most popular Famine text is the earlier *The Black Prophet* (1847). Subtitled 'A Tale of Irish Famine' and published at the height of the crisis, the story is nonetheless set in 1817, during an earlier famine.[7]

The Black Prophet of the title is the dangerous vagrant Donnel Dhu, who foresees the advent of famine and loudly proclaims his prophecies where he goes. As Christopher Morash argues in *Writing the Irish Famine* (1995), 'Donnel Dhu... is the antithesis of both progress and narrative';[8] yet, as Morash himself also points out, although the novel can to a certain extent be read as an allegorical depiction of the political and social tensions that plagued Ireland during the Famine, it is not an unequivocally symbolical rendering of the crisis. The selection below is a good example of Dhu's divinations, which are followed by a harrowing description of the calm before the storm.

From *The Black Prophet: A Tale of Irish Famine*

(London: Simms & M'Intyre, 1847), pp. 20–4.

'Throth, at any rate', replied Sullivan, 'I didn't care we had back the war prices again; aither that, or that the dear rents were let down to meet the poor prices we have now.[9] This woeful saison, along wid the low prices

---

6 W. Carleton, 'Owen M'Carthy; or the Landlord and Tenant', in *Alley Sheridan and Other Stories* (Dublin: P. Dixon Hardy & Sons, 1858), pp. 136–7.

7 In the summers of 1816 and 1817, extremely cold, wet weather destroyed the crops and led to a small-scale famine. See D. MacKay, *Flight from Famine: The Coming of the Irish to Canada* (Toronto, ON: National Heritage Books, 1990), p. 28. As a result, as Henry Mayhew writes in *London Labour and the London Poor* (London: G. Woodfall, 1851), there was a 'great influx of the Irish into London ... in the year of the famine, 1817–8' (p. 12).

8 Morash, *Writing the Irish Famine*, p. 164.

9 As the novel is set in 1817, Sullivan is most likely referring to the Napoleonic Wars (1803–14).

and the high rents, houlds out a black and terrible look for the counthry, God help us!'

'Ay', returned the Black Prophet, for it was he, 'if you only knew it.'

'Why, was that, too, prophesied?' inquired Sullivan.

'Was it? No; but ax yourself is it. Isn't the Almighty in his wrath, this moment proclaimin' it through the heavens and the airth? Look about you, and say what is it you see that does not foretell famine – famine – famine! Doesn't the dark wet day, an' the rain, rain, rain, foretell it? Doesn't the rottin' crops, the unhealthy air, an' the green damp foretell it? Doesn't the sky without a sun, the heavy clouds, an' the angry fire of the West, foretell it? Isn't the airth a page of prophecy, an' the sky a page of prophecy, where every man may read of famine, pestilence, an' death? The airth is softened for the grave, an' in the black clouds of heaven you may see the death-hearses movin' slowly along funeral afther funeral – funeral afther funeral – an' nothing to folly them but lamentation an' woe, by the widow an' orphan – the fatherless, the motherless, an' the childless – wo an' lamentation – lamentation an' wo.'

Donnel Dhu, like every prophecy man of his kind – a character in Ireland, by the way, that has nearly, if not altogether, disappeared – was provided with a set of prophetic declamations suited to particular occasions and circumstances, and these he recited in a voice of high and monotonous recitative, that caused them to fall with a very impressive effect upon the minds and feeling of his audience. In addition to this, the very nature of his subject rendered a figurative style and suitable language necessary, a circumstance which, aided by a natural flow of words, and a felicitious illustration of imagery – for which, indeed, all prophecy-men were remarkable – had something peculiarly fascinating and persuasive to the class of persons he was in the habit of addressing. The gifts of these men, besides, were exercised with such singular delight, that the constant repetition of their oracular exhibitions by degrees created an involuntary impression on themselves, that ultimately rose to a kind of wild and turbid enthusiasm, partaking at once of imposture and fanaticism. Many of them were, therefore, nearly as much the dupes of the delusions that proceeded from their own heated imaginations as the ignorant people who looked upon them as oracles; for we know that nothing at all events so much generates imposture as credulity.

'Indeed, Donnel', replied Sullivan, 'what you say is unfortunately too thrue. Everything we can look upon appears to have the mark of God's displeasure on it;[10] but if we have death and sickness now, what'll become of us this time twelve months, when we'll feel this failure most?'

'I have said it,' replied the prophet; 'an' if my tongue doesn't tell truth, the tongue that never tells a lie will.'

'And what tongue is that?' asked his companion.

'The tongue of the death-bell will tell it day afther day to every parish in the land. However, we know that death's before us, an' the grave, afther all, is our only consolation.'

'God help us', exclaimed Sullivan, 'if we hadn't betther and brighter consolation than the grave. Only for the hopes in our Divine Redeemer an' his mercy, it's little consolation the grave could give us. But indeed, Donnel, as you say, everything about us is enough to sink the heart within one – an' no hope at all of a change for the betther. However, God is good, and if it's His will that we should suffer, it's our duty to submit to it.'

The prophet looked around him with a gloomy aspect, and, truth to say, the appearance of everything on which the eye could rest, was such as gave unquestionable indications of wide-spread calamity to the country.

The evening, which was now far advanced, had impressed on it a character of such dark and hopeless desolation as weighed down the heart with a feeling of cold and chilling gloom that was communicated by the dreary aspect of every thing around. The sky was obscured by a heavy canopy of low, dull clouds that had about them none of the grandeur of storm, but lay overhead charged with those wintry deluges which we feel to be so unnatural and alarming in autumn, whose bounty and beauty they equally disfigure and destroy. The whole summer had been sunless and wet – one, in fact, of ceaseless rain which fell, day after day, week after week, and month after month, until the sorrowful consciousness had arrived that any change for the better must now come too late, and that nothing was certain but the terrible union of famine, disease, and death which was to follow. The season, owing to the causes specified, was necessarily late, and such of the crops as were ripe had a sickly and unthriving look, that told of

---

10   The notion that the Famine was a form of divine punishment for Irish misbehaviour was widespread. A well-known example of this type of rhetoric is the work of the Protestant Revd Hugh McNeile, who in his *The Famine a Rod of God: Its Provoking Cause – Its Merciful Design* (London: Burnside & Seeley, 1847), a religious tract on the Famine in Ireland, fulminated that '[p]lagues, pestilences, famines, wars are used by God as national punishments for sin. Hear the rod' (p. 8). Carleton's novel is steeped in this type of religious language, even though he is much more ambivalent about this question than hardliners such as McNeile.

comparative failure, while most of the fields which, in our autumns, would have been ripe and yellow, were now covered with a thin, backward crop, so unnaturally green that all hope of maturity was out of the question. Low meadows were in a state of inundation, and on alluvial soils the ravages of the floods were visible in layers of mud and gravel that were deposited over many of the prostrate corn fields. The peat turf lay in oozy and neglected heaps, for there had not been sun enough to dry it sufficiently for use, so that the poor had want of fuel, and cold to feel, as well as want of food itself. Indeed, the appearance of the country, in consequence of this wetness in the firing, was singularly dreary and depressing. Owing to the difficulty with which it burned, or rather wasted away, without light or heat, the eye, in addition to the sombre hue which the absence of the sun cast over all things, was forced to dwell upon the long black masses of smoke which trailed slowly over the whole country, or hung, during the thick sweltering calms, in broad columns that gave to the face of nature an aspect strikingly dark and disastrous, when associated, as it was, with the destitution and suffering of the great body of the people. The general appearance of the crops was indeed deplorable. In some parts the grain was beaten down by the rain; in airier situations it lay cut but unsaved, and scattered over the fields, awaiting an occasional glance of feeble sunshine; and in other and richer soils, whole fields, deplorably lodged, were green with the destructive exuberance of a second growth. The season, though wet, was warm; and it is unnecessary to say that the luxuriance of all weeds and unprofitable production was rank and strong, while an unhealthy fermentation pervaded every thing that was destined for food. A brooding stillness, too, lay over all nature; cheerfulness had disappeared, even the groves and hedges were silent, for the very birds had ceased to sing,[11] and the earth seemed as if it mourned for the approaching calamity, as well as for that which had been already felt. The whole country, in fact, was weltering and surging with the wet formed by the incessant overflow of rivers, while the falling cataracts, joined to a low monotonous hiss, or what the Scotch term *sugh*[12], poured their faint but dismal murmurs on the gloomy silence which otherwise prevailed around.

11　Compare the description of Famine-stricken Ireland in W.H. Smith's *A Twelve Month's Residence in Ireland during the Famine and the Public Works, 1846 and 1847* (London: Longman, Brown and Green & Longmans, 1848): 'the very birds of the air were starved, and the crows could scarcely be alarmed upon the road side, or the unfreqeunt corn stack' (p. 44).

12　Scottish Gaelic *sùgh*, juice or moisture.

Such was the aspect of the evening in question, but as the men advanced, a new element of desolation soon became visible. The sun, ere he sank among the dark western clouds, shot out over this dim and miserable prospect a light so angry, yet so ghastly, that it gave to the whole earth a wild, alarming, and spectral hue, like that seen in some feverish dream. In this appearance there was great terror and sublimity, for as it fell on the black shifting clouds, the effect was made still more awful by the accidental resemblance which they bore to coffins, hearses, and funeral processions, as observed by the prophecy-man, all of which seemed to have been lit up against the deepening shades of evening by some gigantic death-light that superadded its fearful omens to the gloomy scenes on which it fell.

The sun, as he then appeared, might not inaptly be compared to some great prophet, who, clothed with the majesty and terror of an angry God, was commissioned to launch his denunciations against the iniquities of nations, and to reveal to them, as they lay under the shadow of his wrath, the terrible calamities with which he was about to visit their transgressions.

Reginald Tierney (Thomas O'Neill Russell)
(1828–1908)

In *Is Ireland a Dying Nation?* (1906) author, linguist and political activist Thomas O'Neill Russell (1828–1908) laments that his native country 'seems to be dying; to be slowly sinking into the grave' if 'change of the most pronounced and radical kind' does not occur.[1] Being 'partially of English descent... and nowise prejudiced against the British people',[2] Russell promoted Home Rule rather than independence and viewed the rehabilitation of Irish Gaelic as vital for the development of a nationalist consciousness. Russell was not a native speaker of Gaelic, but, working for some years as a foreman at his father's farm in Lissanode, Co. Westmeath, learned the language from local farmers and his father's labourers.

In 1854 Russell began publishing pieces in the *Irishman* to stimulate the revival of Gaelic,[3] and around the same time, to emphasize his allegiance to the Irish nationalist cause, Russell adopted O'Neill, the patronymic of his grandmother, as his middle name.[4] In 1867, fearing that he might be persecuted for his non-violent involvement in the Fenian Rising, Russell emigrated to America, where he continued his efforts in support of the Gaelic revival and delivered lectures at gatherings of Irish-American Gaelic organizations based in New York, such as the Philo-Celtic Society and the Society for the Preservation of the Irish Language.[5] Although he occasionally sojourned in Ireland, tried to place Gaelic on the curriculum for Irish state schools and remained a staunch nationalist throughout his self-chosen exile, Russell lived in the US for the next twenty-six years. When at last he returned to Ireland in 1893, he became a founding member of the Gaelic League.[6]

---

1   T.O. Russell, *Is Ireland a Dying Nation?* (Dublin: M H Gill, 1906), p 1
2   Ibid., p. iii.
3   R. Welch and B. Stewart (eds), *The Oxford Companion to Irish Literature* (Oxford: Oxford University Press, 1996), p. 504.
4   S. Ó Saothraí, 'Russell, Thomas O'Neill (1828–1908)', *Oxford Dictionary of National Biography*, 2004, online edn, 2007, http://www.oxforddnb.com/index/35/101035885.
5   K.E. Nilsen, 'The Irish Language in New York, 1850–1900', in R.H. Bayor and T.J. Meagher (eds), *The New York Irish* (Baltimore, MD: Johns Hopkins University Press, 1996), p. 270.
6   P. Maume, *The Long Gestation: Irish Nationalist Life 1891–1918* (New York: St Martin's Press, 1999), p. 25.

Russell was not only acquainted with such authors and intellectuals as Douglas Hyde and George Moore, but was also a prolific writer and translator in his own right. In his work, he regularly touches upon the painful legacy of the Famine. In *Is Ireland a Dying Nation?* Russell emphasizes the impact of the Famine on Irish history, especially on the minds of those who like himself fully remember and know the awful desolation of those years. In his debut novel *The Struggles of Dick Massey; or, The Battles of a Boy*, first published in 1860 under the pseudonym Reginald Tierney, the eponymous protagonist is a Protestant Anglo-Irish younger son who greatly cares for the famishing tenant farmers, while his family's fortunes are also hit severely by the blight. The novel does not simply depict landlords as the source of all evil and does not envisage a landlordless society, even though it champions reform of the system. The novel promulgates a non-sectarian utopian image of Ireland where all factions are united in their devotion to the country and its heritage, as is underlined by Russell's preface to the second edition: 'it would be a great blessing for Ireland if all its inhabitants – Catholics, Protestants, and Dissenters, would leave off sectarian bickerings and ethnological prejudices, and look on it *as their country*.'[7]

From *The Struggles of Dick Massey; or, The Battles of a Boy*

(Dublin: James Duffy, 1860), pp. 66–7, 75–7.

But we, in the full blaze of the light of these marvellous times, are tasting the bitter fruits of their misdeeds; for where there should be love there is hate; where all should be pulling one way, a hundred are pulling a hundred different ways; and where there should be a thousand warm, peaceful hearths, there range innumerable flocks of sheep and herds of

---

7   T.O. Russell, *The Struggles of Dick Massey; or, The Battles of a Boy* (Dublin: James Duffy, 1860), pp. xii–xiii.

cattle over infinite wastes of grass, – *prairies eternelles*, as Beaumont so justly styled the melancholy plains.[8]

And the people are still flying; flying away from the beauteous isle as though it were the hot-bed, the birthplace of some cursed plague that fastened with deadly gripe upon its victims. Multitudes greater than ever shall be known have whitened the great floor of the Atlantic with their bleached bones.[9] Multitudes as great have laid them down in their long sleep by the far off fever and ague-stricken shores of the St Laurence and Mississippi; or lingered out a miserable existence as the dross of humanity amongst those who hated, pitied, feared, or wondered at them.

Terrible it is that men, the real glory of the earth, should beat a discount, and that quadrupeds – sheep and cattle should be at such a premium; and our politicians tell us we are so much better off than we were; and point out all the millions of four-legged things we have now, more than we had ten years ago; and say we are beginning to be great among the nations, by the loss of those which alone can make a nation, namely, our fellows, MEN!

And farms are growing so enormous that they look like German principalities; hundreds of families once occupied them, and were independent, and had houses, even supposing they were small and humble, to turn to in time of sickness or affliction. They did not grow rich, to be sure; but they lived, and were happy; they were not entirely depending on the caprice of an employer who might dismiss them, and would often, just because he was not in good humour, or wanted to shew he had the power to assert his authority over his fellow-clods.

---

8   As Gustave Beaumont (1802–66), a French magistrate and travel writer, observed in *L'Irlande Sociale, Politique et Religieuse*, vol. 1 (Brussels: Hauman and Co., 1839), 'La plus belle nature manque de vie si le soleil ne l'anime pas: ces montagnes élégantes, ces grands lacs, ces prairies éternelles, ces collines aussi fraîches que les vallées, offrent sans doute des aspects pleins de charme à celui qui par accident les voit sous un beau ciel; mais l'atmosphère de l'Irlande est presque toujours sombre et chargée de nuages ou de vapeurs': 'Even the most beautiful nature lacks life if the sun does not animate it: these elegant mountains, these great lakes, these eternal prairies, these hills which are as cool as the valleys offer, without a doubt, views full of charm to whoever should see them unexpectedly under a clear sky; but the climate of Ireland is almost always sombre and overcast with clouds or mists' (p. 221; our translation).

9   This refers to the many passengers who died during the transatlantic crossing. High mortality rates on board were common, as transpires, for instance, from a report in the *Cork Examiner* of 19 July 1847: 'Captain Thain, of the ship Loosthank, 636 Tons, from Liverpool to Quebec, out 7 weeks, had, when she left Liverpool, 348 passengers on board of which 117 have died, and out of the ship's crew only five are able to work.'

And cities are swelling out into fearful dimensions: the poor man, stripped of his little farm, must go somewhere, and do something: he is weak, or he is sociable, or he is depraved; and the city, with its reeking purlieus, gives him a chance of gratifying his desires; he feels for a time the loss of the pure sunlight, and the blessed uncontaminated breeze of heaven; but then he has only to cross the pestiferous lane, and enter the whisky shop; then God's bright, smoke-unclouded sun, and God's glorious breezes, and the joyous carolling of God's birds are all forgotten.

His children, once fat and rosy, though their food was potatoes, become hideous, lanky things; smoke-dried, poisoned and etiolated; they grow up into 'pins and needles of men and women', and make one shudder at meeting them coming out of their dens, all bleared, and filthy, and wretched – human satyrs[10] instead of what they ought to have been, robust and hardy tillers of the soil.

. . .

We will pass over two or three months, and jump from the glorious days of autumn to the early part of winter. The trees are all stripped of their foliage; and Clonderry, though still beautiful, is not what it was in 'leafy June'; the great hawthorns are still majestic, and even in their nakedness afford the cattle a shelter from the winter winds, nearly as grateful as the shade they afforded from the heats of summer. Still the country is not without its charms even at this time of year. There are no piercing blasts to chill one, and no frost has come to turn the yet green fields into hoary wastes, and if it were not for the bareness of the landscape, one might suppose it is still summer, so mild and balmy are the western breezes.

But a calamity of a new and terrible kind has made its appearance, and many fathers of families looked with gloomy forebodings to the future. The potato rot had commenced; in the early part of autumn many

---

10   In Greek mythology, satyrs are flute-playing companions of Pan or Dionysius. In Roman mythology, satyrs were often depicted as goat-like creatures. The reference to the starving Irish as human satyrs is rather enigmatic. Perhaps the association derives from the fact that satyrs were often represented in rural settings.

diseased tubers were found,[11] but no one felt much alarm believing the blackened spots that now and then made their appearance were caused by accident; but as the winter came on, and when the digging commenced, there could be no doubt at all of the fearful nature of the disease, that threatened to sweep away nearly the entire crop, and plunge the country into the horrors of famine.

It would have delighted Cobbett,[12] had he risen from the dead, and seen the blackened piles of the 'damned potatoes', as he blasphemously called them, heaped up in almost every field; he would, no doubt, have considered it the greatest blessing that could have arrived, even supposing a million or so of human beings were cut off for want of them; and he would most likely have said, like scores of persons of the present day, who do not possess the tithe of his talent or shrewdness, that it was a just judgment on the people for being content to depend on the 'lowest possible human food', as they are by some still called.[13] It certainly appears rather strange that the 'lowest possible human food' could infuse such 'bone and sinew' into men as were often possessed by very many of those whose sole, or at least, chief food, was potatoes. Compare the potato-fed Irish peasant of twenty years ago, with his rounded limbs, free, firm tread, and erect carriage, with the English labouring man, strangling along in his smock frock and tremendous laced boots; for ever munching cheese and swilling ale. Set them to

---

11 The *Illustrated London News* first reported on the potato disease on 18 October 1845: 'the disease in the potato crop is extending far and wide, and causing great alarm amongst the peasantry'. As Christine Kinealy writes in *A Death-Dealing Famine: The Great Hunger in Ireland* (London: Pluto Press, 1997), '[t]he potato blight was first identified in Ireland at the end of August 1845' (p. 59), and a fuller understanding of the scale of failed crops became evident in September. At the end of the year 'one-third of the crop had been lost to blight' (p. 52).

12 William Cobbett (1763–1835) was an English pamphleteer, farmer and journalist who opposed the Corn Laws and the borough system which impoverished the farm labourers. His *Rural Rides* from 1830 (London: A. Cobbett, 1853) criticizes the greediness of the landlords and the fact that tenants had to pay extremely high rents while getting low prices for their harvests. Interestingly, Cobbett often draws analogies with the equally distressing land system in Ireland: 'I see, in the Irish papers, which have overtaken me on my way, that the system is working the Agriculturasses in "the sister-kingdom" too!... The best members of the farming classes have got so much in arrear in their subscriptions' (p. 8).

13 It was generally believed, as William Henry Smith, for example, voices in *A Twelve Months' Residence in Ireland during the Famine and the Public Works of 1846 and 1847* (London: Longman, Brown & Green, 1848) that the potato was a 'carbonaceous' crop, 'fattening, but not nutritious' (p. 197), and that therefore the Irish at home were less productive than those who went abroad and consumed different food.

perform athletic sports together, and which would come off victorious? How many clodhoppers[14] out of Leicestershire or Dorsetshire would have been able to jump across the hole in the bridge over the 'Big river' of Clonderry? Very few, indeed, perhaps no one. Or set them to work in hay or harvest field, and which would be most likely to have the greatest quantity of hay 'pitched', or of corn reaped by sundown? The fact is that good potatoes were and are good food; and as good men as ever trod on green grass have been fed upon them.

Things were not going on at all pleasantly at Belville of late;[15] Mrs Massey's health was gradually giving way; the immense number of company continually there was too much for her; and the anxiety of seeing after everything within and without was beginning to tell plainly on her not over strong frame. But there was another trouble, the greatest of all, which she was perfectly aware would kill her outright, if not stopped in some way: William, her darling, her spoiled and pampered pet, was drinking harder than ever. He had already had more than one attack of delirium tremens;[16] and frightful were the yells, and awful the imprecations of the unfortunate youth during these terrible intervals. But not one word of reproof did ever mother or sisters say to him. He was silly and weak-minded, though not naturally of an evil disposition; and had he been properly managed and advised at the commencement of his propensity for drink, he would never have filled a drunkard's grave.

Dick was the only one that ever reproved him; but he, poor boy, did not do it aright. Instead of speaking to him gently and affectionately, as brother should reason with brother, his words were all hot and passionate, and did more harm than good. He saw the error he had committed when it was too late; for William was now in the last stage of his earthly career. His eyes were blood-shot, his hands trembled as if he were afflicted with palsy; and his wild and wandering stare told of a mind disordered, a reason overthrown.

---

14 Derogatory term for agricultural labourers; more generally, clumsy people.
15 The name Belville, derived from French, means beautiful town. In this passage the irony of the name of the Massey estate lies in the fact that the family fortunes are decaying rather than blooming.
16 A severe form of alcohol withdrawal that involves mental and neurological disorders.

He died. The darling of sisters and mother was gone – gone, but where? with what an infinity of misery did that monosyllable *where* overwhelm those who loved him but too well in life! God alone knows the bitterness of the tears that are shed despairingly on the drunkard's grave!

His father did not last long after William. He had not left his room for some years, and for a long time had not taken the least part in anything that was going on at Belville. He hailed the approach of death with joy, for his life had been for a length of time one of intolerable pain and suffering.

Often it happens that troubles will stay away from families for a great length of time, and then come so thick and fast that one is no sooner over than it is followed by another. It was so with the Masseys; woes came quick upon them.

Mrs Massey was going fast also. William's death, especially, had given her such a blow that it seemed utterly impossible she could survive it. She had been weak for a long time, but ever since the sad event she was not only weak but perfectly bowed down in mind and body. Poor woman! Hers was a hard fate; to be killed by work, and not having ever done anything!

Kathleen O'Meara (1839–88)

'Yet another tale from one of the most graceful as well as the most diligent pens at present enlisted in the service of the insatiable reading public.'[1] This is how the fifth yearly volume of the *Irish Monthly* (1877) starts its review of Kathleen O'Meara's *The Battle of Connemara*. According to the review, O'Meara's novel is 'a charming story charmingly told', containing very realistic conversions of peasants and 'well defined character', although 'some touches seem . . . very unreal'.[2] O'Meara's representation of local speech is subject to some disapproval, for 'an Irishwoman should know better than fall into a bit of false brogue, of which English writers are often guilty. Our good people do not call for the "*praste*".'[3] Despite these critical remarks, the review ends on a positive note, giving its 'warm appreciation'[4] for the novel. It is quite surprising, then, that notwithstanding this overall positive review in such an influential journal as the *Irish Monthly*, O'Meara novels 'were not widely read in Ireland'.[5] James H. Murphy attributes this to the radical religious views that are expressed in O'Meara's work, contending that the 'confrontationalism', Catholic 'militancy', or 'ultra-montane' streak of her novels have led scholars to ignore them.[6] In this context, it comes as no surprise that early twentieth-century anthologies such as *The Cabinet of Irish Literature* do not feature O'Meara's work. Murphy sees a connection between O'Meara's strong Catholic sentiments and the fact that she lived abroad for the greater part of her life. Residing in Paris allegedly made O'Meara 'eschew the upper middle-class agenda that [she] might have accepted' if she had spent her life in Ireland.[7]

Kathleen O'Meara (1839–88), granddaughter of Napoleon's personal physician on St Helena, Barry Edward O'Meara,[8] and daughter of Dennis

---

1   'Review of Kathleen O'Meara's *The Battle of Connemara*', *The Irish Monthly: A Magazine of General Literature*, 5 (1877), p. 767.
2   Ibid.
3   Ibid.
4   Ibid., p. 768.
5   J.H. Murphy, *Catholic Fiction and Social Reality in Ireland, 1873–1922* (Westport, CT: Greenwood Press, 1997), p. 58.
6   Ibid.
7   Ibid., p. 55.
8   R. Welch and B. Stewart, *The Oxford Companion to Irish Literature* (Oxford: Clarendon, 1996), p. 446

O'Meara of Tipperary,[9] was born in Dublin and was taken to Paris by her parents when still a young girl.[10] Most likely, O'Meara never returned to Ireland, but the Emerald Isle nevertheless figures centrally in much of her fiction. She wrote under the pen-name Grace Ramsay. Several of O'Meara's novels were serialized in the *Irish Monthly*,[11] and besides fiction, she also authored biographies and was Paris correspondent for the Catholic journal *The Tablet.*[12]

The Battle of Connemara is not O'Meara's only conversion narrative: her earlier 1867 novel *A Woman's Trials* also features a heroine who converts to Catholicism.[13] *The Battle of Connemara* is a conventional Catholic gentry novel infused with 'ardently pro-Catholic' elements,[14] which follows the life of Lady Margaret Blake, a benevolent Protestant landlord's wife, who after going through many ordeals in Ireland leaves for Paris. During her time in Ireland, Margaret is already strongly attracted to Catholicism, but it is not until her time in Paris, during which she becomes disenchanted with French Catholicism and consequentially more enamoured of Irish Catholicism, that she changes her creed.

Besides giving ample religious illustrations, the novel also provides its readers with passages concerning the Irish countryside in post-Famine times. The excerpts displayed below are all told from the Revd Ringwood's perspective, and thus provide an English (though sympathetic) view on the Irish landscape. As Simon Schama suggests, landscapes are often representations of what we experience on the inside,[15] and the same goes for O'Meara's envisionings of the strong link between the Irish countryside and its people. The author paints a picture in which the uninhabitable, empty and even eerie Irish landscape reflects the traumatic disappearance of its rural inhabitants in the wake of the Famine.

---

9   Murphy, *Catholic Fiction and Social Reality in Ireland*, p. 57.
10   J. Sutherland, *The Longman Companion to Victorian Fiction* (London: Longman, 1988), p. 479.
11   Welch and Stewart, *Oxford Companion to Irish Literature*, p. 446.
12   Sutherland, *Longman Companion to Victorian Fiction*, p. 479.
13   Ibid.
14   Welch and Stewart, *Oxford Companion to Irish Literature*, p. 446.
15   S. Schama, *Landscape and Memory* (New York: Vintage Books, 1995), p. 12.

From *The Battle of Connemara*

(London: R. Washbourne, 1878), pp. 15–9.

For the first three miles it was the dreariest ride the Rev. Mr Ringwood had ever enjoyed. He had journeyed over the wildest parts of Wales and Scotland – districts where for miles and miles the hills and the heather had it all to themselves – but nothing he had ever seen came near the desolation of this wild Western kingdom. To the right, the Twelve Pins[16] reared their crests to the sky like twelve giants' tombs in the wilderness; nearer – to the left – a low, irregular line of hills stretched on and on, like a wave flowing from one end of the world to the other; between the hills lay the vast tracts of moorland broken up with marble quarries, some exhausted, others opened and long since abandoned; bogs floated amidst lakes of every size and form, dark sheets of glass locked in by the hills, that seemed rather to flow in and out of the lakes than the lakes in and out of them, so still and silent were their waters. 'A spot of dull stagnation'[17] it looked like the fag-end of the world, where the Master had flung aside His tools, and left a remnant of His work unfinished. The road was the only trace of man's presence to be seen; it was a magnificent highway, wide, and smooth as a billiard table, a monument of human labour strangely out of keeping in that forlorn, uninhabited region. The traveller wondered how it came there. Later he learned that it had been made by Government to give employment to the starving people during the great famine.[18] Where were they now, these same people, whom he had come to minister to? Nothing indicated the existence of a living soul within miles. Did they dwell in the bogs, or down below in the water? The very genius of silence seemed

---

16   The Twelve Bens or Twelve Pins ('Na Beanna Beola' in Irish) is a mountain range in Connemara.

17   From Alfred, Lord Tennyson's 'The Palace of Art' (1832): 'A spot of dull stagnation, without light / Or power of movement, seem'd my soul'. See *The Poetical Works of Alfred Tennyson*, Volume 1 (Boston, MA: Ticknor & Fields, 1864), p. 68.

18   This is a reference to the Famine roads which also figure in other writings included in this anthology. For a more detailed description of these road works, see Emily Lawless's 'Famine Roads and Famine Memories' and the accompanying notes, also in this section.

to have taken up its abode in the place.[19] Now and then the wild-fowl skimming over the lakes called to one another; the plover whistled, or the bittern cried; high up in the air an eagle, poised upon a cloud, screamed to his mate in the eyrie below, and then circling round and round, descended and alighted on a rock, for the hills were cleft in every direction by sharp grey rocks; but no human sound, far or near, broke the stillness. …

The name, as it sometimes happens in Ireland, was finer than the dwelling it was intended to describe. The Towers had once upon a time been a grand, semi-barbaric castle; but it was a very long time ago, and age had swept away every vestige of its ancient splendour, except one solitary remnant of an old tower, which retained for the modern house its original high-sounding appellation. It had been used for generations as a hunting lodge; but Mr Dermot Blake, the grandfather of the present owner, having run through a fine property elsewhere, had been compelled to entrench himself in this lonely refuge, and, in order to make the abode less unbearable, had spent the remainder of his diminished income in adding a wing to it. His son retrieved the fortunes of the family by marrying an heiress, and built another wing to the house, which now presented the appearance of a picturesque though rather eccentric building, smothered in creepers, and leaning its whole weight apparently on the one old tower, which, from beneath its broken crown of battlements, looked down upon the new gables and chimney-stacks, somewhat as a proud crusading ancestor might regard a dwarfish but respectable descendant.

The tower was built of cyclopean blocks of granite, whose colour almost disappeared under a heavy drapery of ivy. The rest of the building was composed of a variety of stones from the neighbouring quarries, dark-blue and predominating. Heterogeneous as the elements were, the whole was not wanting in harmony; and as the English priest[20] walked his jaded steed up the steep ascent leading to Bangmore Park, he thought he had

---

19   This representation of a post-Famine landscape as dominated by an almost unbearable silence is common. For example, in the passage from Margaret Brew's *The Chronicles of Castle Cloyne; or, Pictures of the Munster People*, vol. 3 (London: Chapman & Hall, 1885), incorporated in this anthology, Hyacinth returns to a post-Famine Ireland marked by an uncanny silence due to its depopulation: 'The teeming population that had once made the air resound with the sounds of life and labour, was all gone' (p. 192).

20   The Revd Ringwood.

never seen so charmingly romantic a spot in the entire course of his travels. This impression was heightened as he drew nearer. A background of dark wood, almost forest, set off the peculiar colouring and fantastic form of the mansion with admirable effect. The park was very fine, rather neglected it struck him, but this harmonised with the wild character of the surrounding landscape.[21] The timber was abundant and very old; elms, beeches, chestnuts, and sycamores spread their broad shadows on the bright green turf that sloped gently towards the cliffs above the sea, the grand Atlantic, that rolled in from the New World, dashing its waves upon the shores of the old one, and moaning in loud thunder-music while its foam leapt up in silver spray against the rocks.

The gates of the park stood hospitably open. There was a lodge, but there might as well have been none, for there was no one in it. There it stood, however, a witness to the days of danger and debt, when the untidy old place was kept up with appropriate splendour.

---

21   The foregoing description of the landscape and the castle are a fitting example of the (literary) picturesque. The picturesque was a landscape aesthetic prevalent in the Romantic period which imagined a quintessential unison between the landscape, the architecture in the landscape, and mankind. In contrast to the Burkian beautiful, in which beauty is highly stylized, in the picturesque the decay, incompleteness and ruggedness of a landscape are highly valued. See W.J. Hipple Jr, *The Beautiful, the Sublime, and the Picturesque in Eighteenth-Century British Aesthetic Theory* (Carbondale, IL : Southern Illinois University Press, 1957), p. 210.

Emily Lawless (1845–1913)

> When we remember how many have perished, both of high
> and low, rich and poor, in this calamity, while we remain
> alive, we cannot but be deeply affected with the recollection.[1]

Thus Emily Lawless, herself born in the first year of the Famine, commented on the legacy of that traumatic event which cost the lives of many Irish. During her lifetime, Lawless was considered an esteemed contributor to the Irish literary scene, receiving an Honorary Doctorate in Literature from Trinity College Dublin in 1905.[2] However, she was quickly forgotten after her death in 1913. Being a member of the Protestant aristocracy and a lifelong unionist damaged Lawless's literary reputation after the proclamation of the Irish Free State in 1922. Lawless's writings were more appreciated in England and the United States than in Ireland, where her novels were at times received in a negative light.[3] Lawless was a versatile writer, and besides being a naturalist who published monographs on entomology, she wrote poetry, novels, a biography of Maria Edgeworth, short stories, general histories of Ireland, and historical essays.[4] Her works were published in prestigious magazines such as the *Nineteenth Century* and the *Gentlemen's Magazine,* and she was an amateur botanist, geographer, geologist and marine zoologist.[5]

Heidi Hansson attributes Lawless's quick removal from the literary limelight to the ambivalent political nature of her writings, for in a time of high pressure on nation- and people-building, nationalist literature was privileged. Lawless's 'resistance to political labelling'[6] and the fact that her work 'both laments and celebrates Irish history'[7] did not fit in with the dominant cultural climate. Lawless's rather nuanced approach to history

---

1   E. Lawless, *Ireland* (London: T. Fisher Unwin, 1885), p. 5.
2   H. Hansson, *Emily Lawless 1845–1913: Writing the Interspace* (Cork: Cork University Press, 2007), pp. 1, 3.
3   For examples of these negative contemporary critiques, see H. Hansson, *Emily Lawless 1845–1913*, pp. 65–71.
4   R. Hogan et al. (eds), *Dictionary of Irish Literature: Revised and Expanded Edition* (London: Aldwych Press, 1996), p. 687.
5   Hansson, *Emily Lawless 1845–1913*, pp. 2–3.
6   Ibid., p. 6.
7   Hogan et al. (eds), *Dictionary of Irish Literature*, p. 688.

and society may go back to the fact that her father, Lord Cloncurry of Lyons House, Co. Kildare, mixed with different classes. Though a Protestant himself, he had a longlasting friendship with Catholic statesman Daniel O'Connell.[8]

As Hansson points out, 'the idea that landscape bears witness to history is prominent' in Lawless's works.[9] In the story 'Famine Roads and Famine Memories' Lawless takes us on a tour of the mountains of Connemara and describes in vivid detail the surroundings, the people and their customs, but most importantly, who or what has been erased from the scene. Central to this story is the image of the Famine roads built to provide labour for the victims of blight. These traces of the past are *lieux de mémoire*,[10] symbolic for the fate of the Irish people, and evoke recollections of the tragedy of the Famine and the responsibility of the English for the past horrors.

In *Traits and Confidences*, 'Famine Roads and Memories' is followed by 'After the Famine', an embedded narrative told by an old man and former English estate agent who travels to Ireland in the aftermath of the Hunger to purchase property. Eleanor D'Arcy is the only one left of her family and now owns this ancestral home that she can no longer afford, as the Famine has severely affected the family fortune. At the same time she has to cope with the death of her sister, Ann. Though it remains unclear what Ann died of, the narrator wonders whether Ann and Eleanor's other deceased family members are Famine victims: 'Had this hideous famine swept them all away, as it had swept away hundreds of thousands of humbler victims?'[11] The love story that then follows deals with issues of guilt, a radical transformed society and tense colonial relations.

---

8   V. Mulkerns, 'Introduction', in E. Lawless, *Hurrish: A Study* (Belfast: Appletree Press, 1992), p. vii.
9   Hansson, *Emily Lawless 1845–1913*, p. 51.
10   The term was coined by Pierre Nora. See 'Between Memory and History: Les Lieux de Mémoire', *Representations*, 26 (1989), pp. 7–25.
11   E. Lawless, 'After the Famine', in *Traits and Confidences* (London: Methuen, 1898), p. 180.

From 'Famine Roads and Famine Memories', in *Traits and Confidences*

(London: Methuen, 1898), pp. 142–4, 150–7.

It has sometimes seemed to me as if every great event, especially if it be of the more tragic order, ought to have some distinctive cairn or monument of its own; some spot at which one could stand, as before a shrine, there to meditate upon it, and upon it alone. Such a shrine – though only in my own eminently private mental chapel – the great Irish Famine of 1846–47[12] possesses, and has possessed for more years than I can now readily reckon. Whenever I think of it there rises before me one particular spot, in one particular corner of Connemara; one particular cluster of cabins, or rather wrecks of cabins,[13] for roofs there have been none since I knew it first. There

---

12 Lawless's demarcation of the Famine period differs from contemporary scholarly views, according to which the Famine lasted much longer than the two years mentioned here. Christine Kinealy gives 1845–52 as the beginning and end of the Famine. See *This Great Calamity: The Irish Famine 1845–52* (Dublin: Gill & Macmillan, 2006). Kevin Kenny goes even further, writing about a 'Famine decade' (1846–55). He argues that the direct suffering caused by the Famine exceeded the five or six years in which the blight actually affected the potato crops. See *The American Irish: A History* (New York: Longman, 2000), pp. 89–90.

13 The image of the Irish landscape in ruins or in decay after the Famine is a common figure in Irish and Irish-diaspora literature. James Doran's *Zanthon: A Novel* (San Francisco, CA: Bancroft, 1891) makes repeated use of the element of the ruin, which here becomes a liminal site of contemplation, or marks a transition between two different stages in life or between life and death. In *Zanthon* the protagonist loses his father Marlband in a ruin and afterwards reinvents himself there, while the ruins also mark the rupture between pre- and post-Famine times: 'Coming by the mountain road to the river, a point between the old fort and the ruins of Marlband's house the party stopped to refresh themselves, as the place was secluded and inviting being covered with soft grass ... Young people born since the famine were playing on the hills and the sun was out in full strength, as if exulting over the vindication of supreme law in his case' (pp. 526–7). Ruins, much like the famine roads and the decaying cottages here, signal radical breaks in the landscape and in time, and lay bare a rupture in the seemingly continuous flow of time. Ruins and decay can have an ambiguous meaning, embodying both positive and negative connotations – negative ones because ruins refer to that which is lost. In *The Aesthetics of Decay: Nothingness, Nostalgia, and the Absence of Reason* (New York: Peter Lang, 2006) Dylan Trigg elaborates on this, stating that the ruin at most displays traces, which are not 'substitutes for memory', 'for whatever the event does leave behind, it isn't the memory' (p. 59). Kevin Whelan states that ruins function as 'mausolea of memory' and therefore, in a more positive sense, can also provide a glimpse into an alternative timeline, by pointing to traces of or references to a culture now dominated by another. As such, ruins could even signal the possibility of return or triumph of the subjected culture. See 'Reading the Ruins: The Presence of Absence in the Irish Landscape', in H.B. Clarke et al. (eds), *Surveying Ireland's Past: Multidisciplinary Essays in Honour of Anngret Simms* (Dublin: Geography Publications, 2004), www.ricorso.net/rx/azdata/authors/w/Whelan_K/xtra.htm.

they stand, those poor perishing memorials, and yearly the nettles spread a little further across their hearthstones, and yearly the slope on which they rest crumbles a little nearer to the sea, and yearly the rain batters them a little more down, and the green things cluster more closely around them, and so it will be till one day the walls too will roll over, and the bog from above will overtake them, and the last trace of what was once a populous village will have disappeared, without so much as a *Hic Jacet*[14] to say where it stood.

To get to this very private chapel you must not mind rough walking, neither must you mind trespassing; indeed that last is a mere English fetish, to which the freer-hearted Celt has never been a slave. Leaving the village of Leenane – it stands, as you are probably aware, upon the south shore of the Greater Killary – you keep straight on till you come to a certain white gate on the right hand side of the road. Turn in here – you are trespassing already, but never mind, there are no notice boards – and you will find yourself upon a grass-grown roadway, with the shining level of the fiord below, and above a steep incline of bog, cutting across the sky; a sky which may be friendly at the moment, or may be threatening, but which is sure to be a sky alive with clouds; clouds which are never for a moment at rest; clouds of every form, and of every degree of trans-itoriness, but each one of which has its own separate make and semblance, unlike any cloud had we eyes to perceive that difference – that ever was or ever will be in any sky again.

. . .

But these are high matters. Our walk in life is a different, and a lowlier one. Returning for a moment to our roadway, we presently leave it, and pass across a long stretch of bog, up one incline, and down another, over a stream – how I hardly know, for the last time I went that way there were no stepping-stones – and now we have reached the point for which we set out. We have arrived at our ruined village. We are standing upon the *Famine Road*.

Certain words and certain combinations of words seem to need an eminently local education in order adequately to appreciate them. These two words, 'Famine road', are amongst the number. To other, larger minds than ours they are probably without any particular meaning or

---

14   Latin, 'here lies'.

inwardness. To the home-staying Irishman or Irishwoman they mean only too much. To hear them casually uttered is to be penetrated by a sense of something at once familiar and terrible. The entire history of two of the most appalling years that any country has ever been called upon to pass through seems to be summed up, and compendiously packed into them.

Other mementoes of the Famine, besides its roads, exist, of course, in Ireland. As his train lounges through its flat central counties the intelligent stranger must have more than once observed some erratic-looking obelisk, or other odd development of the art of the builder. If he bestirs himself to inquire what it is, he will be pretty certain to be told that it is a 'Famine work', – as though bad architecture and empty stomachs had a natural connection! There are plenty of such abortive 'Famine works' scattered over the country, but the Famine roads were the official ones; the ones longest persisted in, and in the vast majority of cases, alas! they were the most absolutely futile and abortive of all.

Do not let the word *road* mislead you though. Road, as is plain to be seen, there is none here, nor has been for a long time back. For some years after the Famine, fifteen or sixteen perhaps, for the grass here is not very quick-growing, a road of some sort survived. Nay, I have even been assured that a spirited-minded gentleman once undertook to drive his coach along this part of the edge of the shore, up to the top of the ridge, and so down by the Devil's Gap to Salrock. If he did do so, and survived the entertainment, that divinity that watches over the doings of madmen and drunkards must assuredly have sat upon the coach-box beside him on that occasion. Whether the tale be true or false, it is at least certain that for a few years a road of some sort existed. After that the mountain took it back to its own green bosom, and, save that it survives as a line of exceptional wetness, and that after prolonged rains it reappears in the form of an odd-looking trough or shallow canal, there is no more sign that a road ever ran here than there was when Saint Patrick preached upon Croaghpatrick[15] yonder, or when Saint Fechin[16] paddled past the point of Renvyle to take up his abode upon the sea-scourged rocks of Ard Oilen.[17]

---

15   Croagh Patrick in Co. Mayo is supposedly the mountain on which Saint Patrick, Ireland's patron saint, spent forty days and forty nights fasting. It is now a popular pilgrimage.

16   Saint Feichín or Fechin (600–665), a saint from Connaught who started a religious settlement at Fore, Co. Westmeath.

17   The monastery of Ard Oilen on one of the Aran Islands off the coast of Galway, was commonly believed to have been established by Saint Fechin.

If the Famine road has disappeared, however, other traces of the famine, or rather of the pre-famine condition of things, are still to be seen. Only if you have eyes to see them though, and if the indications – worn almost to invisibility by this time – are sufficiently familiar to make themselves felt as you look around you. Turning towards the higher ground you can count a succession of small humps or projections along the top of the ridge. There is one with a gable end still visible to help the reckoning. Fifty years back those projections were all villages, or groups, at any rate, of from three to ten cabins. In those pre-famine days the rural population throughout Ireland was all but incredibly dense. The fact that nearly four hundred thousand one-roomed cabins are stated by the Registrar-General to have disappeared between the census before and after the Famine,[18] is alone sufficiently indicative of the change. Of such one-roomed cabins these villages probably all consisted. They were apparently unconnected with one another, even by a 'bohereen',[19] yet this now utterly vacant hillside must have hummed in those days with life, and been as busy with its comings and goings as any village green.

Throughout Connemara decent roads were unknown up to the beginning of this century, and even well within that period they were practically non-existent. I can put my hand at this moment upon a bundle of letters describing a visit paid to the Martins of Ballinahinch, somewhere about the middle of the thirties. From the neighbourhood of Tuam the visitor drove to the ferry beyond Headford; crossed it in a very leaky boat – as in fact you do still – found mountain ponies which had been sent by her hosts to meet her upon the other side; rode up-hill and down-hill across some thirty miles of heathery track, and so down to Ballinahinch to pay her visit.

Out of this roadless condition it emerged rather suddenly. The roads over which the tourist of to-day travels, and which are excellent, were all carried out by one enterprising road-maker not long before the Famine. Outlying villages such as these naturally lay beyond the reach of such central highways, and had to be left to nature. Imagine how urgently some way of connecting them with one another and with the outside world

---

18 The text here refers to the pre-Famine census of 1841, which recorded a population of 8,175,124. The post-Famine census of 1851 indicated that Ireland's population had declined by 1,622,739. See R.M. Rhodes, *Women and the Family in Post-Famine Ireland* (New York: Garland, 1992), p. 9.

19 A narrow rural road.

must have been wished for, how badly they must have been wanted until made. Then the need for such means of communication ceased suddenly, and has never returned. Thus the whole irony of the Famine roads stands revealed in a sentence.

The mere bald enumeration of the number of lives extinguished in this one county of Galway during those two years of famine is enough to make one ask oneself how any man or woman living there at the time retained his or her sanity. Many did not. The list of those, well above the reach of actual hunger, who broke down, mind and body alike, from mere pressure upon their vital forces, from pity, from a sense of unutterable horror, is greater than would be believed, or than has ever been set down in print. And can anybody reasonably wonder? Take the mere official reports; the report, for instance, of one county inspector in this very district, and you will find him speaking of a hundred and fifty bodies picked up by himself and his assistants along a single stretch of road. Multiply this fiftyfold, and ask yourself what that means?

And if upon the roadsides, what of the less easily attainable places? Think of the thousands of solitary cabins and sheilings[20] high on the hillsides? Think of the little congeries of similar cabins, such as these whose wrecks lie around us here; of the groups collected round their hearths, so large at first, growing smaller and smaller day by day, until none were left to carry out the dead. Think of the eyes lifted to heaven here upon these very slopes on which we are to-day indolently strolling. Think of the separate hell gone through by each individual father and mother of all that starving multitude. And when all hope was over, when the bitter draught was almost drunk, the end had almost come, that end which must have been so welcome, because there were none left to live for, think of the lying down to watch the vanishing away of this familiar green landscape in the last grey mists of death.

Unhappily we are not driven to piece out such scenes from the shallows of our own moral consciousness, and fifty years after the event. Would that we were! The most matter-of-fact, the most coldly official reports of the time read like the imaginings of some brain-sick poet; to turn over the leaves of your Hansard[21] is like dropping upon the pool of Malebolge.[22] In

---

20   A patch of pasture or a roughly constructed hut adjacent to such.
21   The Hansard is the official printed transcript of both the House of Commons and the House of Lords in Great Britain.

a speech in the House of Commons Mr Horsman[23] – not, I take it, an imaginative orator – speaks, for instance, of the condition of Ireland as follows: 'It is like a country devastated by an enemy; like a country which the destroying angel has swept over… The population struck down, the air a pestilence, the fields a solitude, the chapels deserted, the priest and the pauper famishing together; no inquests; no rites; no record even of the dead; the high-road a charnel-house; the land a chaos; a ruined proprietary, a panic-struck tenantry, the soil untilled, the workhouse a pest. Death, desolation, despair reigning throughout the land.'[24]

---

22   In Dante's *Divine Comedy*, Malebolge is the Eighth Circle of Hell, reserved for procurers, prostitutes, hypocrites, those guilty of political corruption, and similar sinners.

23   Edward Horsman was a Scottish barrister, commissioner of church inquiry in Scotland, Lord of the Treasury from May 1840 until September 1841, and was appointed chief secretary to the Lord Lieutenant of Ireland for 1855.

24   *Parliamentary Debates*, 3rd series, vol. 4 (London: T.C. Hansard, 1845), p. 609. (Lawless's note.)

Priests and Proselytizers

Margaret Percival

Hardly anything is known about the author Margaret Percival, apart from the fact that she apparently wrote three works of fiction. *The Irish Dove* suggests that the author had previously written *Rosa, The Work-Girl*, a novel published anonymously in 1847.[1] Moreover, *The Fisherman's Daughter*, a novel published in 1852, also proves to be by Percival, as it is attributed to 'the Author of "Rosa the Work Girl"'.[2]

As the preface to *The Irish Dove* suggests, the novel is written by a native Irish woman from a Protestant background. The author expresses her concern that '[i]n Ireland, the Bible is still, in most places, bound in chains', because the population is 'deluded' by the Priests into a superstitious rejection of Scripture reading.[3] The writer therefore implores the English readers to 'embrace Erin, prodigal as she is, though not irrevocably lost; and, with the Irish Bible in one hand, subscribe with the other the articles of a lasting union, based on the holy law of God, and sealed with the gift of His sacred Word'.[4] The author's belief that it is necessary to bring the Bible to Irish Catholics is not only voiced in the preface, but is also central to the narrative. Young Helen, who has an Irish mother, cherishes her Celtic roots and speaks Gaelic, travels from India – where her father, Colonel Wilson, was stationed – back to England. The family subsequently relocates to Ireland, where her mother has inherited an estate with tenantry.

As the extract below indicates, to her shock Helen learns that the family's Irish steward and her close companion Corny O'Brien refuses to listen to her reading the Bible, because the priest has forbidden him to do so. Upon her settlement in Ireland, Helen therefore determines to evangelize among the tenants and bring reform to them by setting up a school. While the text thus promulgates the importance of proselytism, it does not endorse the negative stereotyping of the Catholic Irish common in much evangelical literature from the period. Rather, the novel displays

---

1   *Rosa, The Work-Girl; A Tale* (Dublin: Simpkin, Marshall & Co., 1847). In a review in *The Christian Lady's Magazine*, 27 (1847), it is stated that *Rosa, The Work-Girl* was 'published for the benefit of the Society for the relief of distressed Sempstresses' (p. 468) in Famine Ireland who were underpaid by their employers.
2   See the title page of *A Fisherman's Daughter* (Dublin: John Robertson, 1852).
3   M. Percival, *The Irish Dove; or, Faults on Both Sides* (Dublin: John Robertson, 1849), p. vi.

a sympathetic view towards the Irish peasantry and their cultural traditions, criticizes English bias towards the Irish through the representations of heroine Helen and accuses the Protestant Anglo-Irish of neglecting the spiritual welfare of the lower classes and their ill treatment of them: 'the Irish Protestant gentry and landlords have been, for years past, mostly occupied in pressing from their tenants, what have been expressively and justly termed rack-rents'.[5]

The Irish Dove addresses the dire living conditions of the farming classes and particularly points to the responsibility of 'the British crown' for the welfare of the Irish.[6] As James Murphy has observed, the novel fits in with a tradition of evangelical novels dealing with the issue of famine,[7] but it states that this is an earlier famine taking place in 1822. However, as the novel particularly deals with conflicts between landlords and tenants and the religious controversy surrounding the Great Famine, *The Irish Dove* rather appears to consign the harrowing circumstances contemporary with the novel's publication date to a more distant past.

From *The Irish Dove; or, Faults on Both Sides*

(Dublin: John Robertson, 1849), pp. 76–9, 129–31.

'I have often explained all this to you, and proved it from the Bible, which is our only guide to salvation; the best men may err in what they tell us, but every word of God is truth', – and Helen drew forth her pocket Bible, and was about to open it, when Corny threw down the spade he was digging with. 'For the Holy Vargin's sake, don't read to me, Miss Helen! Oh, don't: I'll be ruined entirely by that book.'

'And why not?' asked his young friend, in amazement at the horror depicted in his countenance – 'Have I not read to you out of it a hundred times, and what can be the matter now?'

---

4   Ibid., p. viii.
5   Ibid., p. 152.
6   Ibid., p. 163.
7   J.H. Murphy, *Catholic Fiction and Social Reality in Ireland, 1873–1922* (Westport, CT: Greenwood Press, 1997), p. 153.

'There's no use in denying it; his riverince won't allow me to listen to it any more.[8] He said, when I made so bold as to ask him why, that it wasn't fit for the like of me – that it would put my soul in danger, listening to one word of it, and he was dreadful angry about it entirely; and oh! Miss, I have had such a power of prayers and penances to do, that I'm almost kil't outright. There's no use in hiding the truth from you; the clargy knows what's best for us, poor, ignorant, weak creatures as we are'; and Corny, as if afraid of getting another view of the volume that had cost him so much pain and trouble, took up his working implements, and moved quickly to a distant part of the garden.

'The Bible not fit for him! Oh! the blinding veil they put over the eyes of the poor beings, whose souls are committed to their guardianship; penances for even hearing a few words read, and prayer desecrated to such a service!'

These were Helen's mental exclamations, as she walked towards the house. She had often heard that the Bible was a sealed book to the members of that Church, which asserts herself to be the only true one on earth – out of whose pale none can be eternally saved; but until now, no instance of the animosity with which any attempt to circulate the scriptures amongst the laity is regarded by the ministers of the Romish Church, had come under her personal observation. Popery, at this period, was still (in England) lurking under a cloud;[9] and when it ventured to put forth one of its hydra-heads,[10] it was arrayed in the smiles of gentleness, and clothed in the garb of moderation; glad to find a resting-place in the shade of obscurity, it was quietly acquiring the strength that would enable it to climb round, and stifle, the generous oak that gave it shelter; it fawned in grovelling submission before its unsuspecting protectors, but its feline disposition was unsoftened by favours conferred, and was incapable of giving room to one feeling of gratitude.

---

8   This refers to the priest, Father Moylan.

9   In the Victorian age, it was feared that by the settlement of Catholic immigrants from other nations, such as Ireland, the Roman Church would also gain more ground among the native English. This anxiety is voiced in, for instance, J.C. Hare's *Charges to the Clergy of the Archdeaconry of Lewes*, vol. 2 (Cambridge: Macmillan, 1856), which expresses the hope that God 'will not allow the dark clouds of Popery to spread over the nation that He once delivered from it' (p. 124).

10   In Greek mythology, the Lernaean Hydra is a poisonous serpent-like marine creature that possesses several heads and grows more heads if decapitated. It is here suggested that the Catholic Church is a similarly self-regenerative monster. The image may also suggest that the Catholic Church contains many different factions which are divided amongst themselves.

Helen could number among her acquaintance, several members of the Romish church; the benevolence of disposition, generosity and kind-heartedness, she had seen these persons display on many occasions, had often drawn from her a sigh, as she pondered on what such qualities might have produced, if fostered and encouraged by Scripture principles.

This reflection forced itself powerfully on her mind, now that she discovered all her efforts for Corny's spiritual good were frustrated, and had ended in causing personal suffering to the poor fellow himself. When she recalled his faithfulness, and devoted affection – when she remembered the many noble qualities that were allowed to run to waste – and saw all the evil feelings of his nature that remained unchecked – her spirits fell, and her countenance wore such a desponding expression, that Mrs Wilson became alarmed, and enquired the cause. After hearing it, she exclaimed, 'You forget, my dear Helen, that the interest of the church to which they belong, compels the Roman priesthood to keep back the Scriptures from their flocks; as those among them, who are in any degree enlightened, well know that its tenets would not bear to be tested by the Word of Truth; others of them, conscientiously believing in the doctrines they inculcate, never question whether their church errs or not in withholding the Bible, but implicitly obey its injunctions, no matter what they may be. I feel convinced, that in this latter class, may be ranked a large proportion of the Roman Catholic priests.'

'But mamma, to think what I have been saying to Corny for years, has been thrown away, and all by means of that horrid priest; oh! you cannot imagine how it grieves me.'

'I am sure of it, my dear child; and am fully as much afflicted by it as you can be; but I have long expected this, and think it should prove rather an encouragement to further exertions than otherwise; as if Mr Moylan did not see that your words, or rather the words of Scripture, were beginning to make some impression on Corny's mind, he would not deem it necessary to be so stringent, or to impose such severe penances. With regard to Father Moylan, himself, we should endeavour to imitate his watchfulness and decision, rather than harbour resentment towards him, for acting in accordance with what he believes to be his duty: he has a zeal, but not according to knowledge.

...

94

'For many years', said Mr Burgh, 'a barrier seemed to exist between me and usefulness, so far as regarded them; but at length a flood of light was cast on it from above, and I was made the unworthy instrument of working a change so great, that many who have seen it, have assured me that less than ocular demonstration would not have convinced them; and the weapon that was placed in my hands, is so small that statesmen have over-looked it; yet it is the only one capable of overthrowing error, turning hatred into affection, and changing the course of every natural feeling.'

These words bore so strongly on the subject ever uppermost in Helen's thoughts, that she could not forbear exclaiming, 'Oh! do tell me what is it!'

'My dear young lady, here it is! and believe me, it will do more for your countrymen than all the measures that ever passed through parliament.'

So saying, he drew from his pocket, AN IRISH BIBLE.[11]

Mr Burgh now heard for the first time of Helen's knowledge of the Irish language, and her vain attempts for Corny's spiritual enlightenment; for as these subjects were disagreeable to Colonel Wilson they were seldom alluded to; now, however, seeing Mr Burgh's interest in the recital, he freely joined in the conversation.

'And did you place this book in his hands, and did it fail?' asked the old gentleman.

'I had not one to give, and if I had, he could not read it', answered Helen.[12]

'And most likely would not if he could', remarked her father.

'Trust me, the contrary would be the case', replied Mr Burgh. 'I will answer for it, that when he hears it read, he will not only delight in listening to it, but will in a short time learn to read, in order to peruse it himself. He looks on your English Bible, if not with detestation, at least with fear and mistrust: it is the book of heretics; and is associated in his mind with Saxons and oppressors, which are to him synonymous terms. But give him the same book in the Celtic, and none of these doubts and fears are aroused; the language opens his heart at once, and commands

---

11 A Bible in Gaelic. Anglican churchman Wiliam Bedell commissioned the translation of the Bible into Irish Gaelic. This translation was completed by the Protestant Rector of Templeport parish, Muircheartach Ó Cionga.

12 Many among the lower classes of pre-Famine and Famine Ireland were illiterate. The 1841 census showed that in Ireland's West 'at least three-quarters of the population could neither read nor write'. See T.W. Freeman, *Pre-Famine Ireland: A Study in Historical Demography* (Manchester: Manchester University Press, 1957), p. 133.

the citadel of his affections; its sweet tones, loved in childhood, and hallowed by every sacred and tender association, soften his stony bosom, and the words of inspiration, thus clothed, will distil as dew into his soul.'

'But would it not be much better to instruct the people through the medium of English, and not perpetuate a language which prevents the assimilation of the two countries?'[13]

'Certainly, it would be much better if it were practicable; but time has proved the fallacy of this proposition. The stronger the attempts made to destroy the nationality of a people, the more devotedly they cherish the remnants which are left: no exertions made by a government can possibly eradicate an aboriginal tongue; we know that persecution, either of a sect or party, only increases its strength and numbers; and the same holds good as regards a language. Besides, though instruction in English may penetrate the Irishman's ears, it scarcely ever reaches his understanding; how could it, when his thoughts come into being in another tongue? He recoils from the learning proffered in the obnoxious garb; and the only choice open to us is, either to leave him in his present degraded condition, or attempt his improvement in the way common sense, as well as his inclinations, point out to us.'

---

13   After the Act of Union was passed in 1801, integration between Ireland and England became the main objective. However, throughout the following decades the success of this operation remained questionable, as can, for instance, be read in Richard Congreve's *Ireland* (London: E. Truelove, 1868), which shows that politicians were 'at variance as to the degree of assimilation between England and Ireland which it is desirable to secure, so far as it can be secured by legislation and administration' (p. 7).

'An Irishman'

> Ye privileged inhabitants of free and happy England, little can
> ye form a true and adequate idea of that mystery of terror and
> oppression, the altar curse, as wielded by the Irish Roman
> Catholic hierarchy and priesthood.[1]

These lines from *Poor Paddy's Cabin; or Slavery in Ireland*, written by an
anonymous 'Irishman', expressively convey the criticism of the priesthood
that is central to the novel's plot. Little is known about the male author, apart
from the fact that after the success of *Poor Paddy's Cabin*, he wrote *The Irish
Widow; or A Picture from Life of Erin and her Children* (1855), with the same
'aim to direct his censures against systems, not against persons; and so to
expose what is wrong.'[2] It is clear that the author wrote his texts from a
Protestant perspective, and, like other authors of Famine fiction, such as
W.C. Upton and Thomas O'Neill Russell, was inspired by Harriet Beecher
Stowe's bestseller *Uncle Tom's Cabin* (1852). As the preface to the second
edition reveals, *Poor Paddy's Cabin* is not only similar to Stowe's novel in
its depiction of a hero of humble origins with a 'child-like regard and deep
reverence for the Word of God',[3] but also in the analogy it suggests between
between two systems of slavery: 'Negro Slavery' and the 'mental slavery' of
the Irish people under the yoke of the Roman Catholic priesthood.[4]

The purported tyranny of Catholicism in Ireland is illustrated in a plot
set during the Famine. Rather than seeking to relieve the starving
population, as the Protestant clergy and Bible readers successfully do, the
priests sacrifice the lives of their congregations in an attempt to uphold their
dominant influence on Irish society. Father Moran, initially willing to lend
assistance to the famishing poor, is commanded by his superiors to break off
his friendship with the Protestant ministry. Moreover, he is ordered to
expose the Protestant evangelicals, the 'soupers' who offer food to children
in schools, as unscrupulous hypocrites who only seek to benefit by the

---

1   'An Irishman', *Poor Paddy's Cabin; or Slavery in Ireland*, 2nd edn (London: Wertheim & Macintosh, 1854), p. 43.
2   'An Irishman', *The Irish Widow; or A Picture from Life of Erin and her Children* (London: Wertheim & Macintosh, 1855), p. iv.
3   'An Irishman', *Poor Paddy's Cabin*, p. vii.
4   Ibid., p. x.

Famine by endangering the souls of the poor peasants. While the novel thus implies that the fierce criticism of souperism in Famine Ireland was just a fabricated lie aimed at increasing the priesthood's stronghold over the country, *Poor Paddy's Cabin* also suggests that the way the Catholic clergy deal with the crisis of the Famine is little effective, as is also foreshadowed by the passage below. Priests forbid the suffering Irish to accept food from the Bible-readers, while their prayers are to no avail: 'the praties are as black as ever, although the priest has been blessin the fields'.[5] The novel's hero, Paddy, and his eldest daughter Maureen have converted to Protestantism, but as a result suffer violent assaults by Catholic fellowmen, who also plunder and raze the cottages of other converts. Despite all these trials Paddy remains true to his newly accepted creed, and, thanks to the help given by other adherents of the 'true faith', manages to survive the difficult times.

Upon its publication, *Poor Paddy's Cabin* received a lot of media attention in the Protestant press. *The Church-Warder and Domestic Magazine* called the novel 'a lively and correct picture of the slavery to which Popery has reduced the native Irish' that shows 'how much more cruel is the slavery which white men are under to the False Prophet than Black men are under to the lash of the planter'.[6] *The Christian Lady's Magazine* praised the novel for distinctly setting forth 'principles of Scriptural Christianity', and ably contrasting them 'with the corruptions of Romanism'.[7]

From *Poor Paddy's Cabin; or, Slavery in Ireland,* 2nd edn

(London: Wertheim & Macintosh, 1854), pp. 12–17.

The horror-stricken state of the breakfast-table company may be better imagined than described. But the dear lady, ever fertile in thoughts of benevolence, talented in planning, and prompt and energetic in acting,

---

5   Ibid., p. 4.
6   'Notices of Books', *The Church-Warder and Domestic Magazine*, 8 (1854), p. 222.
7   'Review of New Publications', *The Christian Lady's Magazine*, 10 (1855), p. 120.

immediately said – 'Oh! dearest, 'tis no use to be pitying these little ones, whom the Lord has taken away from the evil to come; but let us this very day plan and build a house of refuge for famine-made orphans[8] – I'm sure the kind English will give funds enough for it.[9] Sit down, dearest, and write at once one of your nice letters, telling how these poor children perished. Not an hour should be lost. You remember how we were told, when we inquired about poor children, and how *they* bore the famine, that those poor little things were the first to perish.'

'Yes, beloved, I remember when, on my making that inquiry of James Rourke, he said, "Oh! Sir, the little things died off almost at once when the food failed." It struck me that perhaps the dreadful pangs of famine hardened even the warm and affectionate hearts of Irish parents, to take an undue share for themselves of what was got.'

'Oh, dear husband, you ought not to say this; here, I have the written statement of the Scripture reader,[10] whom we sent the day before yesterday to visit the cabins. It shows that the poor parents are as badly off as their children, and perishing alike; and, besides, remember how the poor

---

8   In Ireland, asylums for Famine orphans were established, and these were often supported financially by Protestant institutions. An example is the Donoghmore Refuge for Famine Made Orphans in Cork, which took in Catholic children with the aim of training them 'for useful employments and situations in future life' (p. 7), and to instruct them in Scripture. See *Report of the Donoghmore Refuge for Famine Made Orphans in the South of Ireland for the Year Ending March 31, 1850* (Cork: George Nash, 1850).

9   A poem such as Sarah Revell's 'Sorrow's Benison', 'written at the time of the Famine in Ireland', suggests that England, as a 'Sister Island' acting according to its 'firm … fair' and 'loving band' with Erin will help the country in its sorrow. *Verses that Would Come; or the Five Worlds of Enjoyment* (Sudbury: Henry S. Pratt, 1873), pp. 105–6. Indeed, many English individuals and organizations, such as the Society of Friends, offered money and relief to Ireland's starving population, but, as Edward Lengel points out, English charity for Ireland collapsed after 1847. The Quakers, moreover, ended their relief programme in the summer of 1847. See *The Irish Through British Eyes: Perceptions of Ireland in the Famine Era* (Westport, CT: Praeger, 2002), p. 114.

10   Scripture readers were Evangelicals aiming to 'read the Bible and converse' with the Catholic Irish population and 'send the word of God' among them ('Missionary Records', *The Church of England Magazine*, 25 [1848], p. 366). In *A Twelve Months' Residence in Ireland during the Famine and the Public Works, 1846 and 1847* (London: Longman, Brown & Green, 1848), William Henry Smith champions the British evangelicals who 'well becoming their holy vocation, labour[ed] in the universal cause of charity' (p. 42) by offering relief to Famine victims. These proselytizing Bible-readers were also called Soupers, because they offered soup to the famishing Catholics on condition of conversion, as Donal Kerr explains in *The Catholic Church and the Famine* (Blackrock: Columba Press, 1996), p. 86. These Soupers are often represented in very hostile terms in Famine literature. Elizabeth Willoughby Varian's poem 'Proselytizing' pictures a relentless Evangelical who only offers food in exchange for conversion to the Protestant faith: 'Thou shalt have food, but first thou most renounce / Thy erring faith, and yield these children up'. *Poems By Finola* (Belfast: John Henderson, 1851), p. 41.

parents of those two orphans died first – I suppose they gave everything to the children, and so left them alive; if the children die first it must be because they are not so well able to bear it – but let us read the Scripture reader's account –

"'*March* 14, 1847.[11] – Called at the house of a man named Scanlan – on opening the door saw three little famished-looking children sitting on the ground, about a little fire, and close by them at the other side their poor father lying dead; his clothes were on – his head rested on a little sop of straw – and his legs were drawn up and crippled, just as he died. I went into the bed-room; there I saw the poor mother lying on the bed, quite dead also. I turned and went away, to call at the other houses, and send relief to the little ones.

"'No. 2. Called at Nicholas Brew's house; found the poor man and three of his children had died and been buried this week; saw his two boys, of about nine and twelve, lying dead upon the table covered with an old cloth, – the poor mother was there with her legs dreadfully swelled from famine.[12]

"'No. 3. Called at Michael Hearlihy's house; saw a man dead, lying by the wall, in his clothes, with a sheaf of straw under his head, and just near him a coffin in which his son lay dead. Was informed that he had gone for the coffin for his son, was bringing it home, and fell and died under it on the way.

"'No. 4. Called at another house, – saw a woman, Mrs Regan, a few days after her confinement, lying in bed not able to get up; her infant child lay dead near her in the bed; it had been lying there dead three days; her old mother was there and two starving children; the old mother could scarcely stir from age: the woman in bed told me she had buried her husband a few days before. I told her to put her trust in the Lord Jesus, who died for her, and that he would forgive her her sins; she seemed to listen attentively, and said she would; I left the little money I had with her.'

---

11   Note in the original text: 'As literally reported.'

12   As Stuart McLean and others have pointed out, victims of starvation often displayed signs of famine dropsy (medically known as hunger oedema), when limbs and body swell, 'often to several times their normal size'. *The Event and Its Terrors; Ireland, Famine, Modernity* (Stanford, CA: Stanford University Press, 2004), p. 124. Elihu Burritt writes in *A Journal of a Visit of Three Days to Skibbereen and its Neighbourhood* (London: Charles Gilpin, 1847) that he 'had seen men at work on the public roads with their limbs swollen almost to twice their usual size', and he describes a starved child as having a 'body … swollen to nearly three times its usual size' (p. 10).

'Isn't that dreadful, dearest?' said the lady; 'and these are but a few samples out of hundreds that are similarly perishing all over the country. And you see that parents and children are perishing alike. But it is probable, if there was an asylum to take the poor children into, where we could bring them up in the knowledge of God's word, and teach them to fear God and love their Saviour, as well as to make them orderly and industrious, God might graciously spare the children to such a good purpose. For, otherwise, it is hard to say whether it is not better these little ones should "die *off* at once", as James Rourke said, than live to be brought up in the superstitious bad habits and rebellious bigotry of their parents; or perhaps to go about crying and moaning as those wretched boys and girls we meet every day, half-lunatic with famine, and making use of their little remaining senses to rob and steal; but there I see Mr Moran, the priest, in the lawn, talking very angrily to the poor men who are at work – you had better go and see what it is about.'

'Dear Mr – ', said the priest, 'I called over to tell you of a dreadful thing I've just found out – it is a conspiracy to attack and plunder my house, and take away all I have in the world. I hope you have no objection to my calling these people to an account for it; and I hope, dear Sir, you will join with me in putting it down.'

'Oh! most surely, Mr Moran', and, addressing the men, 'I tell you that I will make the closest inquiry, and if I find any one of you engaged in so villainous and shameful a thing, I will instantly dismiss that man from the charity employment, and leave him and family to sift for themselves.' …

'I hope at all events', said the priest, 'that till the relief-works open in the other barony, you will not cease employing and feeding the people, for if you do, the consequences will be dreadful.'

'I hear great complaints by the landed proprietors', said the rector, 'about the way the relief-money is laid out. They have good reason too to complain. They have themselves, as you know, given large sums (and now they are getting very little of their rents) to the Relief Committee, for the poor. And isn't it hard they should not be consulted about the laying out of the government money, which will, I understand, be a charge on their properties to pay it all back? They say the Board of Works' officers are only spoiling all the roads, and cutting up the land for no purpose in most cases. Many plans have been suggested for laying out the money in a remunerative way, but they have been deaf to all such appeals.[13] I myself, at the beginning of spring, when there was time enough for the thing, forwarded to them a plan for laying out the money under the same machinery of officers and stewards, in sowing the extensive waste lands, with consent of the farmers; which the latter, as well as the landlords, would have been very glad to avail themselves of – and also to agree to insure the repayment out of the land, so tilled and improved, in small instalments – all which could have been managed by an Act of Parliament of sixty or eighty lines. But they would listen to nothing of the kind, but lay all out in useless roads. What an unjust thing it will be if the re-payment of this relief-money shall hereafter be enforced!'

The above fact, of a priest actually seeking protection, to a certain extent, from a Protestant clergyman, not only shows the wonderful blow to priestly tyranny in Ireland, which Divine Providence commenced to give by the famine,[14] but the equally wonderful protection thus afforded to the Protestants, especially the clergy. If the famishing thousands could think of such a thing as ransacking *a priest's house,* in the frantic pangs of famine before their strength was gone and their numbers greatly reduced, what would they not have done to the Protestant clergy as well as the other defenceless Protestant families whom they always were taught from infancy to regard with bigoted dislike?[15] The benevolent English, doubtless, must, as far as aware of this fact, rejoice in reflecting that their generous contributions, in the famine time, not only relieved thousands of heart-rending cases, like those before given, but that, by making the Protestant clergy the almoners of their bounty, they not only preserved their houses from plunder, and perhaps the lives of themselves and families, but gave

---

13   Isaac Butt in *A Voice for Ireland; A Famine in the Land* (Dublin: James M'Glashan, 1847) comments upon the reluctance of 'landed interests' to support 'the demand that railways should be constructed with the labour that Ireland was forced to employ' (p. 17), fearing an appropriation of its property for the general interest.

14   The passage evokes the common representation of the Great Famine as Providence. Compare, for instance, the following passage from C.H. Gaye's *Irish Famine; A Special Occasion for Keeping Lent in England, A Sermon,* 2nd edn (London: Francis & John Rivington, 1847): 'The hand of God has torn away the veil from our eyes, and made itself terribly visible in operation' (p. 8).

15   Some texts from the Famine era suggest that the Catholic Irish held severe grudges against the Protestant clergy and proselytizers, even implying that they used violence against the Soupers. *The Great Famine; By A Friend of Ireland* (Cheltenham: Wright & Bailey, 1847), for instance, claims that Evangelicals 'who have gone preaching salvation by the precious blood of Christ, have been shot at – threatened with death – letters, with coffins painted on the inside, sent to them' (p. 4).

thereby a moral influence over an intensely hostile population, which has been, and with God's blessing will be, turned to the best of purposes – that of emancipating our warm-hearted, but misled and misguided peasantry, from *spiritual bondage*, and enabling them to understand and assert their rights as men, and as British Christians.

Richard Baptist O'Brien (1809–85)

> Well, sir, the time will come. We *have* made a mistake.
> Ireland's clergy must always be the real power.[1]

Richard Baptist O'Brien (1809–85) was born in Carrick-on-Suir, Co. Tipperary. He entered the priesthood, was a staff member of All Hallows College in Dublin, and spent several years in North America.[2] He returned to Ireland in 1859 and from then until his death in 1885 O'Brien was Dean of Limerick.[3] Besides being 'a distinguished priest',[4] O'Brien wrote novels and poems, which were frequently published (in serialized form) in several esteemed journals, including the *Irish Catholic Magazine,* the *Irish Monthly* and *The Nation.*[5]

Although O'Brien's credentials for entering the Catholic Church 'were impeccable', he was also looked upon as 'somewhat of a maverick'.[6] In line with this, O'Brien's novels seem to represent a more radical and at times even militant view of Catholicism than those of many of his literary contemporaries. As a review of *Ailey Moore* in the Catholic periodical *The Rambler* observed, O'Brien manifests himself as 'a zealous and active ecclesiastic' in his writing.[7] The above quote, spoken by the heroic character Crishawn in *The D'Altons of Crag* (1882), illustrates this religious radicalism well, and although the novel does not end with the clergy on top, without a doubt it presents Catholic characters and morals as Ireland's intended future path. In O'Brien's fiction there is a clear ultramontane streak, which could be attributed not only to O'Brien's own individualism, but also to the audience he targeted. Whereas most novelists wrote for the Irish and English market, and had to find a religious middle path to appease both, O'Brien wrote for the Irish and Irish-American market,[8] which was more welcoming of his particular staunch ideas on Catholicism.

---

1   R.B. O'Brien, *The D'Altons of Crag: A Story of '48 & '49* (Dublin: James Duffy, 1882), p. 174.
2   Ibid.
3   J. Sutherland, *The Longman Companion to Victorian Fiction* (London: Longman, 1988), p. 471.
4   S.J.M. Brown, *Ireland in Fiction* (Dublin: Maunsel & Company, 1919), p. 231.
5   J.H. Murphy, *Catholic Fiction and Social Reality in Ireland, 1873–1922* (Westport, CT: Greenwood Press, 1997), p. 55.
6   Ibid.
7   Review of '*Ailey Moore*', *The Rambler*, 5 (1856), p. 156.
8   Murphy, *Catholic Fiction and Social Reality in Ireland*, p.55.

Ailey Moore, set during the Famine, primarily criticizes the corrupt landowning system. The plot centres on Gerald Moore, who is unjustly convicted for murder by the land agent who seeks to avenge himself on the Moore family because their daughter Ailey has rejected his marriage proposal. Populated with Famine fiction stock characters, such as 'soupers, villains, beggars; evicted peasants starving, dying, or driven to exile or desperation',[9] *Ailey Moore* first and foremost seeks to underline the heroic role played by Catholic clergy during the Famine years. When his parishioners look haggard and worn, Father Mick not only prays for and looks after the spiritual needs of his perishing flock; he also uncomplainingy gives away all his possessions and economizes on food in order to provide sustenance for his parishioners. The extract below shows the determination of the Catholic congregation to stand by their faith, even in the face of certain starvation.

From *Ailey Moore, A Tale of the Times*

(London: Charles Dolman, 1856), pp. 263–7.

Inside the house the scene was afflicting. The old man sat over the last embers of a turf fire, on which he looked fixedly. He was sick and spiritless. Young Patrick stood a little inside the door, looking vacantly out on the highway. The two younger children had each a portion of a raw turnip, which they greedily devoured, and the young mother had a baby in her arms, which tossed itself hither and thither uneasily, and wept as it found it could not get its ordinary sustenance. The bloom had faded from the cheek of young Mrs Nolan, and one side of her flaxen hair fell over her face, although she never perceived it. Old Mrs Nolan lay in the place which had once held her bed. She now lay upon some straw – and she prayed. Nearly everything had been disposed of; for the poor people found it hard to break up the old homestead and to go to the poor-house.

---

9   Review of '*Ailey Moore*', *Bronson's Quarterly Review*, 2 (1857), p. 232.

It should be added that the whole family, excepting Patrick, were ragged almost to nakedness. Old James wore a flannel vest, and the remnants of shoes could hardly be called by their original name.

Young Nolan turned round and looked at his wife and child, and a shudder ran through his warm frame. Mary Nolan was fast relaxing her hold of the infant, and falling towards the wall by which she sat.

'God Almighty!' cried her husband, rushing towards her and catching wife and child in his arms – 'God Almighty! she's dead!'

The old man started from the hearth, and the poor children for a moment forgot hunger in their fears. All hurried shrieking towards the young couple, and even the poor cripple in the bed-room, insensible to pain and weakness, flung herself out upon the floor, and there cried in anguish, for she was not able to move further.

'Don't be afeard, Paddy, a vic,'[10] said the old man, when he had taken the shrieking infant from her arms, – 'don't be afeard, a vic, there's nothing the matter yet. Mary is only weak a little, wisha! Darlin' Mary!' said the old man; 'darlin' Mary!' he repeated.

'Weak!' answered the son, 'weak with hunger![11] Mary!' he continued, and he kissed her pale forehead, – 'Mary! a gra ma chree,[12] 'tis for this you joined yourself to Pat Nolan. Oh God! oh God!'

'Hush, Paddy! hush; be a man, a vic, God is good! God is good!'

The old man held a broken bowl to the young woman's pale lips.

'There now', he said, as she gave a sigh, – 'there now, 'tis nothing, 'tis nothing.'

And then two large tears flowed down the wrinkled cheeks of old James Nolan, and he kissed the pale sickly little baby.

Quite gently and without uttering another word, Paddy Nolan took Mary in his arms into a room that was next his poor mother's, for the two rooms halved the floor of the dwelling. He remained a few moments, and appeared to have gone on his knees, for he prayed and his prayer partook of agony. The old man kept the baby in his bosom, and again sat on the hearth. The other little creatures clung to his knees, sobbing.

---

10   Vocative form of *mic*, meaning son.

11   While the narrative here implies that women and children were most vulnerable to the effects of starvation and disease, in reality it was remarkable that 'not only old, or feeble, or specially sensitive people died, but strong men, heads of houses'. E. Lawless, *Ireland* (London: T. Fisher Unwin, 1891), p. 400.

12   Love of my heart.

'I'm better, Paddy, agra[13] – oh, I'm very well. Where's the child? – little Mary – where's the child, eh?' was heard from the apartment.

'Mary, agra, you're sick, and – '

'Oh, no! You'll see yourself, I'll be finely – Ah, Paddy! 't will kill me to see you cryin'.'

The old man entered the room with the infant, and the young man rose up from his knees. He once more kissed the forehead of his devoted wife, and having seized his father's hand for a momentary grasp, he disappeared from the house.

James Nolan had not been many minutes away, when a man named Cusack entered. He was comfortably clad, wore a blue frock and a white neckerchief, and he carried a book in his hand. As he entered, old James Nolan returned from the little room, having left the baby with its mother.

'Good morrow, Mr Nolan', the new comer commenced.

'Good morrow, sir', answered the old man.

Mr Cusack sat down on a 'boss', or straw seat, the single ottoman of the poor.

'Will you listen to the holy word to-day, Mr Nolan?'

'I read it myself', answered the old man.[14]

'Ah, then, don't you see the judgment on the counthry; an' why won't you save yourself and your family?'[15]

'I think I am savin' 'em', answered James.

'Don't you see the whole weight is fallin' on the Catholics?'

'An' so was the whole weight upon Job, an' upon Christ, an' upon the Apostles', answered old James.[16]

---

13 My love.

14 It was often assumed that the Irish Catholics never read the Bible – were even forbidden to do so by their priests – and showed no respect for God's holy word. For instance, in *Poor Paddy's Cabin; or, Slavery in Ireland* (London: Wertheim & MacIntosh, 1854), the impression is created that the Catholic clergy discourages individual Bible reading, for it is only after their 'sincere conversion from Popery' that Paddy and his daughter Maureen start reading the Bible together, 'in a ready and well-pointed application of Scripture, as bearing upon the change from former opinions to the doctrines of Protestantism' (p. 18).

15 Cusack here appears to repeat a common belief of the time that the Famine was brought upon Ireland by God as punishment. See, for example, J. Travers Robinson, *A Sermon Preached in St Leonard's Chapel, Newton Abbot, Devonshire* (Feignmouth: E & G.H. Croydon, 1847): 'it is as though a vial of wrath were being poured out by a commissioned angel over a guilty world' (p. 10).

16 The Book of Job in the Old Testament tells of Job's trials: God deprives him of his possessions and family, but despite these hardships, Job remains steadfast in his faith.

'Always the sharp word. But 'tis plain enough that every other religion in the counthry has plenty; an' all the weight is on *yez*', rejoined the Bible-reader.

'I don't want to quarrel wid you', answered James. 'There is no use in scoulding; an' I'm weak. Once for all, don't think we'll sell ourselves for our stomach – don't think id. 'Tis queer charity to offer me bread an' meal for my conscience, bekase when you ax my conscience for id, by course you ax my sowl for id. Bread an' meal for my sowl! for the little childher's soul!'[17]

'Don't you know you can't stand?'

'Just so then, thank God.'

'And you'll die, while full and plenty is near you!'

'Yis, I'll die, please God.'

'An' you'll see the poor little gran'childhren wasting away and going into the clay for your stubbornness?'

'Just so, then', answered James.

'Ah! God has appeared at last', said the Bibleman, bitterly.

'Yes, indeed', answered James, weakly and slowly. 'Thrue for you – God is appearin' at last. An' I'll tell you – the poor, who have nothin' to keep 'em here, will go with Him to Heaven; an' the people that want the poor to sell their souls, an' that don't give the poor justice, may remain awhile afther, an' they'll go to hell. There's the short an' the long iv it. An' see, Mr Cusack', he said, growing a little warm, 'God is a quiet law-maker, *but sure* – oh, *very sure*. The famine will send thousands to heaven – what more do they want? Is *that* punishment? An' the famine will bring down thousands of hard hearts to want – hearts that 'll feel id – hearts that this same want is hell to, an' that have no heaven on'y their pleasure. God is just, just; an', as you say, is appearin' these times.'

---

17   In his refusal to barter his soul and those of his relatives for food, James Nolan is similar to other characters in Catholic Famine fiction who would rather starve than change their creed. For example, in Mary Anne Sadlier's *New Lights; or Life in Galway* (New York: Sadlier, 1853) Bernard O'Daly refuses to embrace the Protestant Church to protect his family from starvation. Rather, he wishes to have an empty stomach and taste 'the true bread of life' (p. 244) of Irish Catholicism, referring back to his forefathers who were similarly willing to die for their faith: 'Tell them that the O'Dalys are of the ould stock ... an' they can die *for* their faith, as they have lived *in* it, them an' their fathers before them' (p. 248).

Once more the Bibleman went way, and the poor man looked round his cold cabin and his starving grandchildren, and thought of the night – the long night – if his son should fail in obtaining a little loan, for which he had been preparing to go to Kinmacarra, when his beloved wife fainted.

'God is good!' cried the old man. 'God is good!'

'An' how is my colleen, now?' the old man said, entering the bedroom. 'An' how is little Mary?' The good old man spoke half-joyously, though his heart was very sad.

'Och, father', she answered, 'don't be botherin' with that poor Cusack – don't be frettin' yourself with him.'

'An' how is my cushla?'[18] he said, stooping down.

'Oh! very well – just goin' to get up out o' this', she answered.

And Mary Nolan attempted to rise, but immediately fell back.

'Oh, *Iosa*!'[19] she exclaimed.

'Starved!' whispered the old man to himself; 'starved!' said he.

'God ha' mercy on me!' prayed Mary Nolan.

The grandfather stooped down to the wretched bed, and once more raised the baby.

'She is very quiet', said the young mother; 'she is lying there like a little lamb, ever since her father went out. Oh! but my head is queer, daddy Jim.'

He took up the child in his arms. He placed the tiny hands round his neck, and the little head on his shoulder.

'Let me kiss little Mary!' said the mother.

'Lie down, *avourneen*',[20] said the old man.

'*Ochone*!'[21] she answered, 'I feel so queer – my head is so giddy! Daddy Jim, take care of Mary – poor little Mary – Mary', she said.

The child's face fell in towards the old man's cheek, and he trembled from head to foot – the face was icy cold. He ran from the little room to the cradle – night was just falling – the fire was nearly out – the two elder children lay in a little straw beside the ashes.

'O Hierna! Hierna![22] – Lord! Lord!' cried old James Nolan.

---

18 'pulse', from *Cuisle mo croidhe*, endearment meaning 'beating of my heart'.
19 Oh, Jesus!
20 Darling.
21 An interjection meaning 'alas'.
22 Lord.

He ran to a corner, collected a little turf-mould, got together a few sticks, and took some of the straw from beneath the two children. A momentary blaze illumined the cabin, and the grandfather ran to the cradle again. He looked in – turned the cradle round towards the light – looked in again, steadily – steadily.

A groan burst from the old man's heart.

'Dead!' he exclaimed; 'dead!' he repeated. 'Starved!' he cried, and he went down on his knees. Old James's first impulse in every excitement was to go on his knees.

'Glory, honour, an' praise be to God Almighty, an' the Virgin Mother!' prayed old James Nolan. 'I'm a sinner – a sinner, so I am.'

And then the old man prayed over the dead body of the innocent baby, and he wept for the poor young mother; and he stooped over the little skeletons that slept through weariness, and cried in their sleep for bread, and he kissed them gently.

Emily Bowles (1818–1904)

While her novel *Irish Diamonds; or the Chronicles of Peterstown* is set in a 'straggling, up-and-down, in-and-out village' in Co. Meath during the Great Famine,[1] Emily Bowles (1818–1904) was born and bred in Abingdon, Berkshire (England), in a well-to-do Protestant family.[2] While two other brothers, John and Samuel, remained Protestants, Emily and her brother Frederick became Catholics in 1843, inspired by the Oxford Movement. When her brother joined the Oratory with John Henry Newman in 1847, Emily became involved in the foundation of a new religious order for the education for girls in Derby in 1846.[3] Six years later, as a nun in the Society of the Holy Child Jesus, Bowles was sent as superior to found a convent and school in Liverpool. Here she ran the Society into a debt of £6,000, an amount she had borrowed without permission in order to finance a teacher training college. As a result, Bowles was removed from her function as superior in 1854 and was dispensed from her vows in 1856.[4]

In 1850, during her time as a nun, Bowles had anonymously published *The History of England.* After her departure from the Society, Bowles must have opted for a literary career, as she wrote more than a dozen books between 1861 and 1888. These were largely translations from French Catholic literature,[5] but also included original writing, such as *Martha's Home; or, Work for Women* (1864), a collection of tales portraying charity work carried out by Sisters of a religious order. *Irish Diamonds*, described by Stephen Brown as '[a] story of landlord and tenant, of illicit distilling, and of proselytising' with a 'tone strongly Catholic and anti-Protestant',[6] centres on the conflict between Orangist land agent Moylan and farmer

---

1   F. Bowles, *Irish Diamonds; or the Chronicles of Peterstown* (London: Thomas Richardson, 1864), p. 1.
2   E. Short, *Newman and His Contemporaries* (London: Continuum, 2011), p. 180.
3   J.A. Marmion, 'Another Voice: The History of England for Catholic Children of 1850', *Paradigm: Journal of the Textbook Colloquium*, 24 (1997), http://faculty.ed.uiuc.edu/westbury/Paradigm/ Marmion2.html.
4   See R. Flaxman, *A Woman Styled Bold: The Life of Cornelia Connelly, 1809–1879* (London: Darton, Longman & Todd, 1991), pp. 247–51.
5   S.J.M. Brown, *Ireland in Fiction* (Dublin: Maunsel & Company, 1919), p. 39.
6   Ibid.

Randall Molina, who has assaulted the Scripture-reader Israel Brooker. As Bowles apparently never visited Famine-stricken Ireland, she may have been inspired to write a Famine narrative by the stories she heard from the Liverpool Catholic poor – a class including many Irish immigrants who had come off board in that city.

The novel mainly aims to promote Catholic doctrine. Against the background of the Famine the novel draws a strong contrast between the proselytizers on the one hand, who are depicted as wolves in their hunt for new souls to convert; and Father Murphy, who is the concerned shepherd who seeks to protect his congregation from damnation. *Irish Diamonds*, moreover, appears to be directly influenced by the politics of the Devotional Revolution at the time during which it was written, for the novel represents a priesthood which is devoted to the moral principles of its parishioners and which seeks to promote worship and Catholic rituals among the congregation. This is particularly illustrated in the passage below, in which Father Murphy admonishes his congregation to stay true to the Catholic creed even in the dire times of hunger.

From *Irish Diamonds; or, A Chronicle of Peterstown*

(London: Thomas Richardson & Son, 1864), pp. 197–203.

Father Murphy stood at the altar in his alb and stole.[7] He made the sign of the cross slowly and solemnly, and then began to speak. His voice was rich and strong, and poured out so easily through the windows as to be clearly heard to the farthest confines of the churchyard. He told the people in clear, common words that he had thought it well to call them together that night to speak of the state of the village and the surrounding country, and of their own souls. They had a good landlord, an excellent man he might say; but his ears were filled with idle tales, and he seldom saw his own tenants. Men who were prejudiced against the faith, *because*

---

7   A white tunic with a necktie worn by ordained clergy.

they did not know it, represented matters to him in a way contrary to the truth, and he believed what they said. There was but one cure for this – they must pray for their landlord. He was sorry to find and to see that they had not done this, and some of them had indulged evil and bitter feelings against him. He would not name them now, but he knew them all. Others had given a noble example of forgiveness, and they would have a blessing for it. From this very night they must all promise him to pray for their landlord every day. That was one thing he had to say to them.

Another was that some of them had acted worse than these. They had given in to temptation, and had sent their children, or allowed them to be taken, to the parson's school. They had not accepted the sufferings sent them by God; they had not borne with hunger and cold; but they had sold their children's souls for coals, and soup, and bread. If those who tempted them were justly called 'soupers', what kind of name did these deserve but 'soupers' slaves'? Poor, miserable, cowardly slaves, forgetting the life to come, and the beautiful courts of Heaven, and the crown of stars on our Lady's head, and the glorious Face of God, which was to be their everlasting reward; forgetting all this, and their own eternal glory, for a mouthful of bread and a stitch of rags! But he knew they had only forgotten themselves through trouble. They had turned their back on Almighty God for awhile, but they were now ready to return. They would not cast themselves to the devil for ever. He then, in the most powerful though rough way, drew a sketch of bygone times, and carried them all back, as he seemed to see it himself, to be eyewitnesses of what their forefathers had gone through for the faith. How during the 'Hag's War',[8] – when all that country had been laid desolate by Elizabeth's lieutenants, every farm a heap of smoking ruins, every village a street of empty roofless shells, every road strewed with dead horses, cows, and sheep, and with bodies of those who were ploughing their land or tending their flocks – death and destruction had filled the whole province; but where were the souls of those who died? They were gone up with their martyrs' crowns; they were kneeling round the crystal sea with palms in their hands for ever.

---

8   The term 'hag' here refers to Elizabeth I, the Virgin Queen (1533–1603). The Irish represented Elizabeth I not as a nurturing mother, as much English propaganda did, but as a 'calliagh' or old hag denying sustenance to the needy labourer. See L. Hopkins, *Writing Renaissance Queens: Texts by and about Elizabeth I and Mary, Queen of Scots* (Danvers, MA: Rosemont, 2002), p. 140.

And so, when Cromwell's soldiers had swept the country,[9] and, having killed the last of the O'Brian Blakes,[10] had quartered themselves in the old court, well did they know the tradition that the deep pool of Cahir-na-Duigan was then red as blood from the bodies that were thrown into it,[11] and that from that time to this, it is said no beast will drink of it, even on the hottest summer day. Those bodies were the congregation gathered in St Malachi of the Bocks,[12] when the soldiers came and surrounded the chapel, and killed the priest, and every man, woman, and child, there worshipping their God. But they were no 'soupers'. The mothers smiled when they saw their children butchered. They were true Irishwomen, and rejoiced to die for the ancient faith. And it was the same again and again – not many years beyond their memory – when the Orangemen first rose up, and began to search and imprison the Catholics wherever they pleased; and the triangle was set up in every town, and poor Catholics were flogged to death because they would not renounce their religion. There was not a Catholic whose life was safe; not one whose house was sacred, or whose goods were not a prey to the spoiler. But how many of them bought his safety at the price of his soul? But one; but one. Out of all the names recorded, there was but *one* who went back and renounced his God. These were the forefathers, what would they say to their faithless, degenerate children? And what would *God say to them*, but the one terrible word, 'Depart! Depart from Me, ye doubly cursed; cursed in the world by the Church, and in the next before all men and angels. Depart from Me for all eternity! You have chosen the devil; let him be your portion for ever!'[13]

At these words the feelings of the people, which had been raised to the highest pitch by the forcible sketches of past times and glories, towards which the Irishman looks back with a tender and half-sad, half-exulting regret, now burst beyond their control. A shivering sound of sobs and groans ran through the whole crowd; and they all fell on their knees, beating their breasts and kissing the earth. Those especially, like the

---

9   During Cromwell's Wars of the Three Kingdoms (1649–52), Cromwell landed with his Parliamentary troops in Ireland to conquer the land and its people.
10   The clan of the descendants of Brian Boru, King of Munster (c. 941–1014).
11   A stream in Co. Tipperary.
12   The Dominican church of St Malachi at Dundalk.
13   Matthew 25:41.

Sweeneys, Peter Kooney, and others, who had yielded to the storm, and sent their children to Mr Hall's school, were completely broken down by grief and horror at their present position.

Father Murphy saw that there was no resistance of will. He raised his hand, and, turning to the Tabernacle,[14] he promised our Lord, there present in the Blessed Sacrament, that His strayed sheep should return to their duty. He touchingly reminded Him of His long-suffering and mercy, and of His promise that all who repented should be pardoned by Him. And then he went down from the altar steps, and vested for Benediction.[15] The altar blazed with its myriad lights, the organ played softly, and the children of the choir, with Una, sang a few verses of a simple hymn. It was one they much loved to sing and hear, and which is not enough known:

To Our Lady of Sorrows

O Mother, most afflicted,
Standing beneath that tree,
Where Jesus stands rejected,
On the hill of Calvary![16]

Chorus. O Mary, sweetest Mother,
We love and pity thee;
And for the sake of Jesus,
Let us thy children be!

Thy heart is well-nigh breaking,
Thy Jesus thus to see,
Insulted, wounded, dying,
In greatest agony!

Chorus. O Mary, sweetest Mother, *&c.*

---

14   In the Bible the Tabernacle was the portable shrine for the divine presence, carried around by the Israelites from the time of the exodus from Egypt until the conquest of Canaan. See Exodus 40:18: 'Moses erected the tabernacle. He laid its bases, and set up its frames, and put in its poles, and raised up its pillars.' In the Catholic context, the word refers to the box in which the sacred host is kept.
15   A ritual during which the priest blesses the faithful by tracing the sign of the cross with the monstrance held upright before him.
16   This is another name for Golgotha, the hill on which Christ was crucified.

When the Blessed Sacrament had been exposed high above the altar, Father Murphy turned again to the weeping and praying people. He bade them, every one who was there present, – women and children as well as men, – raise his right hand, and promise solemnly that night to God never again, for the love or fear of anything whatever, to tamper with his faith, or to countenance any other in doing so. Thus, and thus only, would he be justified in admitting them to the Sacraments, or could they find prosperity or peace.

It was a wonderful and a beautiful sight. Instantly, both inside the crowded church and outside to the very boundary-walls, every head was raised, and every right hand lifted high above their heads. Then, with streaming eyes fixed on the Mystic Face of their God, did every creature present clearly and solemnly follow the words of the priest, and vow to be henceforth loyal and true.

'Come trouble and want, come sickness or famine, come persecution and beggary of all, I will truly practise the Catholic faith, and renounce all dealings with every false religion. So help me, my God!'

And He heard their vow, and blessed them from His throne.

There was not one among all that bowed and hushed multitude who did not turn to God that night with all his heart. The chains fell off them, and their bonds were broken; and from that hour there was no more tyranny that could hurt those souls. 'Souping' in Peterstown came to an end, and Una had enough to do with her full school and ignorant scholars to deaden the sting of her grief for the time.

T. Mason Jones

Educated at Trinity College Dublin, T. Mason Jones was politically active both in Ireland and in England, where he was a prominent member of the Reform League, which agitated for the reform of suffrage law.[1]

In 1868, he stood for Parliament, but his nomination was controversial and eventually he surrendered his candidacy.[2] In the 1850s, he served as the editor of the short-lived Dublin-based newspaper *The Tribune*.[3] Although a Protestant, he was opposed to the established Church in Ireland, and in the excerpt from *Old Trinity* (1867) reproduced here, the rector of the local Anglican parish, the Reverend Henry William de la Poer Beresford, is given short shrift.

As a review of *Old Trinity* suggests, the direct manner in which Jones addresses his subject matter raised eyebrows in some circles; in the anonymous reviewer's terms, 'Mr Jones is terribly unconventional, both in idea and expression.'[4] As the same reviewer remarks, Jones's plot functions mostly as 'a thread on which to hang some of his vivid pictures and able dissertations on men and things'.[5] Although the novel can be read as a 'bleak assessment' of Trinity College as an educational institute,[6] the friendship between two students on which the narrative centres is mainly a vehicle for the life story of one of them, Thomas Stead Butler. This rambling narrative encompasses a great number of themes related to the condition of Ireland in the first decades of the nineteenth century, such as the Famine, religious issues and the landlord question. The following passage details how Butler's mentor, the Dissenter preacher Doctor Young, assisted in relief efforts during the Famine, for which he is extolled by the local village priest, Father Brady. The contrast between the self-centred Beresford on the one hand and Dr Young and Father Brady on the other reflects Jones's dislike of the established Church.

---

1   For an overview of Jones's involvement with the Reform League, see A.D. Bell, 'Administration and Finance of the Reform League, 1865–1867', *International Review of Social History*, 10 (1965), pp. 385–409.

2   E. Larkin, *The Consolidation of the Roman Catholic Church in Ireland, 1860–1870* (Dublin: Gill & Macmillan, 1987), pp. 607–10.

3   S.J.M. Brown, *Ireland in Fiction* (Dublin: Maunsel & Company, 1919), p.149.

4   Review of T. Mason Jones, *Old Trinity*, *Christian Spectator*, 8, 3 (March 1867), p. 192.

5   Ibid.

6   T. Brown, *Ireland's Literature: Selected Essays* (Mullingar: Lilliput Press, 1988), p. 32.

From *Old Trinity: A Story of Real Life*

(London: Richard Bentley, 1867), vol. 2, pp. 135–43.

'With all his learning, experience, and ability, the doctor[7] was as innocent of the ways of the world as a child. He was so simple and unsuspecting, that you might deceive him twenty times a day. Truthful and straightforward himself, he was slow to suspect others of falsehood and duplicity. He had little or none of what is commonly called worldly wisdom, and was ignorant of all that cunning and self-seeking on which men of the world too often pride themselves. His ear was open to every tale of sorrow and distress. Those who wished to dupe him found an easy prey, for he has often said he would rather give to ninety-nine impostors than that one case of real want should go unrelieved.

'The divine instincts of pity and compassion were so strong in the man, that his hand and purse were constantly open. He was frightened at the condition of the peasantry, and the events of the famine years almost broke his heart. It was upon such a man as this, "an Israelite indeed, in whom there was no guile,"[8] that the lordly rector of the parish looked down with scorn, and treated with an indifference bordering close on contempt.

'The Reverend Henry William de la Poer Beresford was the incumbent. The parish of Ossory was worth about £1100 a year, and Mr Beresford obtained it. He paid a poor curate, named Scott £80 a year, to do the duty, and cure the few souls committed to his care. He was away from his living nine months in the year, and spent the three months that he remained at home, shooting, coursing, and fox-hunting.

'The rector kept his dogs and horses in splendid style, and did credit to the church militant at the hunt. He has been known to break a quartern loaf in two, and pouring over the bread a bottle of port wine, give it to his greyhounds before starting for a coursing match, while the people around

---

7   Dr Young, a Dissenter preacher.

8   John 1:47. 'Jesus saw Nathanael coming toward him and said of him, "Behold, an Israelite indeed, in whom there is no deceit [var. guile]!"'

him were dying of fever and famine.[9] He seldom preached. He left that duty to the curate. He was, however, a fine reader; and, as he stood robed in his white surplice in the reading-desk, or by the grave, his tall graceful figure looked to great advantage; and he rolled out in a full deep voice the sentences of the Burial Service with an air of satisfaction that said plainly enough, "You may well admire me, my good people. I do this kind of thing well, and I quite enjoy it."

'In '46, a local committee was formed for the relief of the poor of the village.[10] Mr Beresford was appointed chairman, and Dr Young and Father Brady, the parish priest, were hon. secretaries. The chairman headed the subscription list with a donation of five pounds, and what was his vexation when Dr Young and Father Mat put down their names for twenty pounds each. The chairman was not surprised that the priest should subscribe largely for the relief of his own flock, but he could not understand why twenty pounds should be given for the purpose by a poor dissenting preacher. He would have been still more astonished if he had known that Dr Young had sent and carried wine and food to the cabins of the poor; that, in order to relieve his sick, starving neighbours, the good doctor had placed his own small household on short – almost starving allowance; that everything, not merely of luxury, but of comfort, was excluded from his table, and nothing allowed on it, but what was necessary for mere subsistence. Even then, he was pained and grieved to know how utterly inadequate his means were to meet the existing distress.

'In these ministrations of mercy, the doctor came into frequent contact with Father Brady. They met each other daily on their rounds, and a warm friendship sprung up between the puritan and the priest. "Do you know, Mr Young", the latter said one day, "I am beginning to feel jealous of you?

---

9   Intriguingly, dogs feature frequently in Famine fiction, often as well-fed animals that form a stark contrast with starving people or as creatures that deprive the hungry of their last morsels. See, for example, a harrowing scene in Charles Joseph Kickham's *Sally Cavanagh; or the Untenanted Graves* (Dublin: W.B. Kelly, 1869), which depicts Brian Purcell's well-fed greyhounds Bran and Gazelle munching away at a 'large piece of the Bread' (p. 155) while starving Sally comes to beg for food at the door.

10 Local relief committees were one of the three central components of the government Famine relief policy from 1846 onwards, the other two being public works and workhouses. According to Christine Kinealy, '[t]heir main functions were to raise subscriptions for a local relief fund, to provide small works of local utility, and ... to promote works of more general improvement such as drainage or land reclamation.' *This Great Calamity* (Dublin: Gill & Macmillan, 2006), p. 82.

I am, indeed. My poor people are getting fonder of you than they are of me. I hear your praises sounded wherever I go. I only ask you not to make Protestants of them."

"'Ah, Mr Brady, do not fear. The Samaritan did not inquire what religion the man wounded by the wayside was of.[11] It matters little what we call ourselves if the heart be right. Mercy is of no sect."

"'Right, sir! very true! I think I am nearer being a Protestant than ever I was before. And to tell you the truth, if it would make a better Christian of me, I should not be sorry. God help me."

"'You surprise me, Father Brady.'

"'It's all your fault, sir. You put us to the blush. If we were all like you, Doctor Young, it would not matter by what name we were called, Protestant or Catholic. Although I am a priest, I read my Bible, and I know that you practise what it calls 'religion, pure and undefiled',[12] and if that doesn't take a man to Heaven, nothing will."

'And the two men, representatives of antagonistic creeds, shook each other cordially by the hand. Father Brady took a pinch of snuff, blew his nose violently, and went on his way.

'The Reverend Mathew Brady had been a distinguished student at Maynooth,[13] and was now a contented parish priest. He was a large, stout man; with a corporation, a regular Celtic head, sanguineous complexion, a jolly beaming face, and a roguish blue eye, that sparkled with drollery and good-humour. There was nothing of the anchorite or hermit about "Father Mat", as his flock universally called him. On the contrary, he enjoyed the good things of this life, and was not ashamed to own it. "Fasting", he said "did not agree with him." He was never so happy as after a good dinner, followed by five or six glasses of whisky-punch. Then his eye grew still brighter, his face shone with satisfaction, and his stories set the table in a roar.

---

11   Dr Young here refers to the New Testament parable of the Good Samaritan (Luke 10:25–37), in which a Samaritan helps an injured Jewish man fallen by the roadside, despite the discord between Jews and Samaritans, while two Jewish priests walk by without tending to the man. By drawing this parallel, Dr Young emphasizes that charity should not be restricted by sectarian boundaries.

12   James 1:27. 'Religion that is pure and undefiled before God, the Father, is this: to visit orphans and widows in their affliction, and to keep oneself unstained from the world.'

13   St Patrick's College in Maynooth, Co. Kildare. The college was established in 1795 by an Act of the Irish parliament to educate Irish Catholic priests, and became the largest seminary in the world.

'He kept a brace of greyhounds, and enjoyed a good course. He winked roguishly at the girls as they passed, and they laughed and called him "the funny Father Mat". He spoke of Doctor Young in the highest terms from the altar; eulogized him for his charity to the poor, and told them to be sure and carry home his turf. To all of which there was a ready and general response. I was standing one morning at the library window with the doctor, when we saw coming up the avenue and along the road, a long cavalcade of seventy or eighty cars laden with turf, and before the doctor could recover from his amazement, it was stacked in the yard, and his year's fuel secured, without costing him a sixpence. No people more gratefully remember benefits conferred upon them than the Irish peasantry.

'The perplexity in the doctor's face was a perfect study, as he watched the long line of horses and carts filing into the yard, and saw the crowd of men and boys, women and girls, that had taken possession of his premises, and, without leave, asked or obtained, began with laughter and joking to pile and clamp the turf. He walked from the sitting-room to the library and back again with a puzzled look in his face.

'"I cannot understand all this", he cried, "I gave no orders to have the turf brought home. I thought next month would be time enough."

'"If you gave no orders, Father Brady did", I answered, "this is his work."

'"Father Brady! Is it possible? How much shall I have to pay them?"

'"Pay them! Nothing at all. I should like to see you offer them payment."

'"Not pay them. Am I to take their time and labour for nothing?"

'"Certainly. They will not take a farthing. This is a compliment to you."

'I could see he was touched with this proof of the people's gratitude.

'"What", he asked, "might not be done with such people, by a little kindness and justice?" Soon after, the spokesman of the party, a young farmer, came in, hat in hand, to tell us what they had done, and to wish his honour long life, health, and happiness; and after three cheers for the doctor, they departed.'

Section 4

Landlords and Tenants

William Carleton (1794–1869)

William Carleton's *The Squanders of Castle Squander* (1852) is a typical Big House novel in that it focuses on a single upper-class family and their mansion and traces the dissolution of the house against the background of an Irish crisis[1] – in this case, the Great Famine. The novel does not only focus on the suffering of the poor, but also traces how a combination of factors such as the obligations laid upon landlords under the Poor Law and the diminution of rental income – combined with reckless spending habits and bad business decisions – brought low many landlords. Unlike Carleton's earlier *The Black Prophet*, which was published in 1847, when the eventual scale of the 1840s famine was not yet fully clear, *Squanders* was written with the benefit of hindsight. Written after the event, it lacks the urgent tone that characterizes *The Black Prophet*, whose purpose was activist as much as literary. Nevertheless, the work is highly moralistic; as a contemporary reviewer pointed out, '[t]his is a socio-didactic novel, where a particular family is chosen as the type of a class, and their characters, conduct, and fortunes are exhibited, less perhaps to adorn a tale than to point to a national moral.'[2]

Although Carleton's depiction of Irish life was generally considered first-rate, many reviewers took issue with the author's tendency to intersperse his narratives with lengthy disquisitions on sociopolitical issues. As one reviewer complained, '[w]e get a brief glimpse here and there of true Irish life: the rest is all about tenant-right and a multitude of other topics connected with politics and political economy...The sermons...are neither well written nor very well seasoned, and they swarm with small inaccuracies in statements of fact.'[3]

---

1   As Vera Kreilkamp writes in her seminal *The Anglo-Irish Novel and the Big House* (Syracuse, NY: Syracuse University Press, 1998), 'Big House novels represent a major tradition in Irish fiction. Set on isolated country estates, they dramatize the tensions between several social groups: the landed proprietors of a Protestant ascendancy gentry; a growing, usually Catholic middle class; and the mass of indigenous, rural Catholic tenantry. In the course of two centuries, these novels reveal recurring themes and conventions, most notably the setting of a beleaguered and decaying country house collapsing under the forces of Anglo-Irish improvidence and the rising Irish nationalism of the Irish society outside the walls of the demesne' (pp. 6–7).

2   'Carleton's *Squanders of Castle Squander*', *Spectator*, 25, 1253 (1852), p. 638.

3   P. Murray, 'Traits of the Irish Peasantry', *Edinburgh Review*, 69, 196 (1852), p. 403.

The novel's narrator, Randy O'Rollick, is an initially dissolute hedge scholar who is employed as a tutor for the Squander sons, Dick, Harry and James. With the exception of James, his sister Emily, and their uncle Tom, the Squanders are all profligate spenders, and the house is serviced by an excessively large retinue of conniving servants. As Mrs Squander reminds the baker in the excerpt printed below, she is the daughter of a peer, and demands that Mr Squander support her in a way suitable to her class, even though this means that Mr Squander has to rack up huge debts. Eventually, Mr Squander is flung into debtors' prison, and shortly upon his release, he dies. Dick, his heir, then installs his brother Harry as manager of the estate, which is suffering heavily under the effects of Famine. Harry shows himself a ruthless and even cruel manager, evicting scores of tenants without managing to improve the family's financial position. His cruelty sparks rebellion, and ultimately he is shot by a tenant. Dick loses the estate and becomes a poor-rate collector instead. At the end, it is suggested that Emily's father-in-law might buy the estate following the passage of the 1849 Encumbered Estates Act, heralding the rise of a new and more conscientious ruling class.

From *The Squanders of Castle Squander*

(London: Illustrated London Library, 1852), vol. 2, pp. 76–80, 87–8.

One day about this time the baker came as usual, but refused to leave bread unless the amount was settled. This was the first time that such a circumstance ever occurred, or was even dreamt of. The family had been for some time forced down to the closest limit. The housekeeper had been gone long ago, and no servants were retained unless such as were indispensably necessary. The duties of housekeeper Emily took upon herself, for under no circumstances could Mrs Squander be prevailed upon to look into or undertake the management of her own domestic affairs.

'Ma'am', said Nogher the old butler, who was now forced to act in a manifold capacity, 'ma'am', said he, approaching his mistress with a face of dismay, 'will you allow me to say a word to you?'

'Certainly, Nogher; why should I not allow an aged and faithful servant to speak to me on all becoming occasions? I suppose it is concerning the arrear of your wages, Nogher, which Miss Squander spoke to me about. I am truly sorry for your daughter's illness and that of her family; but until the rents come in she can have bread and other matters from this house. The wealthy and high-born, Nogher, should not overlook the distresses of their dependants. I except against mere tenants and cases of sickness or contagion – cases in which, I am sorry to say, Miss Squander, from a mistaken principle, runs foolish and unjustifiable risks. Let your daughter then and her children have bread and other provisions from this family until the rents come in.'

The old man was touched by this unexpected instance of generosity from his mistress, and the tears stood in his eyes as he spoke.

'I scarcely know how to tell you, ma'am', he replied; 'but I'm glad that the old master's gone, for it would break his heart; it's hard enough upon myself, ma'am', and the tears fairly ran down his cheeks.

'What is it, Nogher?' she asked; 'I am not now what I have been. I cannot bear suspense or agitation. What is it?'

'The baker's below, ma'am, and he says he won't lave any more bread, unless his masther's account is settled. You'll excuse me, ma'am, but if he doesn't lave the bread – '

Mrs Squander rose up, and swept through the drawingroom with great dignity, and greater passion. 'You don't tell me, Nogher – you can't presume to tell me, that this man – this insolent fellow – this plebeian baker, refuses to leave his bread?'

'Don't blame me, ma'am, but I'm forced to tell you so.'

'I must see him', she replied; 'I must see this ungrateful creature; does he know – '

She went down in a high state of indignation to the hall, on the steps of which the baker was standing.

'What is this', she exclaimed, 'which the butler has told me? It cannot surely be true that you have refused to leave bread as usual?'

'Don't blame me, ma'am, but my master', said the man; 'I'm acting only according to his orders.'

'Who is your master, my good man? Nogher, who is the person that has been serving this family with bread?'

'Mr Brennan, ma'am', replied the butler; 'an honest man by all accounts, and a good baker as you know.'

'Does your master, my good man, know who *I am*?' she asked, with a swell of pride that was rather ludicrous. 'Does he know that my father was a peer? that I am the daughter of a nobleman? Does he know all this?'

'It's more than I can say, ma'am', replied the baker; 'but he knows that there's nearly two hundred pounds due, and I know that he forbid me to lave any more bread unless I was paid. It's not my fault, ma'am; but he says the times is hard, and that he can't afford to lie any longer out of the money.'

'Does he know, sir, that I am the daughter of the late Lord Gallivant? Does he know that my noble father was the particular friend of the great statesman, Lord Castlereagh?[4] Go home, my good man, and tell him who I am, and see then if he will presume to – '

'I beg your pardon, ma'am', said the baker; 'but I'm afeard that if I tould him all this, it would only make him worse.'

'The thing's impossible, my good man; explain yourself.'

'Bekaise, ma'am, my masther's a Repaler,[5] and he hates the very name of Castlereagh, because he brought about the Union; and I'm sartin, ma'am, that if he had suspected you to be the daughter of any friend of his, he'd have stopped givin' credit long ago. It's upon the strength of the ould Squire himself, ma'am, that he gave credit so long as he did. At least, so he says – '

'Oh, yes', she replied, 'I can understand that – I raised the position of my husband, and brought him high connection, my good man. The character of his wife was reflected on him, and being son-in-law to a distinguished nobleman, his memory is yet, as such, treated with respect.'

---

4   Robert Stewart, 2nd Marquess of Londonderry (1769–1822), commonly known as Lord Castlereagh, was Chief Secretary for Ireland between 1797 and 1801. In this capacity, he played an important part in the quenching of the 1798 United Irishmen Rebellion and the passing of the Act of Union in 1800. Because of this, he was not exactly popular among Irish nationalists.

5   Repealers supported the campaign of Daniel O'Connell for the repeal of the 1801 Act of Union, and the re-establishment of an Irish Parliament. See for instance the poem 'O'Connell's Warning', printed in *The Repealer Repulsed!* (Belfast: William M'Comb, 1841): 'And your clan of Repealers are scattered in fight, / Who burn to restore to our Island its crown' (p. 145).

'Am I to be paid for the bread, ma'am?' replied the blunt baker; 'bekaise if I'm not, I can't lave it. I was forbid to do so.'

'I never enter into domestic matters', she replied; 'but, in this instance, I desire you to let your master know that I am the only daughter of the late Lord Gallivant, and that he ought to consider it an honour to have such a lady, or the son of such a lady, his debtor. If he is ignorant of the honour we have conferred upon him by allowing him to give us such liberal credit, I can only say that I shall transfer my patronage and the influence of my name to some baker who may be better acquainted with the Peerage.'

...

In this state of things, the landlords arose one morning and found themselves bankrupts. They had forgotten that in conniving at or encouraging, for political purposes, the subdivision of land, they were also increasing a pauper population. The fatal facility of producing the potato crop rendered the means of life easy to a class of persons, whose standard of comfort was based only on slavery and wretchedness. They forgot, that a young married couple in the poorest hut, will generally breed with a fertility in proportion to their poverty. They forgot that, by suffering such a mass of national misery to accumulate under their eyes, they were throwing these creatures into the hands of the agitator and the dema-gogue, who, in point of fact, cared as little about them as the landlord did, and only made a political use of them as a stock in trade, precisely as the landlord himself had done before them. There they were, however, a gigantic and multitudinous Frankenstein,[6] created by corruption, and their unholy creators saw that their own safety as landowners consisted only in their destruction. Hence the unnatural and inhuman crusade against their very existence into which these landowners have considered it their duty to combine; and hence those horrible and terrific outrages, in the name and under the sanction of law, against the rights of life, and the claims of common humanity to live, so long as the individual is not stained with crime.

---

6   This is a reference to Mary Shelley's famous monster, rather than his creator, Victor Frankenstein himself. Intriguingly, in the British media Ireland was often likened to the monster of Frankenstein. For example, in May 1882 *Punch* published a cartoon entitled 'The Irish Franken-stein', depicting a monstrous ruffian holding a knife.

Charles Lever (1806–72)

If a nation is to be judged by her bearing under calamity, Ireland – and she has had some experiences – comes well through the ordeal. That we may yet see how she will sustain her part in happier circumstances is my hope and my prayer, and that the time be not too far off.[1]

Thus writes Charles Lever in the preface to *The Martins of Cro'Martin*, a novel first published in 1856,[2] and as such written shortly after the Famine. The narrative takes place partially in the west of Ireland and partially in Paris, and is set in pre-Famine times, in the late 1820s and 1830s. Nevertheless, the text clearly resonates with the hardships of the period of the Great Hunger. Lever's hope painfully exposes the fissure between the understanding of the Famine and its impact on Irish life in its immediate aftermath and the irreversible and far-reaching consequences the Famine was to have in the long run.

W.J. Fitzpatrick wrote that *The Martins* was a 'thoroughly Irish book' which was 'tinged by the sadness of his [Lever's] own experiences when ministering to the suffering of cholera patients in Clare'.[3] Lever was the son of Irish Julia Chandler and James Lever, an English carpenter and builder, who helped build the Bank of Ireland and Maynooth College. He practised medicine for a number of years, which led him to work with cholera patients in Clare.[4] Once he started writing, Lever became quite prolific. Many of his novels were first published in serialized form, and his articles and stories were printed in journals, including *The National Magazine*, *Blackwood's*, *The Cornhill* and *Dublin University Magazine*,[5] which he edited from 1842 to 1845.[6] Lever spent much of his time abroad, taking his family with him to places such as Brussels, where he practised

1   C. Lever, *The Martins of Cro' Martin* (London: Ward, Lock & Company, 1872), p. 4.
2   S.J.M. Brown, *Ireland in Fiction* (Dublin: Maunsel & Company, 1919), p. 143.
3   W.J. Fitzpatrick, *The Life of Charles Lever* (London: Ward, Lock & Company, 1884), p. 312.
4   C.A. Read and T.P. O'Connor, *The Cabinet of Irish Literature*, vol. 4 (London: Blackie, 1880), pp. 78–9.
5   S.J.M. Brown, *Ireland in Fiction*, p. 140.
6   M. Kelleher, 'Prose Writing and Drama in English, 1830–1890: From Catholic Emancipation to the Fall of Parnell', in M. Kelleher and P. O'Leary (eds), *The Cambridge History of Irish Literature*, vol. 1 (Cambridge: Cambridge University Press, 2006), p. 453.

medicine; Florence, La Spezia (Italy), where he was appointed British vice-consul; and Trieste, where he became consul[7] and lived until his death in 1872.

Lever was well-known in his own time as a novelist and Tory, and Brown describes him as 'by far the greatest of that group of writers, who by education and sympathies are identified with the English element in Ireland'.[8] *The Martins* is a multifaceted novel, depicting societal hardships from both the perspective of the landlord classes and the impoverished tenants. Although showing both sides of the divide, critics felt that Lever's depictions of lower-class characters – due to his middle-class English background[9] – were one-dimensional, even bordering on the 'offensive', and that his peasants 'are more than half stage-Irishmen'.[10] This awareness caused bad feelings among other Irish writers, and Yeats even stated derisively that Lever 'wrote ever with one eye on London'.[11]

The landlord of Lever's novel, Richard Martin, is a good-hearted man, who unfortunately has made bad decisions in life, is not fit to be a landlord and is not very strong-willed. The estate – especially after Richard Martin becomes chronically ill – is run by his wife Lady Dorothea, a cold, indifferent and, because of her pride, even cruel mistress, who blames the tenants for all their hardships, and refuses to help them, to the point of evicting them because they speak up against her and her class. Mary Martin is the opposite of her aunt Lady Dorothea: a pure-hearted and benevolent young woman who will spare no effort or expense to alleviate the tenants' sufferings. As Richard and Dorothea Martin leave the country, they become absentee landlords, leaving the governing of the estate to their agent and Mary. Even abroad, Lady Dorothea counteracts all of Mary's plans for innovation and the improvement of the tenantry's conditions. The excerpt below starts with a conversation about upcoming evictions between Lady Dorothea and her servant, Kate Henderson, and functions as an apt illustration of the landlord – tenant divide in mid-nineteenth-century Ireland.

---

7   Kelleher, 'Prose Writing and Drama in English, 1830–1890', p. 468.
8   Brown, *Ireland in Fiction*, p. 140.
9   Kelleher, 'Prose Writing and Drama in English, 1830–1890', p. 466.
10   The late-nineteenth-century American critic Horace Sheafe Krans, quoted in Brown, *Ireland in Fiction*, p. 140.
11   W.B. Yeats, 'Popular Ballad Poetry of Ireland', *The Leisure Hour*, 38, 11 (1889), p. 106.

From *The Martins of Cro' Martin*

(New York: Harper & Brothers, 1856), pp. 100–2.

'Have you made out the list I spoke of?'

'Yes, my lady, in part; some details are wanting, but there are eighteen cases here quite perfect.'

'These are all cottiers[12] – pauper tenants', said Lady Dorothea, scanning the paper superciliously through her eye-glass.

'Not all, my lady; here, for instance, is Dick Sheehan, the blacksmith, who has worked for the Castle twenty-eight years, and who holds a farm called Mullanahogue on a lease.'

'And he voted against us?'[13] broke she in.

'Yes; and made a very violent speech too.'

'Well, turn him out then', said Lady Dorothea, interrupting her. 'Now, where's your father? Send for Henderson at once; I'll have no delay with this matter.'

'I have sent for him, my lady; he'll be here within half an hour.'

'And Scanlan[14] also. We shall want him.'

'Mr Scanlan will be here at the same time.'

'This case here, with two crosses before it, what does this refer to?' said her ladyship, pointing to a part of the paper.

'That's Mr Magennis, my lady, of Barnagheela, who has been making incessant appeals for a renewal of his tenure – '

'And how did he behave?'

'He seconded Mr Massingbred's[15] nomination, and made a very outrageous speech on the occasion.'

'To be sure, I remember him; and he had the insolence – the unpar-

---

12   Cottiers were smallholders, peasants renting and farming very small plots of land.
13   The Martins entered in the most recent local elections, and because their tenants did not vote for them, underwent a great and humiliating loss.
14   Maurice Scanlan is the Martins' attorney.
15   Jack Messingbred, an upper-class character who ran against the Martins in the recent local elections and won.

alleled insolence – afterward to address Miss Martin, as she sat beside me in the carriage, and to tell her that if the rest of the family had been like her, the scene that had been that day enacted would never have occurred! Who is this Hosey Lynch? His name is so familiar to me.'

'He is a post-master of Oughterard, and a kind of factotum in the town.'

'Then make a note of him. He must be dismissed at once.'

'He is not a freeholder, my lady, but only mentioned as an active agent of the Liberal party.'[16]

'Don't adopt that vulgar cant, Miss Henderson – at least when speaking to me. They are not – they have no pretensions to be called the Liberal party. It is bad taste as well as bad policy to apply a flattering epithet to a faction.'

'What shall I call them in future, my lady?' asked Kate, with a most admirably assumed air of innocence.

'Call them Papists,[17] Radicals, Insurgents – any thing, in fact, which may designate the vile principles they advocate. You mentioned Mr Nelligan,[18] and I own to you I felt ill – positively ill – at the sound of his name. Just to think of that man's ingratitude – base ingratitude. It is but the other day his son[19] was our guest here – actually dined at the table with us! You were here. *You* saw him yourself.'

'Yes, my lady', was the quiet reply.

'I'm sure nothing could be more civil, nothing more polite, than our reception of him. I talked to him myself, and asked him something – I forget what – about his future prospects, and see if this very man, or his father – for it matters not which – is not the ringleader of this same movement! I tell you, child – and I really do not say so to hurt your feelings, or to aggravate your natural regrets at your condition in life, but

---

16   The Liberal Party grew out of the Whig Party and although it already existed in the 1830s, had its first big success in 1868 under the leadership of William Gladstone. Liberals were in favour of '[e]conomic freedom, in the form of free enterprise at home and free trade in international relations', which they believed would 'result in economic growth and benefit to all'. M. Pearce and G. Stewart, *British Political History 1867–2001: Democracy and Decline*, 3rd edn (London: Routledge, 2002), pp. 28–9. Because the Liberal Party was not an independent political party in the time of Lever's narrative, and because the Liberal ideals go directly against Lady Dorothea's station and ideas, she refuses to call them anything else than a 'faction'.

17   Roman Catholics, a term which – like 'Radicals' and 'Insurgents' – is clearly adopted unjustly by Lady Dorothea to describe the Liberal Party.

18   Pat Nelligan is a humble and hard-working local shopkeeper.

19   Joseph Nelligan, a local law student who has befriended Mr Massingbred, the Martins' political opponent.

I say it as a great moral lesson – that low people are invariably deceitful. Perhaps they do not always intend it; perhaps – and very probably, indeed – their standard of honorable dealing is a low one; but of the fact itself you may rest assured. They are treacherous, and they are vindictive!' . . .

Lady Dorothea was too deeply occupied with her own thoughts to waste a second's consideration on either of them, and promptly said,

'I want you, Henderson, to inform me who are the chief persons who have distinguished themselves in this outrageous insult to us in the borough.'

Mr Henderson moved from one foot to the other, once more stroked down his hair, and seemed like a man suddenly called upon to enter on a very unpleasant and somewhat difficult task.

'Perhaps you don't like the office, sir?' said she, hastily. 'Perhaps your own principles are opposed to it?'

'Na, my leddy', said he, deferentially, 'I ha' nae principles but such as the family sanctions. It's nae business o' mine to profess poleetical opinions.'

'Very true, sir – very just; you comprehend your station', replied she, proudly. 'And now to my demand. Who are the heads of this revolt? for it is a revolt!'

'It's nae sa much a revolt, my leddy', rejoined he, slowly and respectfully, 'as the sure and certain consequence of what has been going on for years on the property. I did my best, by warning, and indeed by thwarting, so far as I could, these same changes. But I was not listened to. I foretold what it would all end in, this amelearating the condition of the small farmer – this raising the moral standard o' the people, and a' that. I foresaw that if they grew richer, they'd grow sturdier; and if they learned to read, they'd begin to reflact. Ah, my leddy, a vara dangerous practice this same habit of reflaction is, to folk who wear ragged clothes and dine on potatoes!' . . .

Before Mr Henderson had completed that hesitating process which with him was the prelude to an answer, the door opened, and Mary Martin entered. She was in a riding-dress, and bore the traces of the road on her splashed costume; but her features were paler than usual, and her lip quivered as she spoke.

'My dear Aunt', cried she, not seeming to notice that others were present, 'I have come back at speed from Kyle's Wood to learn if it be true – but it can not be true – however the poor creatures there believe it – that they are to be discharged from work, and no more employment given at the quarries. You haven't seen them, dear Aunt – you haven't beheld them, as I did this morning – standing panic-stricken around the scene of their once labour, not speaking, scarcely looking at each other, more like a shipwrecked crew upon an unknown shore than fathers and mothers beside their own homesteads!'

'It was I gave the order, Miss Martin', said Lady Dorothea, proudly. 'If these people prefer political agitation to an honest subsistence, let them pay the price of it.'

'But who says that they have done so?' replied Mary. 'These poor creatures have not a single privilege to exercise; they haven't a vote among them. The laws have forgotten them just as completely as human charity has.'

'If they have no votes to record, they have voices to outrage and insult their natural protectors. Henderson knows that the worst mobs in the borough were from this very district.'

'Let him give the names of those he alludes to. Let him tell me ten – five – ay, three, if he can, of Kyle's Wood men who took any share in the disturbances. I am well aware that it is a locality where he enjoys little popularity himself; but at least he need not calumniate its people. Come, sir, who are these you speak of?'

Kate Henderson, who sat with bent-down head during this speech, contrived to steal a glance at the speaker so meaningful and so suppli-cating, that Mary faltered, and as a deep blush covered her cheek, she hastily added, 'But this is really not the question. This miserable contest has done us all harm; but let us not perpetuate its bitterness! We have been beaten in an election, but I don't think we ought to be worsted in a struggle of generosity and good feeling. Come over, dear Aunt, and see these poor creatures.'

'I shall certainly do no such thing, Miss Martin. In the first place, the fever[20] never leaves that village.'

'Very true, Aunt; and it will be worse company if our kindness should desert them. But if you will not come, take *my* word for the state of their destitution. We have nothing so poor on the whole estate.'

'It is but a moment back I was told that the spirit of resistance to our

---

20 Famine fever. According to R.T. Lyons, '[a] contagious fever, generated by starvation, chiefly met with among the poorer classes, and occurring as an epidemic during seasons of scarcity and famine.' See *A Treatise on Relapsing or Famine Fever* (London: Henry S. King, 1872), p. 1.

influence here arose from the wealthy independence of the people; now, I am informed it is their want and destitution suggest the opposition. I wish I could ascertain which of you is right.'

'It's little matter, if our theory does not lead us to injustice', said Mary, boldly. 'Let me only ride back to the quarries, Aunt, and tell these poor people that they've nothing to fear – that there is no thought of withdrawing from them their labour nor its hire. Their lives are, God knows, not overlaid with worldly blessings; let us not add one drop that we can spare to their cup of sorrow.'

'The young leddy says na mare than the fact; they're vara poor, and they're vara dangerous!'

'How do you mean dangerous, sir?' asked Lady Dorothea, hastily.

'There's more out o' that barony at the Assizes,[21] my leddy, than from any other on the property.'

'Starvation and crime are near relatives all the world over', said Mary; 'nor do I see that the way to cure the one, is to increase the other.'

'Then let us get rid of both,' said Lady Dorothea. 'I don't see why we are to nurse pauperism either into fever or rebellion. To feed people that they may live to infect you, or, perhaps, shoot you, is sorry policy. You showed me a plan for getting rid of them, Henderson – something about throwing down their filthy hovels, or unroofing them, or something of that kind, and then they were to emigrate – I forget where – to America, I believe – and become excellent people, hard-working and quiet.[22] I know it all sounded plausible and nice; tell Miss Martin your scheme, and if it does not fulfil all you calculated, it will at least serve for an example on the estate.'

'An example!' cried Mary. 'Take care, my lady. It's a dangerous precept you are about to inculcate, and admits of a terrible imitation!'

---

21   The assizes was a civil and criminal court which periodically held session in each county in England, Ireland and Wales.

22   Many Irish pre-Famine and Famine emigrants were just as much marginalized socially and economically in diaspora as at home. As nationalist Jeremiah O'Donovan Rossa wrote in 1898: 'I cannot feel that America is my country ... I am made to see that the English power, and the English influence and the English hate, and the English boycott against the Irishman is to-day as active in America as it is in Ireland.' *Rossa's Recollections, 1838–1898* (New York: Mariner's Harbor, 1898), p. 262. Therefore, Lady Dorothea's outlook on migration is far too rose-coloured. For a concise history of Irish America, see K. Kenny's *The American Irish: A History* (New York: Longman, 2000).

'Now you have decided me, Miss Martin', said Lady Dorothea, haughtily.

'And, good Heavens! is it for a rash word of mine – for a burst of temper that I could not control – you will turn out upon the wide world a whole village – the old that have grown grey there – the infant that clings to its mother in her misery, and makes a home for her by its very dependence – '

'Every one of them, sir,' said Lady Dorothea, addressing herself to Henderson, who had asked some question in a low whisper. 'They're cottiers all; they require no delays of law, and I insist upon it peremptorily.'

'Not till my uncle hears of it!' exclaimed Mary, passionately, 'a cruel wrong like this shall not be done in mad haste.' And with these words, uttered in all the vehemence of great excitement, she rushed from the room in search of Martin.

Anthony Trollope (1815–82)

Although Anthony Trollope was an Englishman, many of his fictional works are set in Ireland and concern important Irish themes such as the Famine. Born in London on 24 April 1815, Trollope was educated at various prestigious public schools, including Harrow and Winchester. In 1834, he became a clerk at the London headquarters of the Post Office. He was anything but a dutiful employee, and also had trouble supporting himself, running up debt as a result. In 1841, he applied for the position of postal surveyor in Ireland to escape his failed London life, and was appointed to a post in Banagher, Co. Offaly. In Ireland, Trollope was much more successful, both professionally and privately, and began writing in earnest, publishing a number of (Irish-themed) novels such as *The Macdermots of Ballycloran* (1847) and *The Kellys and O'Kellys* (1848). As Owen Dudley Edwards states, '[h]is view of Ireland from first to last was that of a participant: Ireland made him'.[1] In Ireland, Trollope's productivity increased due to the strict writing habits he developed, and with the publication of *Barchester Towers* (1857) his popularity took flight. In 1867, Trollope resigned from the Post Office, as the income from his literary endeavours was sufficient for him to live on. He wrote a total of forty-seven novels, and was one of the most popular English authors of the nineteenth century, although his popularity has since waned. He died in London in 1882.[2]

As Trollope lived in Ireland during the Famine and had to travel around extensively because of his professional duties, he witnessed the horrors of famine at first-hand, and commented on the state of the country in seven letters published in the *Examiner* in 1849–50. In these letters he showed great sympathy for the plight of the Irish who, he felt, manifested a great potential to improve their country, but were brutally beaten down in their efforts by the Famine: 'No Irishman ever lacks the ability, when he can muster the will, to put his shoulder to the wheel; many good men have

---

1   O.D. Edwards, 'Anthony Trollope, the Irish Writer', *Nineteenth-Century Fiction*, 38, 1 (1983), p. 1.
2   This biographical sketch is based on N.J. Hall, 'Trollope, Anthony (1815–1882)', *Oxford Dictionary of National Biography*, Oxford University Press, 2004, online edn, 2006, www.oxford dnb.com/view/article/27748; and V. Glendinning, *Trollope* (London: Hutchinson, 1992).

been formed during the last three years; but in the spring of 1847 the energies of the country were expended in petitions for relief.'[3]

Trollope's 'big house' novel *Castle Richmond* (1860) is set in Co. Cork during the Famine and contains extensive descriptions of starvation, class conflicts, and relief efforts. Trollope comments in detail upon the past situation in Famine Ireland, drawing upon the providentialist discourse about the causes of the calamity to present the Famine as a relief for the poor tenants, since it would 'result in the renewal of the land system that had been neglected by lazy landlords':[4]

> But though I do not believe in exhibitions of God's anger, I do believe in exhibitions of his mercy. When men by their folly and by the shortness of their vision have brought upon themselves penalties which seem to be overwhelming ... then God raises his hand, not in anger, but in mercy, and by his wisdom does for us that for which our own wisdom has been insufficient.[5]

The main plot focuses on the romantic entanglement between Clara, the daughter of the Earl of Desmond, and her two suitors, Owen Fitzgerald and his cousin Herbert Fitzgerald, the heir to Richmond Castle. The plot is spiced up by a number of subplots, the most important of which concerns the blackmailing of Sir Thomas, Herbert's father. In the novel, Herbert's relentless efforts on behalf of his Famine-stricken tenants render him more eligible in Clara's eyes, and the crisis, represented in painstaking detail, thus has an important function in the romantic plot.[6] The passage reproduced below describes the efforts taken by Herbert to distribute meal to the poor, and shows his sisters and Clara Desmond visiting the shop that has been established by the relief committee.

---

3   A. Trollope, 'The Real State of Ireland', *The Examiner*, 30 March 1850, p. 201.

4   J.H. Murphy, *Irish Novelists and the Victorian Age* (Oxford: Oxford University Press, 2011), p. 126.

5   A. Trollope, *Castle Richmond* (London: Chapman & Hall, 1860), p. 64.

6   For an extensive and convincing analysis of the role of the Famine in the novel's plots, see M. Kelleher, 'Anthony Trollope's *Castle Richmond*: Famine Narrative and "Horrid Novel"?', *Irish University Review*, 25, 2 (1995), pp. 242–62.

From *Castle Richmond*

(London: Chapman & Hall, 1860), vol. 1, pp. 152–7.

The morning was very cold. There had been rainy weather, but it now appeared to be a settled frost. The roads were rough and hard, and the man who was driving them said a word now and again to his young master as to the expediency of getting frost nails put into the horse's shoes. 'I'd better go gently, Mr Herbert; it may be he might come down at some of these pitches.' So they did go gently, and at last arrived safely at Berryhill.

And very busy they were there all day. The inspection of the site for the mill was not their only employment. Here also was an establishment for distributing food, and a crowd of poor half-fed wretches were there to meet them. Not that at that time things were so bad as they became afterwards. Men were not dying on the road-side, nor as yet had the apathy of want produced its terrible cure for the agony of hunger. The time had not yet come when the famished living skeletons might be seen to reject the food which could no longer serve to prolong their lives.

Though this had not come as yet, the complaints of the women with their throngs of children were bitter enough; and it was heart-breaking too to hear the men declare that they had worked like horses, and that it was hard upon them now to see their children starve like dogs. For in this earlier part of the famine the people did not seem to realize the fact that this scarcity and want had come from God. Though they saw the potatoes rotting in their own gardens, under their own eyes, they still seemed to think that the rich men of the land could stay the famine if they would; that the fault was with them; that the famine could be put down if the rich would but stir themselves to do it. Before it was over they were well aware that no human power could suffice to put it down. Nay, more than that; they had almost begun to doubt the power of God to bring back better days.

They strove, and toiled, and planned, and hoped at Berryhill that day. And infinite was the good that was done by such efforts as these. That they could not hinder God's work we all know; but much they did do to lessen the sufferings around, and many were the lives that were thus saved.

They were all standing behind the counter of a small store that had been hired in the village – the three girls at least,[7] for Aunt Letty had already gone to the glebe,[8] and Herbert was still down at the 'water privilege', talking to a millwright and a carpenter. This was a place at which Indian corn flour, that which after a while was generally termed 'meal' in those famine days, was sold to the poor. At this period much of it was absolutely given away. This plan, however, was soon found to be injurious; for hundreds would get it who were not absolutely in want, and would then sell it; – for the famine by no means improved the morals of the people.

And therefore it was found better to sell the flour; to sell it at a cheap rate, considerably less sometimes than the cost price; and to put the means of buying it into the hands of the people by giving them work, and paying them wages. Towards the end of these times, when the full weight of the blow was understood, and the subject had been in some sort studied, the general rule was thus to sell the meal at its true price, hindering the exorbitant profit of hucksters by the use of large stores, and to require that all those who could not buy it should seek the means of living within the walls of workhouses.[9] The regular established workhouses, – unions as they were called, – were not as yet numerous, but supernumerary houses were provided in every town, and were crowded from the cellars to the roofs.

It need hardly be explained that no general rule could be established and acted upon at once. The numbers to be dealt with were so great, that

---

7   Women from the Ascendancy class played a significant role in relief and charity works during the Famine years. As Margaret Kelleher has observed, women in landowner's families were often involved in private charity, providing 'soup and clothing to tenants, visiting their homes' and carrying our the administration of local schools. See *The Feminization of Famine: Expressions of the Inexpressible?* (Cork: Cork University Press, 1997), p. 91. Asenath Nicholson's *Ireland's Welcome to the Stranger; or an Excursion through Ireland in 1844 and 1845* (New York: Baker & Scribner, 1847) also shows that Anglo-Irish women were actively involved in bettering the conditions of the Famine-stricken tenantry; she discusses the works of Lady Wicklow who 'has established three schools among the cottagers, which she supports; and she visits from house to house, inquires into their wants, and gives them premiums for cleanliness' (p. 56).

8   Although glebe is used to refer to land or soil or sometimes, more specifically, '[a] portion of land assigned to a clergyman as part of his benefice' (*OED* online, 2011, www.oed.com), it is here used synecdochally to refer to Reverend Townsend's parsonage.

9   As Maria Luddy writes in *Women and Philanthropy in Nineteenth-Century Ireland* (Cambridge: Cambridge University Press, 1995), '[d]uring the famine the number of workhouses was increased to 163' (p. 15) which were soon overcrowded. By 1849, 200,000 people were in workhouses, while 800,000 had to rely on outdoor relief.

the exceptions to all rules were overwhelming. But such and such like were the efforts made, and these efforts ultimately were successful.

The three girls were standing behind the counter of a little store which Sir Thomas had hired at Berryhill, when a woman came into the place with two children in her arms and followed by four others of different ages. She was a gaunt tall creature, with sunken cheeks and hollow eyes, and her clothes hung about her in unintelligible rags. There was a crowd before the counter, for those who had been answered or served stood staring at the three ladies, and could hardly be got to go away; but this woman pressed her way through, pushing some and using harsh language to others, till she stood immediately opposite to Clara.

'Look at that, madam', she cried, undoing an old handkerchief which she held in her hand, and displaying the contents on the counter; 'is that what the likes of you calls food for poor people? Is that fit 'ating to give to children? Would any av ye put such stuff as that into the stomachs of your own bairns?'[10] and she pointed to the mess which lay revealed upon the handkerchief.

The food, as food, was not nice to look at; and could not have been nice to eat, or probably easy of digestion when eaten.

'Feel of that.' And the woman rubbed her forefinger among it to show that it was rough and hard, and that the particles were as sharp as though sand had been mixed with it. The stuff was half-boiled Indian meal, which had been improperly subjected at first to the full heat of boiling water; and in its present state was bad food either for children or grown people.

'Feel of that', said the woman; 'would you like to be 'ating that yourself now?'

'I don't think you have cooked it quite enough', said Clara, looking into the woman's face, half with fear and half with pity, and putting, as she spoke, her pretty delicate finger down into the nasty daubed mess of parboiled yellow flour.[11]

---

10   Children.

11   In fact, many among the poor were uncertain as to how to prepare the Indian meal, as an anonymous lady testifies in *Christmas 1846 and the New Year 1847 in Ireland* (Durham: G. Andrews, 1847): 'I have found out that, in cases where there was no absolute want of food, the anxiety of considering what was best to buy, and how it was best to prepare it, was painfully felt' (p. 15).

'Cooked it!' said the woman scornfully. 'All the cooking on 'arth wouldn't make food of that fit for a Christian – feel of the roughness of it' – and she turned to another woman who stood near her; 'would you like to be putting sharp points like that into your children's bellies?'

It was quite true that the grains of it were hard and sharp, so as to give one an idea that it would make good eating neither for women nor children. The millers and dealers, who of course made their profits in these times, did frequently grind up the whole corn without separating the grain from the husks, and the shell of a grain of Indian corn does not, when ground, become soft flour. This woman had reason for her complaints, as had many thousands reason for similar complaints.

'Don't be throubling the ladies, Kitty', said an old man standing by; 'sure and weren't you glad enough to be getting it.'

'She'd be axing the ladies to go home wid her and cook it for her after giving it her', said another.

'Who says it war guv' me?' said the angry mother. 'Didn't I buy it, here at this counter, with Mike's own hard-'arned money? and it's chaiting us they are. Give me back my money.' And she looked at Clara as though she meant to attack her across the counter.

'Mr Fitzgerald is going to put up a mill of his own, and then the corn will be better ground', said Emmeline Fitzgerald, deprecating the woman's wrath.

'Put up a mill!' said the woman, still in scorn. 'Are you going to give me back my money; or food that my poor bairns can ate?'

This individual little difficulty was ended by a donation to the angry woman of another lot of meal, in taking away which she was careful not to leave behind her the mess which she had brought in her handkerchief. But she expressed no thanks on being so treated.

Allen H. Clington (David Power Conyngham) (1825–83)

A prominent figure on both sides of the Atlantic, David Power Conyngham was born in Crohane, Co. Tipperary, as the eldest son of well-to-do tenant farmers John Cunningham and Catherine Power. Educated at local 'hedge-schools' and later at Queen's College Cork, where he left without a degree, Conyngham became associated with the Young Ireland movement in the 1840s.[1] Like his cousin Charles Joseph Kickham, Conyngham participated in the Young Ireland rebellion of 1848.[2] He served as a local leader in the rising, and was indicted for his part in it, but managed to escape prosecution by mysteriously disappearing for several years.[3]

When he reappeared in the mid-1850s, Conyngham contributed articles to the *Tipperary Free Press,* and he had his first novel, *The Old House at Home,* published anonymously in 1859. It appears that between 1861 and 1862 Conyngham travelled back and forth between Ireland and the United States, where he worked as a war correspondent for *The Dublin Irishman.* After his brief, failed marriage to Anne Corcoran, Conyngham returned to America at the end of 1862. There he joined the Irish Brigade, which had just fought the Battle of Fredericksburgh, eventually rising to the rank of major.[4] Although he had only served in the Brigade from Christmas 1862 till spring 1863, when he started working as a war correspondent for the *New York Herald,* Conyngham would later write a history of the brigade in which he not only emphasized its accomplishments in arms, but also underlined the Irish soldiers' commitment to the American principles of democracy that were in turn rooted in the Irish nationalist struggle for independence: 'the great principles of democracy were at issue with the aristocratic doctrines of monarchism. Should the latter prevail, there was no longer any hope for the struggling nationalists of the Old World.'[5]

---

1 L.F. Kohl, 'Introduction', in D.P. Conyngham, *The Irish Brigade and its Campaigns* (New York: Fordham University Press, 1994), p. xviii.
2 A.M. Brady and B. Cleeve (eds), *A Biographical Dictionary of Irish Writers* (Gigginstown: Lilliput Press, 1985), p. 43.
3 Kohl, 'Introduction', p. xix.
4 Ibid., pp. xix–xxi.
5 D.P. Conyngham, *The Irish Brigade: Its Campaigns* (Glasgow: Cameron & Ferguson, 1866), p. iii.

During the last twenty years of his life, until his sudden death in 1883, Conyngham made a career in the New York newspaper world. After working for the New York Fenian paper *The Helm* in 1866, he became managing editor and owner of *The Staten Island Leader* and *The New York Tablet*.[6] At the same time, Conyngham produced novels that recollected formative events in Irish history, such as *The O'Mahoney* (1879) which is set in Waterford during the '98 rebellion.[7] His most famous work, *Frank O'Donnell*, was a republication of *The Old House at Home*, issued under the pen name of Allen H. Clington. Upon the publication of a specific American edition, *The O'Donnells of Glen Cottage* (1871), the novel became a transatlantic success.[8] The narrative, which is set during the Famine of 1845, aims to show 'how the people are made the catspaw of aspiring politicans and needy landlords'.[9] It focuses on the O'Donnells, a tenant family afflicted by the blight. Though unable to pay their rent, the O'Donnells are not granted an extension by Lord Clearall, and are brutally evicted during a snowstorm by the unprincipled agent Mr Ellis. Broken-hearted by the subsequent death of his mother, Frank leaves for America, only to return some years later, wealthy enough to buy back his family home. The extracts printed below depict the greed of the landlord and his agent and their cowardice in the face of tenant resistance.

From *Frank O'Donnell*

(Dublin: James Duffy, 1861), pp. 280–5, 421–2.

Local committees were appointed throughout the country for the management and distribution of public money – grants, rates, and the like. Useless public works were fast setting in. Of course Lord Clearall was the manager of one of these committees. Mr Ellis had a grist-mill near the

---

6   Kohl, 'Introduction', p. xxiii.
7   R. Welch (ed.), *The Oxford Companion to Irish Literature* (Oxford: Oxford University Press, 1996), p. 114.
8   Kohl, 'Introduction', p. xix.
9   S.J.M. Brown, *Ireland in Fiction* (Dublin: Maunsel & Co., 1919), p. 69.

village. There was a small private house adjoining; in this the committee held their deliberations. Lord Clearall was in the chair. Several of the neighbouring gentry and respectable ratepayers were also present.[10]

'I have', said his lordship, 'got about a thousand pounds, which we are to spend on some public work, such as levelling a hill, or tilling up a hollow, or the like; now, this will give a great deal of employment, and I hope it's only the forerunner of more. We have now to select what work we will commence at – our selections, of course, to be approved of by the Board of Works; but this is a mere matter of form, as one of the commissioners is my particular friend.'

'I think, my lord, there is no work more necessary than to level Knockcorrig hill; it is almost impassable it is so steep, and it is a regular thoroughfare to the village.'

'I think so, too, Mr Ellis', said his lordship; 'but then, we must take the opinions of these gentlemen – what do you say, gentlemen?'

Now, as all the gentlemen present were more or less dependent on his lordship for favours, patronage, and the like, it was not reasonable to expect that they would oppose him, though they well knew the levelling of Knockcorrig was of no earthly benefit to any one save his lordship and Mr Ellis, for it was on the road to his lordship's residence and to Mr Ellis's mills, so they all bowed their assent.

'Will ye agree to that, gentlemen?'

'Yes, my lord.'

'Now, we have to nominate a pay-master, overseer, and clerk; as there must be a great deal of money intrusted to the pay-master, he must be a person well secured; I think Mr Ellis would be a very fit person; I will be his security.'

They all, of course, nodded assent.

'What's the salary, my lord?' asked a broken-down gentleman, that expected it for himself.

---

10 Such meetings of landlords were common. *The Cork Examiner* of 14 September 1846 carried an article on the topic: 'Last week, a meeting of the wealthiest landlords took place at Fermanagh, for the purpose of considering the state of the poor and the late ministerial measure for their relief. Entertaining with the rest of the landlords of the country some objections to the Labour Rate Bill, they have come to a timely resolution of taking the matter into their own hands, and, by providing employment and sustenance for the distressed population on their own properties, diminishing the taxation which should necessarily press on them for the promotion of Public Works.'

'Why, I can't exactly say; perhaps ten pounds a week.'

'Oh! My lord', groaned the other.

'I think we should also nominate Mr Pembert and Mr Burke as overseer and clerk; their wages are low; one has but thirty shillings a week, the other a pound.'

There was a nod of assent, followed by a stifle of disappointment from the members. 'There will be several other clerks and gaugers wanted, I shall be happy to get appointed any worthy person you should recommend, men.'

There was a general vote of thanks to his lordship.

'Now we have to see about a house for our meetings, and for giving out-door relief; I think this a very suitable one, indeed', and his lordship looked about the comfortable room, with its blazing fire.

The others thought so too.

'Now, Mr Ellis, what might be the rent of this?'

'Oh! whatever your lordship choose.'

'No! no! I haven't the selection ; name your rent, for these gentlemen to consider?'

'Would ten shillings a week be too much, my lord?' said Mr Ellis, with the air of one making a great sacrifice for the cause of humanity.

'Really I think not, considering its appearance and usefulness', said his lordship.

'Would not a cheaper house do?' timidly suggested one of the committee. 'I merely ask it for information's sake, my lord', said he, correcting himself.

'Well, perhaps so', said his lordship; 'but then, where is the great saving in a few shillings a week: besides, look at the comfort of this house, and the safety of having it so near the mills, within a call of the police; you know such houses have been attacked already.'

'We agree with you, my lord', said the others.

A vast crowd of half-starved, half-naked wretches were collected outside the door, awaiting the issue of meeting. Some were living skeletons, tottering with disease and weakness. Some looked like scarecrows dressed up in rags, and moved by some inward machinery.

'Arrah! shure it would be dacenter for ye to kill us intirely', said a wretched-looking woman, crouched beside a wall, with a child at her breast.

'Thrue for you, Peg', said another; 'sorra a morsel I ate these two days but turnip-tops and cabbage, and there is Jack dying with me at home.'

'Lord help us', said another; 'they are the terrible times intirely.'

'I haven't a bit nor a sup, nor a spark to warm myself, and my four children', said another poor wretch.

'Will we bear to be stharved this way?' said the men; 'shure it's better for us to be kilt , boys, and our poor wives, and the childers.'

'Let us thrown down the house over them; there's male inside', shouted another.

'Arrah! don't ye', said another, with a scornful laugh: 'ye'll get a great deal from Lord Clearall, that hunted us out of the houses himself, and his skinflint divil of an agent; shure tell him ye are stharving and that will do.'

'Success, Jim, you're right', shouted the crowd.

'Give us something to eat, or we'll pull down the house over ye', shouted the mob.

'Let us brake in the door!'

Some heavy stones were flung against the door, and wild yells rang from the men, and a wail of hunger and despair from the women and children.

'We are going to commence work on Knockcorrig on Monday next', said his lordship from the window .

'What will feed us until then?'

'Pull in your head, you tyrant you, that threw my poor ould father out of the house, and he dying, and wouldn't lave him the house over him to gasp in.'

'Och! Shure that's his thrade; 'tis he knows how to quinch the poor man's fire; but he'll get into a warm corner for it some fine day himself.'

'Bad luck to the tyrant; let us drag him out, himself and his d—d bastard of an agent.'

'Break in the house. Give us male! Ye have it inside there, ye old cadgers.'[11]

'It is better to divide what meal is in the house, Mr Ellis', said his lordship, turning very pale; 'you'll be paid for it.'

'I think so, too', said Mr Ellis, who feared that it would be taken without his leave.

---

11 Attacks by the starving poor were not only launched on the outhouses of landlords where Indian corn was stored. Often 'flour and bread shops' were also destroyed and rifled, as *The Cork Examiner* reported on 23 September 1846.

'If you keep quiet', said his lordship, addressing the crowd, 'what meal is in the mill will be divided upon you, and you will all get work at the hill on Monday next.'

A wild cheer echoed from the crowd. Lord Clearall and Mr Ellis slipped away backwards.

Mr Ellis returned home satisfied that he had made good use of the day. He had set his house to advantage; he had also got a handsome salary for himself for doing nothing. He had been lately appointed a justice of the peace, so that he could now sit on the bench equal in magisterial power with his lordship. His lordship was the sheriff for the ensuing year, and he was to be his deputy. He had cleared off the Ballybrack tenants, and had pocketed a thousand pounds by the event; so, all things considered, Mr Ellis ought to be a happy man. Yet, he did not feel too happy. He knew there was a wild spirit of revenge abroad; he knew that he was a marked man. Only a few months ago an assassin fired at him, but missed.[12]

He now began to cling to life; he would wish to enjoy the sweets of hard-earned wealth and honours; so, in his soul, he resolved, if he had but a few more estates cleared, to change his life, and become a different man altogether.

Though a bold man, Mr Ellis was wavering in his resolutions. He felt that life was sweet, and that it was possible to lose it by the hand of an assassin. Besides, it was terrible to be hurled before his God, without a moment's preparation, for Mr Ellis felt that he was no saint; in fact, he had the reputation of being as gallant a widower as he was a bachelor.

. . .

Mr Ellis and Mr Sly, under the impression that they would hear a good many things not to their advantage, withdrew.

'Arragh, bad luck to ye, hould yer tongue!' said a fierce, gaunt-looking fellow elbowing his way through the crowd. 'Shut yer mouths, and let us

---

12   At the height of Famine crisis, violence was directed to landlords and their agents. Landlord Denis Mahon of Strokestown Park House, Co. Roscommon, was officially the first landlord to be assassinated, on the evening of 2 November 1847. In the previous months he had evicted 600 families who had refused to leave for America. During that winter, six more landlords were murdered in Ireland. See C.E. Orser, *A Historical Archeology of the Modern World* (New York: Plenum Press, 1996), p. 101.

make smiderheens of the door. There is meal and flour enuff widin for the soupers.'

'That's true, Jem; let us smash it.'

'I will order the police to fire at you, if you do', shouted Mr Ellis.

'To the divil wid you! Where yers goin' every day? Put out your mug, until you see what you'll get!'

About ten of the strongest bore over a large log and forced it against the door.

The door shook and creaked upon its hinges.

They struck it again and again. The door was giving way. Mr Ellis read the Riot Act[13] from the inside of a window, as well as he could, with the shower of stones and dirt that was flying at him.

'Fire on them!' said he to the police, as soon as he read it.

'Stop!' said their officer. 'Mr Ellis, it would be throwing away the lives of my handful of men. All I can do until the military come, is to protect you.'

'You're a coward, sir!' said Mr Ellis, vehemently. 'If you fire at them, the dogs will run for their lives.'

'Coward, sir!' said the officer, indignantly 'Coward! You shall answer for that, Mr Ellis.'

'I repeat it, sir. If the men were under my command, I'd have every dog of them either dead or scampering away in a minute.'

'Heaven knows', said the officer, 'you have a surer method for killing them.'

---

13   As Cormac Ó Gráda writes in *The Great Irish Famine* (Cambridge: Cambridge University Press, 1989), many famishing Irish participated in food rioting, which included violent attacks on property (p. 36). The Riot Act, drawn up by Lord Clare in 1787 to contain rebellious violence, was read during such food riots before the police opened fire. *The Illustrated London News* of 7 November 1846 reported extensively on 'the late Food Riots in the south of Ireland – Youghal and Dungarvan'.

Lalla McDowell

While virtually nothing is known about Lalla McDowell, who seems to have slipped into oblivion,[1] her novel *The Earl of Effingham* (1877) offers a multifaceted portrayal of the Great Famine. Although the novel gives the perspectives of both the Anglo-Irish ruling classes and the deprived tenants and labourers, Brown nevertheless felt that '[t]he bias is somewhat Protestant'[2] in this novel. *The Earl of Effingham* tells the tale of Major Effingham, a nobleman of half English and half Irish descent, who, after the death of his father and brother, becomes the Earl of Effingham. The title of the novel led *The Spectator* to question whether the writer knew 'that this is an actually existing title, and that it would have been in far better taste to invent one?';[3] a criticism also expressed in a review in *The Academy*.[4] Brown remarks that McDowell had succeeded in writing a narrative with 'much humour', which brings out the 'good points in the Irish character', and felt that McDowell aptly reproduced the brogue.[5]

The plot centres on the new Earl of Effingham, who buys the property of the destitute Major Burk, an Anglo-Irish absentee landlord.[6] Major Burk is represented as an upper-class character of old Anglo stock who is not cut out for his position, cares little for his tenants, is more interested in his own luxurious lifestyle and makes several bad decisions, which lead to his downfall. His daughter Nelly Burk, on the other hand, is a quintessentially virtuous Irish maiden, loved by all the tenants. McDowell's depiction of Nelly is ambiguous, however, as she embodies these virtues, but is also depicted as being subservient to the extreme; although her father always treats her badly, McDowell writes that Nelly still had for him 'a spaniel kind of affection, that loves, and clings, and follows, despite hard usage and neglect'.[7] Nevertheless, the critic of *The*

1   S.J.M. Brown, *Ireland in Fiction* (Dublin: Maunsel & Company, 1919), p. 187.
2   Ibid.
3   Review of *The Earl of Effingham*, *The Spectator*, 9 February 1878, p. 192.
4   Review of *The Earl of Effingham*, *The Academy*, 9 March 1878, p. 208.
5   Brown, *Ireland in Fiction*, p. 187.
6   In the opening pages of the novel, a tenant remarks to the Earl of Effingham that 'yer honour won't see the Major, anyhow, for he has not been at home for two years'. *The Earl of Effingham* (London: Tinsley, 1877), p. 10.
7   Ibid., p. 194.

Academy states that 'her heroine [Nelly] is a charming study of an Irish girl'.[8]

The first excerpt reproduced below concerns a short contemplation on the murder of the previous agent O'Brien, who was killed by the side of the road – a murder which Nelly witnessed as a young girl and which is illustrative of both the dangerous social climate in Ireland in the mid-nineteenth century and the mindset of good-hearted Anglo-Irish upper-class characters. Because the tenants feel that their new landlord, Lord Effingham, has taken away the estate from Nelly, they oppose him at first, which culminates when he is shot by one of his cottiers, as can be seen in the second excerpt. However, Effingham's honesty, bravery, merciful nature, and good intentions as a landlord – as voiced in the speech he makes after being assaulted – win over the tenantry.

By displaying an Anglo-Irish landlord who replaces an absentee landlord and is extremely committed to his tenantry, McDowell's novel carries a message for real-life absentee landlords: they should 'turn from the error of their ways'.[9] As the critic of *The Academy* notes, the novel is written with 'the intention of showing the evils that result from absentee landlords in Ireland, and the good which they might work by living at home'.[10]

From *The Earl of Effingham*

(London: Tinsley, 1877), pp. 121–2, 130–2.

L ady Clifford[11] had been sobbing for some time.

'Oh! Lord Effingham!' she cried, 'is this not dreadful? To think of that child[12] going through such a scene of horror!'

'It is terrible, very terrible, Lady Clifford.'

---

8   Review of *The Earl of Effingham*, *The Academy*, p. 208.
9   Review of *The Earl of Effingham*, *The Spectator*, p. 192.
10   Review of *The Earl of Effingham*, *The Academy*, p. 207.
11   A friend of Nelly Burk and later of Lord Effingham.
12   Nelly Burk.

'Don't think of me, aunty; what was my suffering? Ask yourself, who was the real murderer; the treble murderer? Lord M., the man who is petted and courted by society – he caused Mr Clarke's death, O'Brien's, and Mary's. He and all absentee landlords, are the true cause of much of Ireland's wretchedness and crime; had he lived on his estate, he must have known that famine, and fever had made it impossible for the tenants to pay. His agent was not a hard, or a bad man, nor was he disliked by the people; but he, like them, was harassed and driven to use force to supply his master's needs; forced to deeds of absolute cruelty, as in O'Brien's case.

'For every talent committed to us there will come a day of strict reckoning. Landlords should bear in mind that with their lands they inherit vast responsibility; that God will hold them accountable for every life sacrificed through their neglect of duty.[13]

'It has been very painful to me, my lord, to tell you this. If my doing so, will induce you to deal justly and mercifully with the poor ignorant people, whose happiness and welfare are committed to your care, I will not have suffered in vain. I know how faithfully they will serve you – repay you in love tenfold for all you do for them; and you will be doing your duty. That will be your best reward.'

...

'Are you hit? Oh, you are!' he cried.[14]

'Yes, my friend, but it does not signify. Now let me speak.'

There is nothing the Irish admire and reverence more than pluck and courage. Their new landlord won their admiration now. He had not moved an inch; his left hand had fallen to his side; that was all the sign he gave that the bullet had not quite missed its mark. He stood with his proud head erect, regarding them with a smile.

---

13 This idea appears to reflect the criticism that was directed to neglectful landlords during and immediately after the Famine years. For instance, *What Have the Whigs Done for Ireland? Or The English Whigs and the Irish Tenants* by 'A Barrister' (Dublin: E.J. Milliken, 1851) states about the landlords: 'it was their own reckless and extravagant habits in private life – their narrow and obstructive policy in public affairs – their systematic inattention to the duties they owed their country and their countrymen – that has left them humiliated, impoverished, pitied, or abused' (p. 38). Similarly, in *Ireland, The Late Famine and the Poor Laws* (London: Hatchford & Son, 1848), Sir Lucius O'Brien wonders whether the landlords have adequately taken care of good living conditions for their tenants: 'are his arrangements so perfect, and on such a liberal scale, that his tenantry are able to give full effect to the productive power of their farms?' (p. 5).
14 Mr St John, Lord Effingham's close friend.

'If the man who fired that shot is not a coward as well as a would-be murderer, let him come forward and speak to me.'

There was a whispering and shuffling of feet, then the crowd fell back on either side, leaving a narrow lane, up which, gun in hand, walked Larry Lynch, the shoemaker.

'Larry, oh Larry! can it be possible it is you?' exclaimed Mr St John in dismay. 'You a murderer!'

'Don't be too hard on me, Mr St John', he replied; 'how could I help it? How could I stand by an' see him, or any one, rob the dear young lady[15] of her home? No one knows', he went on, in a loud voice full of passion, 'what she did for me. Who but her closed the eyes of poor Biddy and the little lad? Didn't she follow me about until she drew me from the drink? Was I to see him do her this wrong? I wish I had killed him that I might die for her, so I do!'

'You have done her the greatest wrong you could do her this day, Larry,' said Mr St John sadly. 'I tell you, man, her heart will be breaking when she hears of this.'

Larry hung down his head; he did not speak.

'Sit down there', said Lord Effingham, pointing to a seat near where he stood; 'I will talk to you by-and-by.'

The man did as he was desired, then Lord Effingham spoke again, addressing the people in front of him.

'When I first heard of this property it was advertised for sale in the public papers. I came to see it, and soon after purchased it. In so doing I wronged no one; I paid Major Burk the sum he asked. I don't say you might not have got a better landlord – you might have got a worse. For the last fifteen years of my life I have served my Queen; and I am going to quit her service, and for the half of every year God spares me, live among you. I have enrolled myself under my Saviour's banner; I mean to serve Him as I have never done before. I will help you to do the same by every means in my power. Mr St John has promised to be my friend and guide. He has taken me on trust, can't you do the same? I will be your friend if you will let me. Suffer me to go in and out among you, to find out your wants, to lighten your troubles, without fear of such a welcome as Larry has given me this evening. There will be plenty of honest work

---

15   Nelly Burk.

for every one, and I hope more prosperous days in the future for all present.'

He had become very white as he spoke, and Mr Short saw with horror there was quite a pool of blood at his feet.

'I hope you will all enjoy your dinner. I must ask my kind friends here to make you welcome, for Larry's bullet has made me rather uncomfortable.' He moved – staggered a little. 'Will you help me into the house?' he said, holding out his uninjured hand with a smile to Larry.

This was a master-stroke of policy. The crowd cheered and cheered again with the greatest enthusiasm, while Larry, who was now weeping bitterly, tenderly supported his wounded master into the Castle.

Hester Sigerson (1828–98)

Hester Varian was born in Co. Cork, and was the sister of the poet Ralph Varian. According to the *Cabinet of Irish Literature* (1903) her family was 'devoted to literature and music, all thinkers and all thoroughly Irish in feeling'.[1] She married Dr George Sigerson, a man of science and letters who was a member of 'several learned societies at home and abroad' and who was 'at the forefront of medical thought and progress'.[2] As such, Sigerson lived in an environment that was very conducive to intellectual and cultural development. The Sigersons had four children, two boys and two girls. Their son William Ralph died in childhood and their other son, George Patrick, died at the age of 36.[3] Their daughters Hester and Dora both also became well-known writers;[4] the latter became a well-known figure of the Irish Literary Revival.[5] The Sigerson family lived in Dublin, and upon her death in 1898 Sigerson was buried at Glasnevin cemetery.[6]

Sigerson primarily wrote poetry and short stories. For *The Harp of Erin* (1869), a collection of poetry edited by her brother Ralph, she wrote 'Under the Snow', a melancholy poem about a mother grieving for her deceased infant,[7] and she regularly contributed to newspapers and journals, such as *Cork Examiner, Irish Fireside, The Gael, Young Ireland* and *Irish Monthly*.[8] *The Cabinet of Irish Literature* describes Sigerson as a 'woman of fine literary talent'.[9] *A Ruined Race*, her only novel, is set in the imaginary town of Fortmanus. The plot relates the downfall of Dan and Mary MacManus, an Irish small-farming couple, who initially have ample means to live comfortably in their pretty little cottage. They are archetypal

---

1   C.A. Read and K.T. Hinkson (eds), *The Cabinet of Irish Literature; Selections from the Works of the Chief Poets, Orators, and Prose Writers of Ireland*, vol. 4 (London: Blackie, 1903), p. 32.
2   Ibid., p. 30.
3   A.U. Colman, *Dictionary of Nineteenth-Century Irish Women Poets* (Galway: Kenny's Bookshop, 1996), p. 229.
4   T. O'Toole (ed.), *Dictionary of Munster Woman Writers, 1800–2000* (Cork: Cork University Press, 2005), p. 277.
5   K. Tynan, 'Dora Sigerson, a Tribute and Some Memories, by Katharine Tynan', in D. Sigerson Shorter, *The Sad Years* (London: Constable & Co. 1921), pp. vii–xii.
6   Colman, *Dictionary of Nineteenth-Century Irish Women Poets*, p. 229.
7   H. Sigerson, 'Under the Snow', in R. Varian (ed.), *The Harp of Erin: A Book of Ballad Poetry and of Native Song* (Dublin: M'Glashan & Gill, 1869), pp. 106–7.
8   O'Toole (ed.), *Dictionary of Munster Woman Writers*, p. 277.
9   Read and Hinkson (eds), *Cabinet of Irish Literature*, p. 201.

hard-working, virtuous and benevolent Irish characters, but when their potato crops are 'rotting in the wet mud'[10] they cannot avert destitution, starvation and illness. As the narrative unfolds, the couple lose more and more loved ones, culminating in the death of their young daughter Eily. When Mary dies in hospital, Dan becomes 'the Last MacManus of Drumroosk', before he perishes with hunger and disease himself.

In *A Ruined Race* the grievances experienced by these lovable Irish Catholic characters are much exacerbated by the deeds of a merciless Protestant landlord and his equally uncompassionate middleman Billy Finnigan, an Irishman with English loyalties. The excerpt below describes an eviction scene, a common element in fiction that recollects the Great Famine. The passage shows a clear dichotomy between Protestant land-lords and Catholic tenants and foregrounds the problems surrounding the Land Question, which were particularly central to political debates of the early post-Famine era. It comes as no surprise, then, that *A Ruined Race,* which was dedicated to Mrs Gladstone 'in grateful recognition of her sympathy with the peasantry of Ireland',[11] was seen as offering 'firm support' to the ideals and actions of the National Land League regarding the Land Wars of 1879–1903.[12]

---

10   H. Sigerson, *A Ruined Race; or, the Last MacManus of Drumroosk* (London: Ward & Downey, 1889), p. 71.

11   Ibid., p. i.

12   S. Deane, A. Carpenter and J. Williams (eds), *The Field Day Anthology of Irish Writing, vol. 5: Irish Women's Writing and Traditions* (New York: New York University Press, 2002), p. 926.

From *A Ruined Race; or, the Last MacManus of Drumroosk*

(London: Ward & Downey, 1889), pp. 178–85.

'Here's the police an' Billy Finnigan[13] coming down over the hill, they'r afther bein' above at Mick Byrne's an' throwin' every ha'porth[14] out upon the road, an' ould Mrs Byrne is like a mad woman, roarin' and tearin' the hair out o' her head!'[15]

Mary turned deadly pale, and sat down again without saying a word; but she soon recovered her self-possession and hastened across to Dan, who was still leaning upon the ditch, gazing upon the plumy oat crop as it waved and nodded before him, as if in a very commotion of joy and gratitude at all the care which he had bestowed upon it. She laid her hand softly upon his shoulder, and whispered gently:

'They're comin', Dan.'

'The police?' responded he.

---

13 The narrative's malevolent middleman. A middleman was usually a native Irishman who, having come into money, rented a 100 or a 1,000 acres of an estate. He was responsible for the payment of the half-yearly rent to the landlord, be he a resident or an absentee, and often strove to get as much as possible from the impoverished tenants. See C. Woodham-Smith, *The Great Hunger: Ireland 1845–1849* (New York: Signet, 1991), p. 22. The middleman features regularly in Famine fiction; for example, in John McElgun's Irish-American novel *Annie Reilly; Or, The Fortunes of an Irish Girl in New York* (New York: J.A. McGee, 1873). John G. Ryan, tellingly a former 'Pig-Jobber and Hog-Slaughterer' (p. 28), is a prime example of the malignant, greedy middleman: a 'false-hearted hypocrite' (p. 21) alternately siding with Protestants and Catholics for maximum gain, he 'could commit the most base and grievous wrong on any of his fellow-men and at the same time shed tears in the fulness of his heart over that man's sufferings' (p. 33).

14 Halfpennyworth, signifying something of very small value.

15 Due to consecutive potato crop failures, many tenant farmers were no longer able to pay rent to their landlords. Arrears in payment eventually led to the eviction of entire families. An article in *The Illustrated London News* of 16 December 1848 speaks of 'the ejectment, by wholesale, of the wretched cottiers'. Between 1849 and 1854 an estimated 250,000 people were forced out of their homes. See C. Ó Gráda, *The Great Irish Famine* (Cambridge: Cambridge University Press, 1989), p. 56. Eviction was a also recurrent theme in nineteenth-century Irish and Irish diaspora literature. For example, Mary Anne Sadlier's *New Lights; or, Life in Galway* (New York: D. & J. Sadlier, 1853) contains a dramatic eviction scene in which the once prosperous O'Dalys are brutally thrown out of their homestead. Unrelentingly, landlord Ousely refuses to accept the payment of arrears by Phil Rooney, who then offers to take in the O'Dalys as a sign of true friendship: 'the friend in need is the friend indeed' (p. 260).

'Yis, darlin', said she, taking his hand in hers and holding it with a clinging, yet almost protecting pressure.

'Very well', muttered he. 'Let them do their worst; they can't drag the hearts out of our bodies anyhow.'[16] But he retracted that assertion before the night closed over him.

'Won't you come out to 'em?'

'Divil a foot.' And he added: 'Maybe 'twould be the worst for some of 'em if I did – only for you.'

They had not long to wait till the sergeant of the police came out into the yard and called out: "Tis better for you to come and take these things out if they're any good to you.' And Billy added: 'Bedad![17] they got notice enough and had plenty of time to be cleared out. So if there's anything broke now 'tis you own fault, an', begob, 'twould be a pity to spile any o' your beautiful furniture!' said he with a grin, as he commenced throwing the few things out with the help of the police, while the sergeant dashed the burning turf[18] off the hearth and scattered it over the floor; then he again called out: 'You have no right here at all. This place is no longer yours. Out with ye!' he cried roughly.

'Bedad we can't have much without paying for it in this world', said Billy.

'Nor in the next either', said Dan fiercely. He was roused at last, and strode rapidly out, but, not losing any of his presence of mind, he led Mary with him, guiding her round to avoid the hot turf, and cautioning her to 'mind her feet'.

They stood side by side in the middle of the roadway. Half the village was gathered on the spot for they were both respected, poor as they were. The cat had taken refuge on top of the roof, and was sitting by the chimney with a terrified look as she gazed down upon the crowd. Mat, Katey, and

---

16 The stoic pride that Dan displays in this eviction scene is very similar to the heroism generally manifested by tenant characters in Irish Catholic Famine fiction. For example, in W.C. Upton's *Uncle Pat's Cabin; Or, Life Among the Agricultural Labourers of Ireland* (Dublin: Gill, 1882), while armed policemen and a 'wagon laden with crowbars, sledges, etc.' drive up to the house, Davy McMahon tells the policemen that 'I and my family are not going to resist the law you have come to enforce' (20). Davy McMahon is presented as a sympathetic, law-abiding citizen who preserves a heroic dignity under the circumstances, which contrasts with the savage brutality of the officers who completely destroy their cottage.

17 Exclamation, derived from 'by dad' or 'by God', alternatively also 'begad'.

18 In Ireland, indoor fires were and still are mostly made with dried peat or turf.

little Patsy Farrell were standing in a row looking on with sad and frightened faces. As the old straw chair was put out Katey whispered:

'That's poor Eily's[19] chair.'

'An' dat's hur pusheen',[20] said the little Patsy, looking up.

Mat's irresistible love of sport got the better of his feeling and he lifted a stone to shy at her, but Katey reproved him sharply:

'Don't throw at poor Eily's pusheen; 'tis a shame for you, sir!' and he dropped the stone silently.

'Bedad! they won't bring very much at an auction, anyhow!' said Billy, viewing the few old things on the road.

'No! nor they won't take long to put in again', said Dan.

'Och! is that your game? Wait awhile an' we'll see', said Billy; and he went over and said a few words to the sergeant, who turned to some of the police, who carried crowbars as well as their other weapons.

''Tis well you brought over the Yorks,[21] Mary', whispered Mag.

Mary was bearing up bravely – now that it came to the worst – and stood pale and calm by the side of her husband. But the first blow of the crowbar beneath the roof seemed to strike her heart. It had also the effect of making poor puss spring from her exalted position down the back of the house, through the hedges, and up the boreen[22] towards a little wood on Mr Jones's land. Bouncer,[23] who was also one of the spectators of the scene, along with the couple of half-starved curs, made a slight chase, in which Mat seemed inclined to join; but they soon gave up and returned.

A portion of the roof still remained intact at one corner, and Dan, lifting a crowbar that one of the men had just put down, proceeded to drive it in.

'There', he said to Mary; 'I said I wouldn't lave it until the roof was off, an' them that she loved could come after her.'

---

19 The little daughter of the MacManuses, who died of Famine-related disease earlier in the narrative.
20 Her little cat.
21 The term 'Yorks' could refer to cabbages (as this excerpt shows, the MacManuses had a cabbage patch). Mag is probably implying that if Mary had not taken the cabbages, the middleman and his men would have.
22 A narrow rural road.
23 The family dog.

He turned to look at her shrine, the old straw chair,[24] and, to his utter indignation and disgust, who would be sitting in it but Billy Finnigan smoking a short pipe. He was before him in an instant, and fiercely commanded him to 'Get up out o' that!'

'The Lord preserve us!' said Billy, coolly turning and knocking the ashes out of his pipe on the back of the chair, and drawing the bowl up and down over it.

'Get up, will you!' roared Dan, deadly pale with anger and excitement.

'I beg your honour's pardon, Mr MacManus sir', said Billy, with an impudent leer; 'but I'm not going to hurt myself be hurrying either.'

'By G— then you will hurry yourself!' cried Dan, taking a strong grip of his collar.

Billy turned purple with rage, and slowly rising, he spat upon the chair and kicked it over, muttering – but loud enough to be heard:

'I had no right to sit in it, anyhow, afther the likes o' you and your sickly brat!'

Dan suddenly caught up the old stool that lay at his feet and dealt him a powerful blow of it on the side of the head, which laid him senseless and bleeding upon the ground.

'Ho! ho! I'm afraid you've done yourself now, by George!' cried the sergeant, seizing him, and calling to his men to bind him, while he turned to Billy, who was bleeding profusely – fortunately for the state of his brain – after the violent concussion he had received.

'Bedad', said one of the police, as he tied Dan's hands behind his back, 'you wouldn't think he had the strength in him to give such a blow – and he so worn looking.'

Dan stood like one petrified, offering not the least resistance. He was gazing earnestly at his wife, who had fallen fainting upon the ground, and was surrounded by a group of villagers.[25] At length he cried in a broken voice, 'Mary!' and struggled hard to get to her, but he was quickly held

---

24 Eily's chair, which – as the word 'shrine' implies – is cherished by her parents as the last object reminding them of her.

25 The image of the mother figure who swoons during the eviction scene is quite common in Famine fiction. For example, in David Power Conyngham's *Frank O'Donnell* (Dublin and London: James Duffy, 1861), Frank's mother collapses when the family is to be forced from their home, and never recovers. Likewise, in John McElgun's *Annie Reilly*, upon being evicted from their cottage Mrs Reilly faints into 'her daughter's arms, while a stream of blood poured from her nose and down over her face and breast' (p. 66).

down by a number of police. He continued struggling fiercely, muttering, 'Let me go to her! Let me go to her!'

Jim Treacy and others of his neighbours mingled themselves with the police, and assured him she was only in a faint, and would soon recover; and even while they spoke she came struggling through the crowd with the look of a maniac on her white face.

'Dan! Dan! don't lave me!' she cried in a voice so unlike her own that Dan shuddered to hear it. She clung to him with a grip like that of a drowning person, while he in broken words attempted to console her, though his own heart was breaking at the thought of leaving her unprotected, a pauper, houseless and homeless!

'Don't fret, Dan! we'll keep her. Never fear, Nora will take good care of her till you're back again to her', said Jim, with the tears running down his sunburnt face. 'Run up an' tell me wife to come down', said he, turning to Mag Farrell, who with streaming eyes stood clapping her hands in a storm of sympathy for her friend, not unmingled with terror at her own prospects.

Poor Dan and Mary were at length forcibly separated by the police, who, to do them justice, were themselves not unmoved by the scene. A car was procured, and Dan was carried off to Knocknevin jail securely bound, a policeman at each side of him. Mary had again fainted, and the last Dan saw of her was her insensible form being carried away to be laid on the 'family bed' in Farrell's cabin. Billy Finnigan also was tenderly conveyed home by his wife and son, who were sinfully vindictive and piously indignant at the dreadful state of Fortmanus morals and their own long-suffering.

William Francis Barry (1849–1930)

Canon William Francis Barry was born in London to Gaelic-speaking Irish immigrants. He was educated at Hammersmith Training School, Segley Park School, and Oscott College, an influential seminary. The highly gifted Barry was then awarded a scholarship to study at the English College and the Gregorian University in Rome, where he was priested and made a Doctor of Divinity. Upon his return to England he became a professor, first teaching philosophy at Olton Seminary, and then, from 1877, at his alma mater, Oscott College, where he held a chair in Divinity. Due to friction with the administration of the college, Barry surrendered his post after three years. In 1883, he was sent to the mission of St Birinus in Dorchester-on-Thames, where his tasks were light, allowing him to devote much of his time to writing. Barry was influenced by Cardinal Newman, about whom he wrote *Newman* (1904). Apart from his non-fictional writings, he also published a number of story collections and novels, the best-known of which is *The New Antigone* (1887). Like his contemporary Canon Patrick Sheehan, Barry was not only interested in ecclesiastical matters but also published widely on political and social questions, and was an outspoken supporter of Irish nationalism.[1]

Barry's activist streak can also be discerned in his novels, particularly *The Wizard's Knot* (1901), a gothic tale of landlords, tenants and magic set during the Famine that, according to a reviewer, 'could hardly fail to be stirring, effective and vivid'.[2] John Sutherland claims that the novel 'is comic at the expense of the Celtic Revival',[3] but his suggestion that *The Wizard's Knot* satirizes the late nineteenth- and early twentieth-century interest in the Celtic past of Ireland is hardly countenanced by the work itself. On the contrary, as Sheridan Gilley points out, Barry's engagement with his Irish heritage was characterized by 'a yearning for the lost glories of a dying Celtic world'.[4] Moreover, the novel is dedicated to Douglas

---

1   This biographical sketch is based on S. Gilley, 'Father William Barry: Priest and Novelist', *Recusant History*, 24 (1998–99), pp. 523–51.
2   See the review in *The Living Age*, 229 (1901), p. 400.
3   J. Sutherland, *The Longman Companion to Victorian Fiction* (London: Longman, 1988), p. 50.
4   Gilley, 'Father William Barry: Priest and Novelist', p. 525.

Hyde, founder of the Gaelic League, and Standish Hayes O'Grady, an important antiquarian known for his work on medieval Irish manuscripts. Though, according to a review in *The Athenaeum*, the author intended his novel to be 'neither political, nor sectarian, but a pure tragedy, shot through with the April lights of frolic, folklore and old customs',[5] the narrative combines fierce social criticism and supernatural elements, placing the landlord question in a folkloric context.

The excerpt reproduced here depicts a discussion between members of two landholding families, the Liscarrolls and the O'Connors, and the agent Mr Nagle. The agent's contribution to the discussion reflects the British argument for the modernization of Irish agriculture. His points about overpopulation and the problems associated with potato-based agriculture echo the dominant progress-oriented philosophy informing the British response to the Famine, Political Economy, an amalgamation of advanced socioeconomic theories – particularly those of Thomas Malthus and Adam Smith – and Christian doctrine. Clearly, Barry does not subscribe to Nagle's ideas; rather, the passage emphasizes that such rationalization can only exacerbate the problems facing the tenants.

From *The Wizard's Knot*

(London: T. Fisher Unwin, 1901), pp. 173–81.

'And the throngs of beggars round this door every morning, hungry as fieldfares in the snow', concluded Miss O'Connor. 'But we still get our rents. How can I take them with a clear conscience? What return do I, Elizabeth Charlotte O'Connor, make to the five thousand wretches that earn them?'

'More than your absentee neighbours', said the agent, smiling, 'not that I yield to the popular fallacy regarding absentees. Many of the great

---

5   *The Athenaeum*, 83 (January–July 1901), p. 84.

English noblemen's estates are exceedingly well managed. Over-population is the national scourge.'[6]...

'What can't be cured must be endured', he[7] said; 'there's an old song for you we have sung time out of mind. Candid should I be? Well, then, Miss Lisaveta,[8] the fortune of Ireland is before you in O'Reilly's piece of statuary.[9] The soldier will be killed out, as you see him there – poor, proud, improvident boy – and the woman will raise a keen over his corpse till one grave swallows them both. The country is doomed.'

'Oh, you have watched the shadow growing larger – as I have watched it. The end – it is the end of our nation, if not of our race', she exclaimed, heart-stricken. 'We are all to blame; none of us can get off. But the people, who have sinned a thousand times less than ourselves, will suffer most.'

'There is every hope of an excellent crop this year, at any rate', said Mr Nagle; 'from all parts I am told the potatoes were never looking better.'

'They failed last season, and the season before, did they not?' inquired Lisaveta, turning on the polite man almost savagely. He bowed.

'To a lamentable extent they did. Our peasants' farming is, I regret to say, ignorant and careless. The land is burnt up, overrun with weeds, exhausted by bad cropping, against every rule – in short, a good harvest is a miracle, for which we must thank the mercy of God.'

'Suppose that miracle did not happen this year? What would be the consequence, Mr Nagle?'

'God forbid, madam. The consequence would be too awful for human language to describe.'

---

6   This is a typically Malthusian statement. Following *An Essay on the Principle of Population* (1798), many political economists argued that Ireland was overpopulated, and that the balance between population increase and food supply needed to be restored – for instance, by rationalizing agriculture, forced emigration, or a famine. This view is, for instance, expressed by William Pulteny Alison, who in *Observations on the Famine of 1846–47* (Edinburgh and London: William Blackwood, 1847) argues that 'the positive checks' (p. 6) given by nature in the form of Famine have solved the problem of Ireland's overpopulation; and that management of the crisis should give 'the least encouragement to redundancy of population' (p. 3).

7   Edmund Liscarroll.

8   Miss O'Connor, whose mother was Russian, spent part of her youth in Russia. She is often called Lisaveta, a Russian form of Elizabeth.

9   Mentioned repeatedly in the novel, the statue represents the mythological heroine Deirdre of the Sorrows, whose lover Naoise was killed at the behest of King Conchobar mac Nessa. When Deirdre failed to warm to the king, he decided to give her away to Naoise's murderer, upon which Deirdre committed suicide.

'You, Edmund, with your vivid imagination, could at least picture it in outline. Would it not be famine, wide as the land, deep as the depth of those numbers living from hand to mouth? I had some trial of it in the year past, among these woods and lawns of Eden. To you stay-at-home Irishmen it is familiar as your changeable sky; a matter of course. Not so to me. I have lain awake, night after night, in fancy travelling over the land smitten with the plague – its crops lying in pestilential heaps, the people dying above them; fathers, mothers, children ghastly in their nakedness – the country a stricken battle-field, its dead unburied. The dream – or is it real? – will not leave me. I walk in it even as I say these words to you. Tell me, in God's name, you men, what am I to do?' ...

'My mother had strange notions. I was taught by her that I never could do anything as I ought until I saw it in visible shape before my mind's eye. The habit is formed in me; *you* will not think it hallucination; it is your own gift when you choose to exercise it. Set these millions in their wasted fields, and say what do you see? That is the thing they will do, that will be done to them, in the day of their hunger. They will feed upon nettles and weeds; the mist of fever will rise about them; they will creep into the ditches and die there, by the visitation of God upon the crime and folly of man. Such a white death is my dream, which this very autumn may crown king of our millions – our millions! I see him coming up from the South, passing the rivers; neither stop nor stay does he make on the mountain-crest; he is lord of the Golden Vale,[10] and away with him over plain and pasture until he reaches the Northern Sea. It will be the famine of the century.'

'An excellent crop', murmured Mr Nagle, 'the calculus of probabilities! By Christmas – '

'The crowded mountain-sides may be a cemetery', said Miss O'Connor.

'Or you may be laughing at your own gloomy presentiments', said he.

'Why do the Irish gentry fulfil no part of their contract?' she insisted.

'It is not they but the farmers themselves that drag the life and soul out of the ground, as well as stocking it with a loose population, till it is no better than a snipe-bog', said the agent, severely.

---

10   The Golden Vale, or Vein, is an area covering part of counties Cork, Tipperary and Limerick. Boasting some of the most fertile pastureland in Ireland, it was traditionally considered one of the best areas in the country.

'Can they help it if their boys and girls marry at seventeen?' threw in Liscarroll; 'what else is a man to do with his lads but divide the holding among them?'

'No coercive enactment is palatable to those people', answered Mr Nagle, almost showing signs of temper. 'They will neither be said nor led by their superiors. They murder the good soil; they lament here that we don't permit them to appropriate the sea-rack[11] and burn up the fine land with it.'...

'For God's sake, madam, keep that opinion to yourself', said the agent, alarmed, 'or we will be having the revels of the Rockites as they had in Tipperary.[12] Don't you see them now pulling the heath for sale, and "stealing mountain", so they term it, by the furlong? And there's the bog-stuff they use for manure, to say nothing of the pernicious sea-sand, the burning itself of the soil, and – '

'But I see here', interrupted Lisaveta, 'that we do what Cathal O'Dwyer charged upon us landlords in my hearing, and I would not believe it. We set the wild, sunken rocks in with the land, to get a rent from them.'

'Land is land, whether at sea or on shore', answered the agent; '"he owns all at low tide and at flood", says their own proverb of the landlord. If the natural indolence of our farmers, big and little, did not encourage them to waste five good months of the year,[13] it is long since they would be independent of a thing that one tide brings in and another may carry out.'

'Well, but, Mr Nagle, as we should not be trusting, like our rude ancestors, to the acorns that hang on the oak and the wild honey in crevices of the trees, surely you can tell us how to begin our improvements',

---

11 Seaweed, which was used to fertilize the land in coastal areas.
12 Active during the early 1820s, the Rockite movement was one of the many rural insurrectionary currents that agitated against the landlord system and aimed to thwart British colonial control of Ireland. Perpetrating their attacks in the name of a mythical Captain Rock, these agrarian rebels waylaid and assassinated landlords and agents and burned down houses. See, for instance, Charlotte Elizabeth, *The Rockite. An Irish Story* (London: James Nisbet, 1836): 'Sometimes half a dozen of the Rockites would appear in a detached dwelling at twilight, and ransack every room for ... such was the order of Captain Rock; to whose commands the most unhesitating and implicit obedience was yielded' (p. 23).
13 For a good part of the growing cycle, a potato crop requires little effort. However, in the eyes of the British, this was proof that the Irish mode of life stimulated idleness and therefore needed reform. Charles Trevelyan, assistant Treasury secretary between 1840 and 1859 and responsible for Famine relief, wrote in his infamous 'The Irish Crisis' (1848), that '[t]he domestic habits arising out of this mode of subsistence were of the lowest and most degrading kind.' As such, he punned, the potato is 'the deep and inveterate root of social evil' in Ireland. *Edinburgh Review*, pp. 87, 175 (1848), pp. 232; p. 320.

said Liscarroll, taking up the sketch-map. 'Look at these colours', he went on, pointing them out to Miss O'Connor; 'much of your estate is held in rundale,[14] and it is striped like the coat of the roving Kern[15] – a plaid wouldn't be more so.'

'Take a patch of it from any one of them', rejoined Nagle, 'and they'll get demoralised, and savage, and wild. The man would be every day watching it, though he lost it twenty years back.'

'But if you gave him as good a patch elsewhere?' said Edmund.

'He will not be satisfied but with his own. Double the quantity wouldn't pacify him. Still, I say to Miss O'Connor, in this way we will have to begin. Improvement and ejectment – but without violence or hardship – must go together. Money will be demanded, and that not trifling.' …

'My plan would be this', he said aloud, 'emigrate the cottiers that have no hold on the land. It will cost a few pounds a head, but will repay you. Get possession of the small broken farms; square them to a reasonable shape; plant the houses convenient but not too near to each other; let six acres be the least size of a farm, or maybe seven, so that a man will have enough to sustain his family in comfort. But I have it all down in black and white for your inspection and approbation, Miss O'Connor.'

'Emigrate, eject, clear off the land – I don't fancy the sound of it', said Lisaveta; 'what think you, Edmund?'

'I shouldn't bless the hand that turned me out on the Atlantic', he answered. 'By the crook of Saint Finbarr,[16] it is a queer country altogether. The landlords won't live in it – the tenants can't. Who has bewitched us?'

---

14 The rundale or *clachan* system was a form of communal landholding common in Ireland until the 1840s but almost entirely eradicated by the Famine. Plots of lands changed hands between members of the community by rotation every few years, and much (agricultural) labour was done collectively. Seen as a primitive and pre-modern phenomenon, the rundale system was fundamentally at odds with the British desire to modernize and rationalize Irish agriculture, as is borne out here by Nagle.

15 Kerns were medieval Irish infantry soldiers.

16 There are five Celtic saints named Finbarr, the most famous of whom – and the one presumably invoked here – is the patron saint of Cork, bishop of that diocese in the late sixth and early seventh century. A crook, or crozier, is a bishop's pastoral staff.

Section 5

Young Ireland and Colonial Rebellion

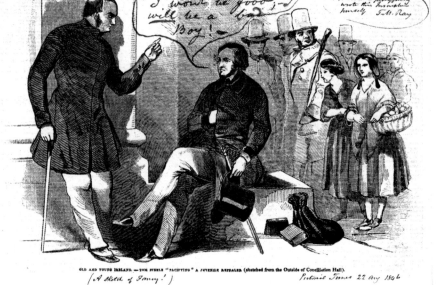

'OLD AND YOUNG IRELAND – TOM STEELE "PACIFYING"
A JUVENILE REPEALER
(sketched from the Outside of Conciliation Hall).'
By T.M. Ray, *Pictorial Times*, 22 August 1846.

The Young Repealer says 'No, Mr Tom Steele, I wont be good;—I *will* be a bad Boy!'
The remark in the top right-hand corner reads 'Mr Steele playfully wrote this Inscription himself
T.M. Ray'; below the caption, the same author has written 'A sketch of Fancy!'

William Gorman Wills (1828–91)

> May the memory of those sickening years soon perish with
> them, when a people's food was turned to poison, and reeked
> by every roadside – when ragged crowds trooped like wolves
> for out-door relief, and the officers who gave it grew faint at
> the stifling pauperstench![1]

Thus the omniscient narrator in William Gorman Wills's *Life's Foreshad-owings* (1859) conjures up the traumatic memory of the Great Famine which continues to haunt the country, rising like 'a pale form' to disturb subsequent generations.[2] As he viewed the novel as a 'large canvas on which you have plenty of room for atmosphere, foreground, middle distance, and vague horizons',[3] the vivid picture of Famine remembrance that he sketches comes as no surprise; and it seems that Wills's skills as a playwright and portrait painter have informed his fiction.

Wills was born on 28 January, 1828 at Blackwell Lodge in Kilmurry, Co. Kilkenny, to Katherine Gorman and James Wills, a well-known autobiographer. Wills studied Art at Trinity College Dublin, but did not take a degree. In 1872, he was appointed 'dramatist to the Lyceum', a position which provided him with a steady income of £300 annually.[4] Contemporaries described him as a man of considerable talent – for example, in *Shadows of the Stage* (1895) William Winter calls Wills a 'genius'[5] – but also states that he was an 'eccentric man'[6] who suffered from 'lapses into "artistic melancholy"' and 'bohemian ways'.[7] His best-known plays are probably *Man o'Airlie* (1867) and *Charles the First* (1872), which ran for over 200 nights at the Lyceum. Although he had considerable success, biographers described Wills as a 'rather pathetic old man' who forced his

---

1   W.G. Wills, *Life's Foreshadowings: A Novel*, vol. 2 (London: Hurst & Blackett, 1859), p. 295.
2   Ibid.
3   F. Wills, *Life of W.G. Wills* (London: Longmans, Green & Co., 1898), p. 60.
4   R. Hogan et al. (eds), *Dictionary of Irish Literature: Revised and Expanded Edition* (London: Aldwych Press, 1996), p. 1252.
5   W. Winter, *Shadows of the Stage: Third Series* (New York: Macmillan & Co., 1895), p. 162.
6   Ibid.
7   Hogan et al. (eds), *Dictionary of Irish Literature*, p. 1252.
8   Ibid.

unpublished verses on unsuspecting visitors and who felt that he had not lived up to his artistic and literary potential.[8] In a more positive twist, Winters attributes Wills's self-deprecating tendency to his not being 'thoughtful of his reputation' or 'careful of his health', but being only concerned with 'doing fine things'.[9] Wills died at Guy's Hospital, London, in December 1891.

While he had addressed the Famine earlier in *Life's Foreshadowings*, Wills revisited the gloomy era in his three-decker novel *The Love that Kills* (1867), which according to his biographer, his brother Freeman Wills, drew 'striking pictures of the relations between landlord and tenant in Ireland, the Irish Famine, and the Rebellion of 1848; and...showed a warm glow of sympathy with the Irish peasantry, which no one would have suspected in a man apparently so wholly out of touch with politics'.[10] The novel describes the life of William Clayton, a man who is blinded by his own idealism and cannot let go of his utopian notions. The narrative is set during the Famine and the following decades. Clayton becomes a supporter of Young Ireland, but quickly realizes that unnuanced idealism and lust for rebellion will not save Ireland, but will be her downfall. The excerpt given below describes a grand rally on the eve of the 1848 rebellion. The scene is infused with historical characters and references, and illustrates Clayton's growing disenchantment with the ideals of Young Ireland. Noteworthy is that Clayton is not represented as anti-nationalist, but simply as embodying a different sort of patriotism. The scene ends with Clayton's resolution to leave for America. Nothing comes of his utopian plans to start a new Ireland in America by incorporating California into the United States as the 'State of Eirinn'. Clayton chooses never to return to Ireland, and lives a disillusioned but relatively happy life in Paris with his only friend Lizzie.

---

9   Winter, *Shadows of the Stage* , p. 163.
10   Wills, *Life of W.G. Wills*, p. 60.

From *The Love That Kills. A Novel*

(London: Tinsley Brothers, 1867), vol. 3, pp. 80–7.

A s Clayton came nearer he perceived that the orator was the youthful Meagher,[11] and the dignified personage was no other than the gentle and well-meaning Smith O'Brien;[12] on his head was a cap encircled with gold lace, and not unsuggestive of a crown; he leant upon a very fine specimen of pike, the spear point on the ground, the characteristic attitude of St Patrick,[13] as chroniclers aver. In one of the priests Clayton recognised his friend and confessor, Father Walshe, with whom he had parted, on the road. Clayton avoided meeting his eye, and took a position in the rear of the party. There he stood as in a dream; the shouting of the orator, and the shouting of the people, and the rush of the fresh west wind, all came to his senses mingled and confused. An isolation, at first slight, but which grew terrible at last, came upon him in the midst of this vast crowd; not that his resolution wavered, – it was rather the presence of that resolution which weighed upon his spirit, confused and overcame him. At one moment he

11   Thomas Francis Meagher (1823–67), also known as 'Meagher of the Sword'. He was a leader of Young Ireland, and played a leading part in the rebellion of 1848. The line 'up with the barricades, and invoke the God of Battle!' is taken from Meagher's 15 March 1848 speech on behalf of the Confederation to congratulate the French on the 1848 Revolution. He was charged with sedition and transported to Van Diemen's Land. Eventually, Meagher escaped to America, settled in New York and lectured on the Irish nationalist cause. See P.R. Wiley, *The Irish General: Thomas Francis Meagher* (Norman, OK: University of Oklahoma Press, 2007).
12   William Smith O'Brien (1803–64) became a member of the Repeal Association in 1843. He and the Young Irelanders formed the Irish Confederation. He was one of the leaders of the 1848 rebellion and was sentenced to be transported to Van Diemen's Land. O'Brien received a full pardon in 1856 and returned to Ireland. See M. Davis and W. Davis, *The Rebel in His Family: Selected Papers of William Smith O'Brien* (Cork: Cork University Press, 1998), pp. 1–2. O'Brien was also very critical of the government policies used to counter the Famine. As he stated, '[i]f, during the Irish famine, for instance, the Government had made liberal advances on loan for railways, embankments, harbors, and other public works to local bodies, many thousands of laboring families might have been saved from the demoralizing and pauperizing tendencies which subsequently resulted from a reckless, aimless, and unprofitable expenditure. The people would have been kept alive in a state of healthy independence; the spirit of the country would have been sustained, and the Government would eventually have lost but a small portion, if any, of the amount so advanced for reproductive employment.' *Principles of Government; or Meditations in Exile* (Boston, MA: Patrick Donahoe, 1856), p. 202.
13   This is a reference to St Patrick's iconic walking staff. According to legend, St Patrick carried with him an ash walking stick which he would thrust into the ground and lean on whenever he was preaching to the people.

thought he was losing his sight, the sea of faces seemed lost in a red haze, and the form of the orator seemed cutting antics against the sky. In a few moments the faces glared out distinct again, but the noise and confusion seemed to sink into a low, thunderous hum. There were moments, too, when every sense grew painfully acute, and the emergency he was about to meet presented itself in all its peril.

Then he would gaze anxiously down the white road which lay below them, expecting to see the glisten of bayonets. Then a wayward reminiscence of his boyhood would take possession of his mind, in which the mood was somewhat akin; that poaching adventure, when he stood on the river bank by the side of his dead and gone friend, poor Jack Sedge, and listened for the steps of the water bailiffs, who stole upon them at last. There was suddenly a great lull in the crowd; the orator was making some important announcement. Clayton's attention awoke.

'Shall we be slaves?' cried the young orator, pushing his fingers through his long hair. 'Republican France cries shame on us! She has offered us her generous example,[14] and my friend, Mr O'Brien, will tell you she will send over fifty thousand of her chivalry to aid us on the field!'

A tempest of applause from those within earshot.

'In public, indeed – lest she might warn the English bloodhounds that the heart-broken stag of Erin[15] had levelled her antlers at last and stood at bay – in public she may possibly stand aloof, but in private she has promised us her heart and her hand!

'Shall we be slaves? The soldiers that garrison our towns cry shame on us! Yet, the military and police are our friends. They will turn and do battle with us as did the glorious National Guard in the streets of Paris. The first that will be shot down would be the officers who gave the word. Shall we be slaves? The whole circumambient universe cries, No! From the North to the South thunders Freedom's invocation; her lessons are read by the light of burning thrones!'

'Shall we be slaves? Nay, rather up with the barricades, and invoke the God of Battle!'

---

14 In his speech, Meagher is referring to the 1848 French Revolution. Mid-nineteenth-century Irish nationalist discourse often alludes to this Revolution; many nationalists, including Meagher, believed that the French could serve as an example for the Irish. It was even hoped that the French might send over troops to Ireland in support of the nationalist movement. See L.M. Geary, *Rebellion and Remembrance in Modern Ireland* (Dublin: Four Courts Press, 2001).

15 Another name for Ireland.

Here there was a sudden alarm in the crowd, and the cry arose, 'The soldiers are coming!' Mr Meagher got down from the table precipitately. Mr O'Brien, trailing his long pike, asked the people would they allow him to be taken; and on their assurances that they would not permit it, he anxiously appealed to them to gather around and guard him. But in a few moments it was found to be a false alarm, and only the arrival of a faithful band of patriots under the command of Mr M'Manus,[16] who was attired in smart green uniform.

The momentary panic having subsided, Father Walshe sprung upon the table, and calling for silence he proceeded to stimulate the people with a denunciation of England, in fact to flourish his torch over the gun-powder around him. He gave them a highly seasoned exposition of their wrongs and sufferings. The policy of the English Government, he averred, was this: – to crush and trample down the Irish, to decimate and drive them from their native soil, to refuse the daily bread on the land they till.

'Years ago', he cried, 'England foresaw your day of ruin and starvation, and legislated to give it murderous effect; she tempted away your landlords, she reduced you to wretched serfs upon the soil, she drove you to acts of requital, which your Church has always denounced; but, if some famished wretch from among you has been driven to shoot his oppressor from behind a hedge, I tell you that a sheriff's bailiff, with a deadlier weapon called a *habere*,[17] has exterminated a whole country-side in a few hours, and sent a thousand starving families to die in a ditch.

'I am weary of constitutional agitation, and will never lift a finger to help it again. Instead of "Agitate! agitate!" let us cry "Arm! arm!" Instead of register, I tell you to hold your land and eat the fruit thereof, and be filled; – defend your right at the point of your pikes.

'England's policy has worked long enough; it has worked against you through all history and from all times. Have you heard, – if not I will tell you, – how the English Government invited the monks of Clare and Limerick to collect in the Isle of Scattery   their monasteries having been

---

16 Terence Bellew MacManus (1811/12–61) was a Young Irelander who was sentenced to death for his part in the Young Ireland rebellion, but was transported to Van Diemen's Land instead. He escaped to San Francisco and died there in 1861.

17 In UK law, *habere facias possessionem* was a writ issued 'in order that the plaintiff might have full and clear possession according to his judgment', enabling the sheriff (and his agents) to legally eject tenants on behalf of their landlord. See J. Reeves, *History of the English Law*, vol. 4 (London: n.p., 1814), p. 167.

burnt to the ground – and promised them a safe passage to some European port: four hundred of the holy monks sailed in a ship from that island, and were scarcely a league from shore when they were torn from their berths and thrown overboard into the sea!

'Have you heard, – if not I will tell you, – how Cromwell in Wexford murdered three hundred men, women, and children around the cross?' (Immense sensation among the crowd, and out-cries for vengeance).

'Have you heard, – if not I will tell you, – how the same Cromwell induced the Irish defenders to Drogheda to come outside the walls, lay down their arms, and receive quarter at his hands; and then, when they came out, that man of blood, having the flower of the Irish chivalry at his mercy, massacred them for five days, so that the streets ran red with their blood?' (Immense sensation and uproar).

'But have you heard, I need not tell you, for you have felt this last treacherous blow England has aimed at your lives. She foresaw it all, I say, – your famine and your ruin.[18] No vulture or carrion crow could have a surer instinct of coming death than she, scenting your misery from afar. People of Ireland, rise! Grasp your arms! Level your pikes! Charge your guns! There's a magic bullet in your pouches, which will go to the heart of this foul scavenger bird, that feeds upon your misery and decay!'

---

18 Some nationalists and their sympathizers felt that England had induced or at least aggravated the Famine to stimulate economic, industrial and social change in Ireland. For instance, the author of 'Another Victim of the Whig Administration', published in the *Cork Examiner* on 29 December 1846, states: 'Political economy is doing its bloody work – slowly, steadily, but not the more surely … Not a single day passes by without abundant evidence of the total inadequacy of the present government, to wield the destinies of this great empire, or to preserve from *actual starvation* the great majority of this long misgoverned and unfortunate country.'

Annie Keary (1825–79)

Annie Keary was the youngest of six children born to an English mother and Irish father at Bilton Rectory in Yorkshire. Her father, Galway-born William Keary, became a clergyman there after he had lost his property in Ireland.[1] The Kearys were Irish Protestants, but it has been argued that Annie later 'developed "Catholic tendencies"'.[2] With the exception of a sojourn of only two weeks in Ireland,[3] during which she wrote *Castle Daly*, Keary lived in England her entire life and died in Eastbourne, England, on 3 March 1879.[4] She is best known for her work as a novelist, but she also wrote children's stories, such as *York and Lancaster Rose* (1876), and a collection of poems entitled *Enchanted Tulips* (1914), written together with her sisters Maud and Elizabeth and published posthumously.[5] She also wrote non-fictional works such as *Early Egyptian History* (1861) and a study on the peoples bordering Israel, *The Nations Around* (1870).[6]

Castle Daly, Keary's only Irish novel, was mostly founded on Keary's reading on the Irish rebellion of 1848, as well as her 'collecting... through friends and relations in the country, details of the terrible famine preceding it'.[7] First published in serialized form in *MacMillan's Magazine*, it is regarded as one of the best 'so-called Irish novels' of her time.[8] The novel goes back to the 1840s, and gives in-depth accounts of the Great Famine and, according to critics of the time, such as Matthew Russell, 'refers in no ungenerous spirit to the Young Ireland movement'.[9] This period of upheaval is represented as a transitional

---

1   E. Keary, *Memoir of Annie Keary, By Her Sister* (London: Macmillan, 1882), p. 2.
2   Review of A. Keary, *Castle Daly, Irish Monthly,* 14 (1886), pp. 455–6.
3   Keary, *Memoir of Annie Keary,* p. 148.
4   R. Hogan et al. (eds), *Dictionary of Irish Literature: Revised and Expanded Edition* (London: Aldwych Press, 1996), p. 647.
5   A.U. Colman, *Dictionary of Nineteenth-Century Irish Women Poets* (Galway: Kenny's Bookshop, 1996), pp. 125–6.
6   Hogan et al. (eds), *Dictionary of Irish Literature,* p. 647.
7   Keary, *Memoir of Annie Keary,* p. 149.
8   Colman, *Dictionary of Nineteenth-Century Irish Women Poets,* p. 125; S. Deane, A. Carpenter and J. Williams, (eds), *The Field Day Anthology of Irish Writing, Vol. 5: Irish Women's Writing and Traditions* (New York: New York University Press, 2002), p. 951.
9   Review of A. Keary, *Castle Daly,* p. 211.

stage between social and economic modernization and older, feudal ways of life. As Margaret Kelleher points out, the novel was well received by English reviewers and Irish intellectuals alike. *Castle Daly* is an apt illustration contesting the assumption that the latter half of the nineteenth century was a period of silence around the Great Famine in literature. Keary created her nuanced view by incorporating rounded Irish and English characters and representing them in dialogue with each other.

Although Keary provides various alternative views on the Famine and Ireland's future course, it is clear that *Castle Daly* privileges English reformist ideas, as embodied by the benevolent English agent, John Thornley. The novel narrates the story of the Daly family who, following the advice of their English cousin Sir Charles Pelham, leave their Irish property in the hands of estate agent Thornley and move to England. The excerpts reproduced here show a conversation on Ireland's condition between the pragmatic Thornley and the idealist Irish heroine and Young Ireland sympathizer Ellen Daly; and the report of an Irish–English battle including references to the real Young Ireland leader, William Smith O'Brien.

From *Castle Daly: The Story of an Irish Home Thirty Years Ago*

(London: MacMillan & Co., 1875), vol. 2, pp. 214–7: vol. 3, pp. 252–6.

'Mr Thornley, you should not have said that word "play."'
'Why not?'

'Don't you think that when people are miserable, and angered, and desperate, and told their death-struggles are play, it is enough to goad them into terrible earnest? It is just those contemptuous sayings that do so much harm and sow more bitterness than actual wrong.'

'I did not mean it for contempt. I am paying a tribute to Young

Ireland's[10] common sense when I call the threats her representatives are flinging about mere play. I cannot suppose them to be so mad and blind as to be in earnest. To dream of plunging the country into rebellion at such a crisis as this would be greater folly than one can conceive.'

'We don't worship common sense as you do; and for my part I don't believe anything great was ever done except when that idol of yours was tossed away. It is always in crises of trouble, out of great depths, that deliverance comes.'

'Yes; but what you are looking for would not be deliverance, it would be destruction.'

'You don't know anything about it.'

'I shall begin to think you are the "Eva" or the "Speranza" who writes pathetic treason in the *Nation*.'[11]

'Don't sneer at them, please. I have read verses of theirs that I should indeed be proud to have written.'

'For your brother Connor's sake, I am very sorry to hear you say this. I shall hardly blame him for any lengths he may go to now. It is enough to make any one a rebel to hear you talk. You should be careful.'

'Can one be careful when one's heart is breaking? The very blackness of the night forces me to believe that there must be a dawn coming.'

'And so there is; though perhaps you won't recognize it as such when it comes. There will come some good out of the present misery, you may be sure. It is good for the country that the surplus population is driven away, even by stress of famine, to seek more prosperous homes elsewhere, leaving the land to be made the best of.'

'Desolated that is, – turned into wide, silent, sheep-walks and great pasture-fields, with only dumb cattle in them from sea to sea. Everywhere

---

10   In 1846 more radical and younger people involved with *The Nation*, such as John Blake Dillon and Thomas Davis, broke away from O'Connell's Repeal Association. There were great differences between O'Donnell, who discouraged the use of violence, and for whom 'Ireland and the Roman Catholic Church were indissolubly associated in his mind' (*Cassell's Illustrated History of England, From the Accession of George IV to the Irish Famine of 1847* [London: Cassell, Petter & Galpin, 1863], p. 27), and the Young Irelanders, who proposed militancy and who sought to unite all Irishmen regardless of religion.

11   Established in 1842 by Charles Gavan Duffy, Thomas Osborne Davis and John Blake Dillon, *The Nation* was the most prominent nationalist weekly, publishing influential pieces on Repeal and the Famine by nationalists such as John Mitchel, James Clarence Mangan and Thomas D'Arcy McGee. 'Eva' is the pen name adopted by Mary Eva Kelly (1826–1910), a major female nationalist poet. 'Speranza' is the pseudonym under which Jane Francesca Elgee (1821–96, later known as Lady Wilde) wrote patriotic and revolutionary poetry and prose. One of her best-known Famine poems is 'The Stricken Land', published in 1847.

roofless villages and deserted homes, only here and there a few of compan-ionless people who have lost all instinct of nationality, guarding riches that are not their own. *That* would be your good; but that is just the fate we Young Irelanders are resolved to make one stand against before it is quite too late – one struggle to keep Ireland and her people together.'

'You might just as well put up your hands and try to stop the sun in the sky. A country can't exist by itself in these days; it must consent to become what the rest of the world wants it to be.'

'I will never agree to that. I think a country is for the people who love it best to live and be happy in, in their own way.'

'Then would you leave America to red Indians for hunting-grounds and wigwams?'

'I shall not answer such an insulting question. We did not come out to quarrel, did we, Mr Thornley? I thought it was to be for rest. We have climbed the hill while we have been arguing, and left Pelham and Lesbia far behind. Let us wait for them here at the top, for this is the view I want Lesbia to admire. Do you see my little lake – my water-lily preserve – down there, looking like a patch of blue sky that has dropped down and been caught and held fast by the hills? I am glad Lac-na-Weel[12] wears his crown to-day; he looks so much grander covered. He might be any height up in the mist.'

'Like Young Ireland's dreams, seen through the mist of eloquence you are wrapping them in. I don't so much wonder at people growing dreamy who live there, for there is glamour over everything. The very beauty of the landscape is made of cloud effects, mist-wreaths, and sunbeams. Through any other atmosphere it would be dreary enough, you must allow.'

'If you will allow that it is some credit to a country to know how to get loveliness, like this we are looking at, out of bare rock and bog lands, and such hopes as we have out of despair.'

'Yes, if you could always be content with shadow instead of substance, and did not dash yourselves to pieces chasing one in mistake for the other.'

'I think I like shadows best', said Ellen; 'such shadows as those on the hills. I pity the people who have to leave them to live in some ugly, flat plain in America or Australia, let it be ever so substantial and fruitful.'

...

---

12   A fictitious mountain range.

'The windows of the white house were full of green-coats,[13] and the crowds with pikes appeared to be besieging the house, trying to make them come out and give up their arms, but nobody seemed to know exactly what was intended, and neither party liked to fire first. I noticed a tall man, who was pointed out to me as Mr Smith O'Brien,[14] come again and again to the windows of the house and then turn and speak to the people, but whether he urged them to attack or keep the peace, I could not say. There were several other young fellows better dressed than the rest trying to put some order into the crowd, and among them I soon espied the two I was in search of. They were well in front, among the small innermost circle, who for the most part carried arms and had more purpose in their faces than the gaping ragged outsiders, and even if I could have forced my way to them and made them listen to me it would have been too late for what I wanted – they had done the worst for themselves they could do. While I stood watching, the first shot was fired, and a volley of stones hurled against the windows, and after that, for about half an hour or so, a brisk exchange of shot went on...While I was there I heard my name called, "Dr Lynch, can that be you?" and turning round I saw O'Donnell staggering up to the wall, through the throng, with some one in his arms. "Yes", I said, "It's me", and I had my heart in my mouth, for I could only see a figure lying across his breast, with an arm over his shoulder, and I thought of Connor at once. "Then it's a lucky chance that brought you", O'Donnell answered. "Here's work for you, the first of the boys that's down yet, the poor lad Malachy, he's breathing still, help me with him over the wall, that he may not be trampled to death in the throng here. He has a bullet in him, I am afraid. It was aimed full at Connor as he stooped to put a light to the little bonfire we had piled up yonder, and if poor Murdock had not started forward at the moment, and thrust his shoulder in the way, it's Connor who would have got it. I think myself he knew what he was about, poor boy, and did it on purpose; anyhow tell them about it at home, and do what you can do for him. I must go back." There were plenty of hands put out to lift the body over the wall, and help me to carry it to

---

13   The Irish nationalists were also called green-coats. See, for instance, the anonymous song 'The Wearing of the Green' which was supposedly written around the time of the 1798 rebellion when it became forbidden to wear the nationalist colour. http://www.ireland-information.com/irishmusic/thewearingofthegreen.shtml (2011).

14   William Smith O'Brien (1803–64). See note 12 to W.G. Wills, *The Love that Kills* in this section.

the next field out of the way of the tumult, and some of the women ran to a cabin a little way off to fetch water; but soon I saw there was nothing to be done!'

'Poor Murdock! was he dead?'

'The bullet had entered just between the shoulder-blades and come out at the throat. It could be only a question of a few minutes, and I did not think he would ever speak again: but he did. As we were bathing his forehead and putting some whisky to his lips there was a minute's consciousness, and he looked full at me. "Mr Connor", he said.'

'"Yes, my poor fellow", I answered. "He's all right, you saved him, I believe, and got this instead of him."'

'"He was always good to me", he answered, "and maybe some day I'll see him and Miss Eileen agin in a better place than Ireland will ever be, when all's done."'

'There was no more talking after that, for the blood rose in his throat and choked him, and I had to lay him down from my arms on the ditch side, for some one called me just then to help a poor fellow who had been pushed out of the crowd with a broken arm.'

'But Connor – did you see nothing more of Connor or D'Arcy? How do you know they were not killed or wounded after poor Murdock left them?'

'By having seen nearly all who were hurt. There was only one other boy killed besides Murdock, and I saw him lying stark among the cabbages when all was over – a tall, lank, famine-stricken shape that would have died of another day's tramp, if a bullet had not found him out and saved him the trouble of going further. There was a withered hag, though, and a couple of skeleton children to hullabaloo over him. To think of clever lads like Connor and D'Arcy, to say nothing of a sober gentleman of forty like Mr Smith O'Brien, proposing to stand up against England with an army composed of material like that.'[15]

---

15   It is believed that the Young Ireland rebellion of 29 July 1848 failed because it had been ill prepared, and because sympathizers were scattered all over the country. Most Irish, encouraged by the clergy, remained loyal to 'Liberator' Daniel O'Connell and his Loyal National Repeal Association rather than the Irish Confederation formed by Young Ireland in 1847. See, for example, L.J. McCaffrey, *Textures of Irish America* (Syracuse, NY: Syracuse University Press, 1992), p. 132.

William C. Upton

Little is known about William C. Upton, and in *Ireland in Fiction*, Stephen Brown only notes that Upton was a carpenter working in Ardagh who later settled in America.[1] Upton's novel, *Uncle Pat's Cabin*, was published in 1882, is set in Fenian times, and in a sense reflects the transatlantic nature of the Fenian movement, for it was modelled on Harriet Beecher Stowe's *Uncle Tom's Cabin* (1852).[2]

Brown notes that *Uncle Pat's Cabin*, set in Co. Limerick and spanning roughly the period 1848–80, was representative of real Irish life, as '[a]ll the facts relative to the agricultural labourer in these pages can be vouched for'.[3] Moreover, Lecky notes that Upton's novel is 'one of the truest and most vivid pictures of the present condition of the Irish labourer'.[4] Although the novel clearly voices a nationalist sentiment, is dedicated to the nationalist poet, republican and agrarian agitator Michael Davitt (1846–1906), and was written when land-war fiction was popular, *Uncle Pat's Cabin* should not simply be categorized as such. Contrary to most land-war novels, Upton's narrative does not focus on Irish tenant farmers, but rather on the agricultural labourers.[5] It is also clearly written in response to the fear of another famine in the late 1870s. Furthermore, instead of stating that Ireland and Irish agriculture will recover (through an adjustment or subversion of the current social hierarchy of Ireland), the novel advises its readers to leave for America.[6] As J.H. Murphy notes, '[t]his, however, might have been a more realistic prognosis for the future of labourers than the tenant-dominated Land League would have cared to admit at the time'.[7]

1   S.J.M. Brown, *Ireland in Fiction* (Dublin: Maunsel & Company, 1919), p. 303.
2   M. Fegan, *Literature and the Irish Famine 1845-1919* (Oxford: Oxford University Press, 2002), p. 226.
3   Brown, *Ireland in Fiction*, p. 303.
4   W.E.H. Lecky, *A History of Ireland in the Eighteenth Century*, vol. 3 (London: Longmans, Green & Co. 1892), pp. 413–14.
5   Fegan, *Literature and the Irish Famine 1845–1919*, p. 226.
6   J.H. Murphy, *Irish Novelists and the Victorian Age* (Oxford: Oxford University Press, 2011), pp. 169–70.
7   Ibid., p. 170.

The excerpt printed below very much focuses on tensions between landlords and tenants, the after-effects of the Great Famine and the omnipresent fear of another period of hunger among the Irish land labourers. The excerpt also displays a fascinating dichotomy between the more radical ideas of the agrarian agitators, such as Michael Davitt, and the actual wants and needs of the poorest of the poor, the Catholic land labourers. In this passage, the former's standpoint is represented by the fictional character Henry Irving, while the latter is voiced by the peasant Tom Harnett. The upper classes are also represented here, in the character of Tom Cassidy, who comes across as a good-for-nothing pompous rake and thief only interested in pursuing his own pleasure and enhancing his property.

From *Uncle Pat's Cabin; Or, Life Among the Agricultural Labourers of Ireland*

(Dublin: M.H. Gill & Son, 1882), pp. 132–4.

After a few gallons of porter had been drunk, and suitable toasts delivered, Henry Irving[8] adroitly turned the conversation on the

---

8   Not to be mistaken for the celebrated English stage actor Henry Irving (1838–1903), since the character of Henry Irving in *Uncle Pat's Cabin* identifies himself as Irish later in the same scene. However, this does not seem to be a merely coincidental use of the actor's name and could be a reference to Irving, who came to Ireland on several occasions and convened with Bram Stoker and Frank Marshall to discuss the writing of a play about Robert Emmet (1778–1803), the Irish nationalist hero and martyr. The play was first commissioned by Irving for London's Lyceum theatre, but after an upsurge in Fenian aggression, was banned by the authorities. In 1884, the play was rewritten (under the title *Robert Emmet*) by noted Victorian dramatist Dion Boucicault and performed in Chicago, where it did not do very well. Upton's fictional Fenian sympathizer Henry Irving was more deeply involved in Irish politics than the English stage actor ever was, for the actor's political ambitions regarding Ireland seem to have been limited to his wish to impersonate Emmet on stage. See J. Richards, *Sir Henry Irving, A Victorian Actor and His World* (Basingstoke: Palgrave Macmillan, 2005), pp. 185–6.

subject of the Fenian Brotherhood.[9] The discussion had not proceeded far when young Cassidy, [10] full of his late election eloquence, began: 'Well, Mr Irving, I don't see what necessity at all there is for men like *you* to lave their homes, and strive to do in such a difficult way what Mister Synan[11] says he will do, and what Father Fitz[12] says he can do. Sure, if we get the Protestant Church disestablished, if we get Tenant Right and Catholic education,[13] haven't we the country then free; and what more, I would like to know, do we want?'

'Tell me', said Henry Irving, rising in an indignant manner from his seat, 'can your intelligence carry you no further than the remedying of those evils? Can your manhood rise to nothing more than provincialism for your country? Are our laws to be for ever made by strangers, who have no feeling in common with us? Must the revenues of our country be ever going to swell the treasury of the strangers? Must our nation's flag' (and here Henry Irving seemed lost in the inspiration that was giving such force to his words) 'be for ever a proscribed thing; and every son of Ireland who would dare to right her, live an outlaw? And must the lot of these poor men' (pointing to Tom Harnett and a few of the labourers), 'who dig and

---

9   The Fenian Brotherhood, founded by John O'Mahony and Michael Doheny, first convened in New York in 1858 and was officially established in 1859. It was the Irish-American sister organization of the Irish Republican Brotherhood in Ireland. The Fenian Brotherhood started out as a secret society, but quickly spread on both sides of the Atlantic. Its aim was to free Ireland from British oppression, and the Fenians did not shy away from the use of excessive force and violence. The convention's address to the people, in which they 'call upon and exhort every true Irishman in America, England, and the British Colonies, to rally around the Fenian Brotherhood, and to aid us in preparing Ireland for freedom's battle' ('An Irishman', *The Fenian Brotherhood: A Few Useful Hints to Irishmen, and Some Valuable Information for Americans, Concerning Ireland* [Boston, MA: Dakin, Davis & Metcalf, 1864], p. 4), is laced with slogans about struggles, inevitability and fight. In 1865, the time in which the scene from Upton's novel displayed here is set, the government perceived the growing threat of the Fenian movement, and government troops were sent into the offices of *The Irish People* to arrest its key contributors, such as Charles Joseph Kickham and Jeremiah O'Donovan Rossa. In 1867, the Fenians attempted a rising and marched towards Dublin, but due to unfortunate weather conditions and a far better prepared government army, the rising failed miserably.

10   The landlord's nephew and a veritable rake. Although his uncle's fortune is dwindling, Tom does not give up his luxurious and amoral lifestyle, causing him to become a thief and a fugitive, as he breaks into the farm of a wealthy but kind farmer with his servant Bill O'Donnell, gets caught, escapes and flees to America, leaving Bill to take responsibility.

11   Mr Synan, the newly elected MP for Co. Limerick in the narrative.

12   One of the priests in the novel.

13   These aims were shared by most nationalist Irish and their sympathizers and were not just goals of the Irish Republican Brotherhood or the Fenian Brotherhood. However, the extent to which these goals were viewed as desirable varied greatly, as many of the poorest Irish labourers had more modest ambitions than the more radical land-war agrarian agitators and Fenians.

delve from morning till night on your grounds remain the same? Are they to be still calculated among your goods and chattels as American slaves used to be? Are they still to subsist on wages that would not give Indian meal to as many dogs? I tell you, young man, you must not reckon on the continual degradation of these men, for there is an intelligence among them that knows their wants, and knows how to remedy them. I must be guarded here', he still continued in a suppressed tone. 'Such language as this endangers my safety; otherwise I would speak sentiments that would put to shame the manless soul within you.'

In a rush, Tom Harnett and every labourer in the room, except Bill O'Donnell, rose to their feet, uttering, 'That's thrue for you, Misther Irving; 'tis you that's telling the truth', 'Hurrah for the Feeneens',[14] and such like impulsive sentiments.

All sat down again except Tom Harnett, who continued, saying: 'We will not bear this thratement always. We are as hardshipped a body of men as there is in the world. We haven't a sod of ground but what we musht pay tin times the value for; and, our bohawns[15] aren't fit for the pigs to live in. Our wages won't allow us to put a rag on our childhern's bones; and some of us has but the wan bed for eight in family to shleep in. We won't get a sup of milk to dhrink but what is pisined; and, when we are sick, or in want, we are tould to go to the workhouse, where the divil will be played to us intirely. And, with Misther Synan, and every wan like him, there isn't a word about the poor labourer. Give me your hand, Misther Irving', continued Tom, raising a pint of porter to his lips; 'here is your health and your song, and may God assisht any cause that will alther our position. Begor, if it was the Rooshians[16] itself, we can't be worse; though, I have nothing to complain myself with Big Ned. Here is your health and your song again, Misther Irving.'

Tom was determined that it should not be considered by those present that he was among that list of human beings situated as he described. No; he should not so wrong Big Ned as to classify him among the landgrabbers of the country; and, to do him justice, he thought it right to say so.

---

14 Fenians. Irving's speech is a telling example of Fenian nationalism, which, as becomes clear in this
    excerpt, was more extreme than the more generally accepted nationalist sentiment expressed earlier
    by Cassidy, for whom emancipation and equal rights are not necessarily linked to Irish independence.
15 Cabins.
16 Russians.

Emily Lawless (1845–1913)

Underfoot, from its caverns, moans
and murmurs the Atlantic,
Moans and murmurs now, as it murmured
and moaned at the dawning.[1]

This depiction of Ireland's West Country may well be rooted in Emily Lawless's recollections of her childhood, when she spent long periods in Galway with her mother's relatives, the Kirwans, who were apparently good landlords. Here she learned to love the rugged West Irish landscape.[2] Lawless's writings are infused with her own observations about the Irish landscape. This is also visible in *Hurrish* (1886), one of her most esteemed novels. The narrative is set in 'a post-Famine Ireland, bitter, resentful, decimated by emigration and riven by agrarian conflict'.[3] Although the story is set against the backdrop of the Land Wars of the 1870s and 1880s, the conflict in the narrative is largely of a personal nature. The novel tells the story of Hurrish, a lovable Irish giant, who, when attacked by his evil and land-grabbing neighbour Mat Brady, accidentally kills him. Hurrish is arrested, but is found innocent, only to be mortally wounded by Mat Brady's brother, Maurice. After an epiphany, Maurice understands his mistake and the novel ends with a typical deathbed scene in which Maurice is forgiven by the dying Hurrish.

Lawless was too young to have consciously experienced the Great Famine herself, and *Hurrish* is set in a later period. Nevertheless, the novel does contain references to the Great Famine, and in combining these references with the novel's contemporary social hardships, the Land Wars, the threat of another famine suggests that (Irish) history is repetitive. The first excerpt below focuses on the old-stock character Phil Rooney, who experienced the Famine. The second excerpt describes the threat of another Famine and the ensuing agrarian unrest, which are eerily reminiscent of that earlier traumatic time.

---

1   E. Lawless, 'Looking Eastward; Written in 1885', in *With the Wild Geese* (London: Isbister & Co., 1902), pp. 48–9.

2   H. Hansson, *Emily Lawless 1845–1913: Writing the Interspace* (Cork: Cork University Press, 2007), pp. 10, 16.

3   V. Mulkerns, 'Introduction', in E. Lawless, *Hurrish: a Novel* (Belfast: Appletree Press, 1993), p. vii.

From *Hurrish: A Study*

(Edinburgh: William Blackwood, 1886), vol. 1,
pp. 80–86, vol. 2, pp. 184–86.

The absorbing interest of the cow's illness over, and its future treatment decided upon, the conversation of the other two lapsed, as a matter of course, to the day's tragedy, which both agreed in regretting, though both held the unfortunate Buggle[4] to be primarily responsible for his own fate, a process-server, as every reasonable person knows, having no more human rights than a stoat, and being liable, like that vermin, to be killed whenever met with.

'I wud wunder a dacent man wud do it, yis indeed', Old Rooney said in his cracked treble (English was a foreign language to him, and at home he never spoke anything but his native tongue, whereas Hurrish, like most of the younger generation, preferred the former – despite its name, by the way, which will doubtless be changed for the better when the new Irish Republic finds time to look about it).

'I'm not sayin' he oughtn't to ha' been shtopped', he observed, in response to his friend's remark. 'Don't mistake me, Phil. But shtones! – they're nasty cruel things shtones is! The blood rins cowld though my body when I think of that cratur al by hisself – rinnin' for the bare life, an' beggin an' prayin' ov thim to let him off, and they throwin' stones at him an' laughin'! Lord! I can see it 's if I'd been there! an' the moon gallivantin' along the sky the way it does, an' not carin' th' half of a ratten pittattee what goes on underneath! An' niver a one nigh him – 'less God, maybe', Hurrish added, with a considerable doubt in his mind as to whether God would have anything to say to a process-server. ''Twas only yesterday one

---

4   The process server, who was killed by bricks while walking on the road. The process server was not a much loved figure, for his job largely consisted of giving people official notice of eviction. Representations of process servers (and other middlemen) greatly varied in Famine fiction. The middleman Billy Finnigan in Sigerson's *A Ruined Race; or, The Last Macmanus of Drumroosk* (London: Ward & Downey, 1889) is a despicable character, while in Keary's *Castle Daly: The Story of an Irish Home Thirty Years Ago* (London: Macmillan, 1875) the English estate agent John Thornley is benevolent and tries to do what is right for his tenants, even at his own expense, staying among his suffering tenants 'but for pity and charity' (p. 83).

of the bhoys told me some wan ax'd him if he wasn't 'feared to be goin' about the counthry servin' writs[5] an' suchlike, an' that he ups an' says no, for he knew they'd niver touch a hair ov his head, 'case of his bein' a cripple an' not able for to defend hisself! Och, Phil! man alive, 'taint that way the counthry's to be righted, howsomedever! What, killin' a man here and killin' a man there, and frightenin' a lot of poor foolish colleens, wid rushin' in to the houses in the dead of the night, cuttin' off their hair, an' makin' them sware[6] – the devil a bit they know what! Disthroying dumb bastes, too, that never did no one any harm. Sure, that's not *fightin'*! D'ye think th' *Inglish* – me curses on thim – care how many of wan anither we dishtroy? Isn't that what they're *wantin'* the bliggards? I'm not spakin', mind ye, agin the Laigue[7] – God defind it – only I wish they'd make thim shtop this potterin' sort of work intoirely, an' pass the word for the risin'.[8] 'Tis fightin' we want, an' fightin' *men*, not cows and colleens!'

Phil Rooney took out his snuff-box – a brass one with a medallion of the Liberator on top. He was a philosopher, and opined that a great deal of fuss was made by young men who had not had *his* experience. *He* could remember the pre-famine days and the rising of '48, and Macmanus,[9] and O'Doherty,[10] and Meagher of the Sword,[11] and most of

---

5   Official notices.

6   Reference to the actions of secret agrarian societies, such as the Whiteboys and Moonlighters. These secret societies–often through the use of violence – caused chaos in Irish rural areas during the agitation for land reform in the 1870s and 1880s.

7   The National Land League. During the late 1870s, feeling the threat of another famine, Irish tenants took matters in their own hands. Michael Davitt (1846–1906), a staunch Fenian who had earlier been convicted for possession of arms, united the disgruntled Irish tenantry under the Land League, which was established for the protection of tenants. Its principal enemies were landlords, who were considered the cause of agrarian hardship and thus seen as representations of the abuse of power. See Cronin, *History of Ireland*, pp. 158–9.

8   Phil Rooney is not forecasting an actual rising here, but alludes to a certain spirit of unease and tension and several past risings, such as the United Irishmen's Rebellion of 1798, the Young Ireland Rebellion of 1848 and the failed Fenian Rising of 1867.

9   Terence Bellew MacManus (1811/12–61). See note 16 to W.G. Wills, *The Love that Kills* in this section.

10 Kevin Izod O'Doherty (1824–1905) was a youth of great promise who joined Young Ireland and became a member of the editorial board of *The United Irishman*. After three court sessions, he was sentenced to be transported to Van Diemen's Land. After completing his medical degree in Paris, he was allowed to return to Ireland in 1855, where he became a successful medical practitioner. He was married to 'Eva' (Mary Eva Kelly), the famous nationalist poet. The couple migrated to Australia, where O'Doherty died in 1905. See A.M. Sullivan and D.B. Sullivan, *Guilty or not Guilty? Speeches from the Dock, or Protests of Irish Patriotism* (Dublin: Lower Abbey Street, 1867), pp. 131–7.

11 Thomas Francis Meagher (1823–67), see note 11 to W.G. Wills, *Love that Kills*, in this section.

the heroes of a generation ago, and it was his opinion that the time had now come when what the country wanted was peace and quietness. Of the modern race of agitators he did not hesitate to profess the profoundest contempt.

'There's bad times and there's good times', he said sententiously in Irish, 'and I don't see that there's so very much amiss with these. If you young fellows had seen the times *I* have, you might talk! Why, I remember in Ballysadare, when there were forty-three corpses lying dead at one time! Forty-three! yes, indeed, and they didn't need to be buried either to be skeletons most of them! The changes too! Why, I can remember when it was all the *masters* the bailiffs was after! Did I ever tell you of the time a bailiff came down to Lugnaskeagh, all the way from London it was, with a writ for the master? A terrible wild man he was, Sir Malachy O'Donel, God rest his soul! but there wasn't a boy on the place wouldn't have died and gone to jail for him, so there wasn't. Well, the bailiff man brought the writ all the way over the sea – a fine upstanding young fellow, with a blue waistcoat, and a gold watch, and a necktie right up to his chin. And he wanted, right or wrong, to get up to the house to serve it on the master. But if he did, the boys caught him just as he was reaching the great front door, and nothing would do them but he must eat it; and eat it he did, sure enough, – paper, and ink, and seals, and all, and the sputtering and the fighting! – oh, wirrastrue, wirrastrue![12] that *was* a sight. And his honour, Sir Malachy, peeping out behind the window-curtains all the while, and laughing fit to split. And when the last bit of paper was eaten, and the young man had gone away, spitting, and swearing to have the law on them, he came out and gave them a glass of whisky all round, and they hurrahed – I was only a slip of a gossoon[13] myself at the time – they hurrahed, so you'd have heard them at Gort! Seems odd to remember now, when it's nothing but killing the landlords will do them', Phil added, with another philosophic sniff out of the brass snuff-box.

Hurrish laughed loud and long at this story, though, as will easily be imagined, he had heard it a few times before. He loved old Phil Rooney's yarns, and often felt a secret regret that he had not himself belonged to an

---

12 Exclamation derived from the Gaelic 'a Mhuire, is trua', meaning 'alas, what a pity'. 'A Mhuire' is the vocative case, addressing the lament to the Virgin Mary.
13 A young boy.

earlier generation. The faction-fights,[14] scrimmages, and 'divarsions' generally of a generation or two ago, seemed to him to be of a much more delectable type than anything which came in a man's way nowadays. Not that there was any lack of fighting or head-breaking either, thank God, but it all seemed to have grown duller somehow. There was too much earnest about it all. Men killed one another for *reasons*, not from pure love and friendliness. You took measures to rid yourself of any one, as you might takes measures to rid your house of rats; there was no risk or 'intertainmint' about it at all.[15] Now Hurrish was sportsman enough to think a game decidedly the better for a spice of danger!

. . .

Two months had gone by since the day of the trial. Other and equally exciting scenes had occurred in the interval, so that it was no longer a matter of much interest even on the spot. It was a bad moment, in a bad year. Though the long nights had not yet come, there was a dangerous spirit abroad. The harvest had in many parts been bad, and a considerable harvest of another sort had been reaped from its failure.[16] All over Ireland there had been scattered crimes, and rumours of coming outbreaks. In lonely cabins, far from roads, far from the possibility of help of any kind, frightened women were lying awake at night, trembling to see the ill-protected door fly open, and blackened faces appear to drag away son, husband, father, to ill-usage, perhaps to death. On the hills around the horns were sounding at the dead hours. The cries of tortured animals – not less audible, perhaps, for being inarticulate – had again and again risen

---

14 It is not clear when faction fighting began, but it had its heyday in Ireland in the nineteenth century. Colonial commentators often saw proof of Irish barbarism in these fights. However, faction fighting was in fact quite organized and included several rituals such as 'the use of particular war cries, insults … challenges … and the practice whereby the faction leaders engaged in single combat before the fight proper'. See J.P. Byrne, P. Coleman and J F King, *Ireland and the Americas: Culture, Politics, and History*, vol. 2 (Santa Barbara, CA: ABC-CLIO, 2008), p. 314.

15 While Hurrish is at first represented as a member of the young generation, in opposition to Phil Rooney who serves as the embodiment of the past, his lament for the loss of sportsmanship and 'friendliness' distances him from the younger more militant generation as well.

16 An interesting reference to the threat of famine of 1879 can be found in Mrs E.M. Berens, *Steadfast unto Death: A Tale of the Irish Famine of Today* (London: Remington, 1880): 'It was the terrible winter of 1879–1880 … In Ireland, the destitution and misery were beyond imagination or calculation. The spectre of famine had not dared to show its ghastly face openly for years' (p. 1).

for vengeance to the sky. The whole country was in one of its periodic fits of excitement, terror, revolt. Vague expectations were everywhere afloat, dreadful or hopeful according to the anticipations of the individual. In the more reckless and desperate spirits, a wild belief in the speedy oncoming of some glorious pandemonium when the torch and carnage would stalk over the country; in the passive, a vague unquenchable expectation of a millennium which would make them rich, happy, prosperous, as by a miracle. In more practical heads, an eager political ferment, – a feeling that old things had passed away, and all things had become new. Brave men were nervous; sober men excited; every one uneasy, uncomfortable, restless. Nowhere stability; nowhere confidence; everywhere a feeling that ordinary routine was henceforward set aside. Of what use, it was asked, was to slave one's self when one might at any moment become rich without doing so? Still more forcibly, who but a fool would 'dishtroy' himself working to pay the rent, when all the world knew that henceforth no rents would have to be paid at all?

Clare had always claimed a prominent position in times of disturbance, and it was not behind its old fame on this occasion. Several barns had been burned, several obnoxious individuals waylaid and chastised, and there were warnings of more vigorous doings still. In no other part of Ireland had Captain Moonlight[17] appeared in greater force or with more absolute impunity. An impalpable reign of terror – invisible, but none the less real – lay upon every one, and every man looked distrustfully at his neighbour.

---

17   Captain Moonlight (or Moonlite) was a mythical persona in Ireland. In his name, rebels performed atrocities during the night, especially in the second part of the nineteenth century.

Mrs E.M. Field (1856–1941)

In the preface to her novel *Ethne* (1887), a historical narrative of the settlement of Ireland by Oliver Cromwell, Mrs E.M. Field, born as Louise Frances Story in Co. Cavan in 1856,[1] emphasizes the significance of history as a source of authorial inspiration. Boxes with 'moth-eaten, worm-eaten, mildewed' papers hidden in 'lofts and lumber-rooms of old Irish country houses' may contain material 'stranger than fiction ... more moving than any work of the playwright'.[2] For the subject of her own novels, which include *Ethne* (1887), *Bryda: A Story of the Indian Mutiny* (1888), and *Little Count Paul* (1893),[3] Field often resorted to the rich cultural and historical legacy of the British Empire, and the past of her native Ireland in particular.

Like other authors who were born after the Famine and therefore had no lived memory of that fateful era, such as Patrick Sheehan and Mildred Darby, Field asseverates that her Famine narrative *Denis* – 'this unvarnished tale' – is not merely a work of fancy but rather the 'relation of actual incidents'.[4] Field's remark suggests careful research of the period, while her dedication of the novel to her 'kinsfolk and friends, among the landowners of Ireland'[5] reveals her own background to be Anglo-Irish Ascendancy.

Denis is primarily a study of the relationship between landlords and tenants, focusing on Captain Mervyn, a reform-minded landlord, and Denis, one of his tenants. However, rather than casting the progressive Mervyn as a hero and concluding with a customary happily-ever-after, the novel ultimately reveals that Mervyn has raped a local girl, Denis's sweetheart, who then dies in childbirth. This sets in motion a downward spiral of mutual reprisal, ending with the eviction of all tenants from the Mervyn estate. Rather than restoring the past by allowing its protagonists to reclaim their idyllic Ireland, the novel ends on an apocalyptic note, with the destruction of an entire way of life: 'Something was gone forever from

---

1   S.J.M. Brown, *Ireland in Fiction* (Dublin: Maunsel & Company, 1919), p. 87.
2   Mrs E.M. Field, *Ethne, Being a Truthful Historie of the Great and Final Settlement of Ireland by Oliver Cromwell* (London: Wells, Gardner, 1887), p. v.
3   Brown, *Ireland in Fiction*, p. 87.
4   E.M. Field, *Denis: A Study in Black and White* (London: Macmillan, 1896), p. v.
5   Ibid.

the heart of the Irish people, something of gaiety and fun which never quite revived after the Black Forty-seven.'[6]

The following excerpt, a political debate among the local gentry, almost reads like a catalogue of mid-nineteenth-century Irish politics, addressing not only parliamentary elections and Daniel O'Connell's Repeal movement, but also Catholic Emancipation, the famous nationalist newspaper *The Nation*, and the friction between Catholicism and Protestantism in the context of nationalism. Darcy O'Hara, a young and idealistic man from the landed classes, delivers a passionate speech, urging the gentry to join the nationalist movement and bring about Repeal. His relatives and acquaintances, however, fail to share his ardour, and among his peers he stands alone in his nationalist sentiments.

From *Denis: A Study in Black and White*

(London: Macmillan, 1896), pp. 268–73.

That is the real fear in Irish agitation after all – it may break this slight thread. And then – well, *then* it is fairly impossible to set down without appearance of exaggeration what the Protestant gentry would expect to happen in such a case. Except in this one word – 'it would be entirely impossible to remain in the country'. The one quarter in which talk about patriotism, Romanism by implication, might be really dangerous was in the minds of the young who could not discern its dangers for themselves. When Mrs Mervyn[7] went into the little school at her gates she found that in every one of the children's reading books two or three pages were carefully pasted over with leaflet hymns. That had been done by Mr and Mrs McGee in evening hours, so that no undesirable emotions might be awakened by 'The Exile of Erin' in verse, or a prose account of the beauties of Killarney.[8]

---

6   Ibid., p. 413.
7   The mother of landlord Captain Mervyn.
8   A poem (1800) by Scottish writer Thomas Campbell (1777–1844), who was inspired by an encounter with Irish exile Anthony McCann. The persona expresses grief at having to leave Ireland because it no longer offers 'refuge from famine and danger'. See *The Poetical Works of Thomas Campbell* (London: Routledge, 2005), p. 125.

So, except for some such little twinge of uneasiness as to this, Mr Darcy's kinsfolk were not much afraid of his notions. They generally met them with mirth, occasionally they turned round in a little outburst of anger, and asked what was the use of trying to deal with people who were not the least grateful when you *did* give them what they asked for.

O'Connell[9] in their name had bothered and bothered till he worried England into granting Catholic Emancipation.[10] What was the result of giving it? Merely that Oliver asked for more.[11] They asked Darcy to account if he could for such base ingratitude; and if he answered that, when a highwayman has stripped you of everything, you are not overwhelmed with gratitude for the return of your small change they either laughed or grew angry, as their mood might be. It was an odd fact that they took a sort of pride in O'Connell; they might call him the Big Beggarman, and his schemes anathema, but there was hardly one of them who would not have walked a mile out of his way any day for a good look at his bullet head and massive features. They were not a bit afraid of him, any more than one is afraid of the child that cries for the top brick of the chimney – one may be a little nervous if the object of the outcry is a razor lying handy on the table. They had put the child in the dark cupboard for a bit when it grew too vociferous, and when it came out again the troublesome shriek

---

9   Daniel O'Connell (1775–1847), often called 'The Liberator', played an important role in bringing about Catholic Emancipation, and his relentless lobbying for the repeal of the Union was crucial for the development of nineteenth-century Irish nationalism. According to John O'Rourke, '[m]oral force, with physical force in the not too dim perspective behind it, was a giant power in the hands of O'Connell, and it won emancipation.' *The History of the Great Irish Famine of 1847, with Notices of Earlier Famines* (Dublin: M'Glashan & Gill, 1875), p. 148. O'Connell organized political monster meetings, at which he spoke before audiences of more than 100,000. See P.M. Geoghegan, *Liberator: The Life and Death of Daniel O'Connell, 1830–1847* (Dublin: Gill & Macmillan, 2010).

10 Until 1829, the legal position of Catholics in the United Kingdom was severely restricted by a number of anti-Catholic laws. Although the majority of the Irish population was Catholic, Roman Catholics could not be elected to Parliament. After intensive lobbying by Daniel O'Connell in particular, the Catholic Relief Act 1829 was passed, allowing O'Connell to take up the seat he had won in a by-election the year before. See F. O'Farrell, *Catholic Emancipation: Daniel O'Connell and the Birth of Irish Democracy, 1820–1830* (Dublin: Gill & Macmillan, 1985).

11 A reference to a famous scene in Charles Dickens's *Oliver Twist* (London: Richard Bentley, 1838), in which Oliver, a young workhouse inmate 'desperate with hunger, and reckless with misery' (pp. 28–9), asks for a second portion of gruel but is rebuffed by the manager and dismissed from the workhouse.

had dwindled to the gentle murmur of Constitutional agitation for Repeal[12] – that quite unreachable top brick!

There had been a little thrill of alarm when the group of young men to whom Darcy O'Hara belonged brought real ability in journalism to bear on the question of Repeal. Some few who condescended to look at their organ, *The Nation*, at closer quarters than the proverbial end of a barge pole, wondered vaguely whether, if real talent were brought to the task of making black seem white, the ignorant and unlearned might not really be led astray. But any such anxieties were now quite set at rest, for it was rumoured that O'Connell had disowned these incendiaries, and Major O'Hara shook his sides as he repeated the squib composed by a bishop of the Established Church:

I do not care a straw for Young Ireland or Old Ireland,
But, as between the two, I rather like old Dan,
And I only wish *The Nation* would let the agitation
Die a humbug, as it first began.

So things had gone on, but now a climax had come, and two events were the cause. First, famine stared the country in the face. A Minister of the Crown might – and did – get up in Parliament and say that there was at present an unprecedented scarcity; every landowner in Ireland knew better. The poor remained as yet in a dull apathy, but the landlords asked themselves what was to be done; even if they could or would close their eyes to the coming agony of the poor their own existence in many cases depended entirely on rent, and, if not starvation, at least destitution would stare them also in the face before many months were over. Secondly, they had to elect a new member for Moyne, in the place of Mr Crosbie deceased, a worthy person, whose doings in the House had been strictly confined to voting straight, and who had enjoyed the confidence of his constituents for some twenty years. It was thought that Captain Mervyn would now stand, and a preliminary meeting of gentry of the Moyne neighhourhood was held to nominate the candidate.

---

12   Ireland became part of the United Kingdom with the 1800 Act of Union, which abolished the Irish parliament. After his successful bid for Catholic Emancipation, Daniel O'Connell established the Repeal Association to agitate for the repeal of the Union so that Ireland could regain a degree of autonomy.

It was at this meeting that Darcy O'Hara burnt his tents, and with impassioned pleading, which his audience honestly admired as a good piece of eloquence wasted on a bad cause, implored them to fill themselves at the head of the national movement and formally demand Repeal.

'There is no national movement. The thing exists only in your own brain, my dear fellow', cried Mr O'Hara, interrupting him.

'There would be a unanimous assent of the whole nation if only the landowners would take the lead', argued Darcy. 'Why not? Would it be so ignoble a thing to rule their own country? to fill themselves the posts that Englishmen filled now? to gather together in Stephen's Green and concert measures for their country's good – *themselves*, and see that they were carried out? Had not their own caste the immense majority in Grattan's Parliament?[13] Surely they had all to gain and nothing to lose. The Union – was it not forced upon Ireland, and her apparent assent only obtained by flagrant and open bribery – presents of titles, posts, money. Now, in the present distress, what could they not do if the power lay with them?'

'What, indeed?' asked a dozen voices at once. 'For one thing, they could stop the export of food. Corn and cattle were leaving the country daily – still. They could form Government stores of food at once.'

Here a vigorous debate arose, not exactly on Darcy's point, but on the question of what Government might, could, or should do. Lord John Russell might be appealed to. At last it occurred to some one to ask, with a suddenly increased respect for his opinion, if Darcy had any practical suggestions to make.

He would make one at once – an Irish Parliament might impose a tax upon absentees. Four to five millions yearly were computed to be spent by absentees in England alone.

A dead silence fell. He had shown the cloven foot. The idea was not new – and underlying it was the old, old sansculottism,[14] Romanist poverty attacking Protestant possession.

---

13   Grattan's Parliament was the Irish parliament in the two decades before the Union. The epithet refers to Henry Grattan, a popular Irish MP and gifted orator staunchly opposed to Union.

14   'Sans-culottes', 'without-*culottes*', was the term used for lower-class combatants of the French Revolution. *Culottes* were a type of silk knee-breeches worn by upper-class men, while most lower-class men wore coarse *pantalons*, full-length trousers. Here, 'sansculottism' is used more generally to denote class-related resistance.

'Such a gross interference with the liberty of the subject can hardly be discussed by sane men, my dear Darcy', said Mr O'Hara. 'Repeal won't save the potato crop. It's possible, though for my own part I can't fancy it quite, that we should all enjoy being officials at the court of King Dan, and that the crownless harp might make a prettier flag than the Union Jack. But in the present distress I think we'd better give our minds to the object of the meeting and think about returning Captain Mervyn to Parliament. I am sure, gentlemen, we can think of no one better able to put our needs before the House of Commons.'

A hearty assent was given to this little speech.

'I presume – that – that', said Lord Fitzwalter, 'that no one would, there will be no attempt, in short that our – our excellent friend, if I may call him so, Captain Mervyn, would be returned unopposed?'

'Oh certainly, certainly. No question about that, I think', said Mr O'Hara. He glanced towards his young cousin and nodded, awaiting a responsive nod.

But Darcy stood up again; he was very pale and his lips quivered nervously.

'Gentlemen', he said, 'I wish to Heaven I could convince you of the power that lies at your feet, only waiting for you to take it up. Stand for Repeal to-day, and the whole nation will follow you. In your hands it can do no harm to living mortal, it is you who will lead all Ireland. To the Protestant volunteers of 1780 England gave what they asked;[15] she will give it now to you. The sturdy Ulster Orangeman will follow you, the poorest Catholic peasant of the south and west will be your willing slave. England will have a friendly neighbour and no longer a bitter enemy. If the ignorant peasant has wild notions of Repeal – I daresay he has – do you think the Barons at Runnymede had an entirely clear scheme for a Constitution in their minds?[16] Theirs is the need; yours are the brains. The measures you could concert would save the country from famine, for England will listen to you, and believe you. Let Captain Mervyn stand as a Repealer, and the

---

15 When France declared war on England in 1778, a volunteer corps was established to defend Ireland from possible invasion. The 'Volunteers' soon used their well-organized power to acquire political and economic concessions from England, securing Free Trade for Ireland in 1780.
16 The twenty-five Surety Barons, listed in the Magna Carta, who gathered at Runnymede in June, 1215 in support of the Charter.

most distant forty-shilling voter[17] will trudge barefoot his twelve long miles into Moyne to throw up his cap for him. And you, and I, and they, – we all shall henceforth be citizens of a happy country, an Ireland united, and free!'

---

17 This is an anachronism: the Catholic Relief Act of 1829 raised the minimum economic requirement for franchise from forty shillings to ten pounds. At the time of this political debate, therefore, Irish landholders whose land (rented or owned) was worth less than ten pounds could not actually vote.

Justin McCarthy (1830–1912)

> Red tape was allowed to interfere with promptitude in official
> action, and the peasantry were dying by hundreds while the
> authorities were considering how the distribution of relief
> could best be reconciled with the rules of political economy.[1]

Thus Justin McCarthy remembered the Famine years, which he had
witnessed as an adolescent student and beginning journalist. Born in Cork
in 1830 to a Catholic clerk and his wife, McCarthy intended to become a
barrister. Due to financial difficulties, however, his formal education was
discontinued when he was 17. Instead, he became a journalist with the
Cork Examiner, to which he contributed articles on the Famine.[2] In 1853,
he relocated to Liverpool, where he held a post at the *Northern Daily
Times*. In 1859 he moved to London, where he started working for the
radical daily *Morning Star*, becoming the paper's editor in 1864. Between
1868 and 1871 he travelled around the United States, returning to England
in mid-1871 to support the Irish nationalist cause. In 1879, he was elected
to Parliament as a member of Parnell's Irish Parliamentary Party, which he
headed from 1890 to 1896. In 1900, because his health was on the wane,
he resigned his seat in Parliament and retired to the English seaside town,
Westgate-on-Sea, Kent.[3] He died in London in 1912.[4]

Apart from his successive careers as journalist and politician, McCarthy
was also a prolific and popular writer: he published numerous novels,
some of which he co-wrote with Rosa Campbell-Praed (1851–1931). In
addition, he was a productive historian, biographer and anthologist.
Among his non-fictional works are the four-part *History of Our Own
Times* (1879–97), a biography of Sir Robert Peel (1891) and a ten-volume
anthology, *Irish Literature* (1904). Many of his novels share a common
mode; as James H. Murphy writes, 'though upper class *manqué*, he wrote

---

1   J. McCarthy, *Ireland and Her Story* (London: Chatto & Windus, 1903), p. 162.
2   J. Sutherland, *The Longman Companion to Victorian Fiction* (London: Longman, 1988), p. 392.
3   S.L. Gwynn, 'McCarthy, Justin (1830–1912)', revn Alan O'Day, *Oxford Dictionary of National
     Biography*, Oxford University Press, 2004, online edn, 2009, http://www.oxforddnb.com/view/
     article/34681.
4   Ibid.

within the conventions of upper middle-class fiction'.[5] However, in the novel here excerpted, *Mononia* (1901), he abandoned this way of writing 'in order to give voice to a more nationalist perspective'.[6] Subtitled 'A Love-Story of 'Forty-Eight', the novel was first serialized in the Dublin *Freeman's Journal*,[7] and concerns Irish-English tensions on the eve of the 1848 Young Ireland Rebellion. However, as McCarthy states in his autobiographical *The Story of an Irishman* (1904), the novel can also be read as 'message of encouragement to the living National cause'.[8] Although it is strongly opposed to the British presence in Ireland, James H. Murphy argues that it 'retains the upper middle-class yearning, if not to conciliate, then at least to explain English and Irish differences'.[9]

The first passage reproduced here reflects the thoughts of Kathleen Fitzwilliam, who believes herself in love with the rebel Maurice Desmond because he is a revolutionary. Later in the novel, she gives up her pseudo-revolutionary ambitions, focusing her attention on a British officer instead. The second passage concerns the ways rebels endeavoured to procure and hide firearms, as the British had outlawed the possession of such weapons by the Irish in an effort to discourage and contain the development of insurrectionary movements.

From *Mononia: A Love Story of 'Forty-Eight*

(Boston, MA: Small, Maynard & Co., 1901), pp. 150–1, 224–7.

Kathleen, however, had gained something more than even the love of Maurice from the events of that evening so memorable in their lives. She had long known that she was a girl with a lover. Now she knew that

---

5   J.H. Murphy, *Catholic Fiction and Social Reality in Ireland, 1873–1922* (Westport, CT: Greenwood Press, 1997), pp. 23–4.

6   Ibid, p. 24.

7   See J. McCarthy, *The Story of an Irishman* (London: Chatto & Windus, 1904), p. 406.

8   Ibid., p. 407. See also J.H. Murphy, *Irish Novelists and the Victorian Age* (Oxford: Oxford University Press, 2011), p. 145.

9   Murphy, *Catholic Fiction and Social Reality in Ireland*, p. 69.

she was not merely a girl with a lover, but also a heroine and a patriot. When she made up her mind that she would not renounce Maurice's love, whatever domestic or other troubles the resolve might bring upon her, she felt that she had suddenly become transfigured into a very heroine of romance. The other day she was only a happy, spoiled, wilful girl, with a certain gift, no doubt, for the fascination of admirers, and with a genuine delight in conquering the admiration of men, whether young or elderly; but she now felt that she had suddenly become a sort of Joan of Arc.[10] Only the other day she had regarded the national movement in Ireland with almost total indifference; and, if Maurice Desmond had not been in the way, she would probably have set it down as an absurd and rather vulgar sort of business, in which young women of good education and of good position, young women who could go to balls, who could sing and play to admiring listeners, and who had been in London and in Paris, could not be expected to take any manner of interest. She had not in the mean time made any study of the political question, and yet was now a devoted Irish patriot, consecrated to the national cause; and she saw herself already, in visions of wrapt self-admiration, the heroine of many a breathless moment of danger by her lover's side. She was already forming wild and rapturous plans for concealing her lover from arrest by hiding him in some mysterious place of safety, known to her alone, and where she could visit him in stolen hours and keep him well supplied with food and with news of all that was going on in the outer world. There were passages in old romances and poems which told her how a heroine should behave under such conditions, and keep the man she loved from the grasp of his enemies until the hour should come for him to emerge from his place of concealment and show himself at the head of his patriotic hosts and march to battle against the foes of his country. There was an old ruined castle, not far away, which had still some rooms deep under the earth, once used as the prison-holds of captured enemies; and she had many a time thought that one of these rooms might well be used as a sheltering-place for her young hero until the propitious hour should sound when he might come forth and summon his followers around him, and march to the chosen

---

10   Saint Joan of Arc, also known as the Maid of Orléans (c. 1412–31), is a national symbol in France. Aged 19, she commanded a French army, gaining important victories against the forces of House Plantagenet, Franco-English claimants to the French throne, during the Hundred Years' War (1337–1453).

field of battle. The one difficulty which she foresaw in the way of all these dear, delightful plans was the difficulty of inducing Maurice to put himself completely under her guardianship, and consent to be hidden while his friends and comrades were arrested above ground, until the right moment should arrive for him to come forth and do or die, or, if it must be so, to do and die. Even this last she felt she could have borne; for it might be the part of a true heroine to see her lover do and die in a great cause, and, if it might not be her happy fate to share his end, yet to live bravely on and cherish his memory to the close of her earthly existence. These thoughts filled her mind and sustained her with a sort of happiness, establishing her already as a true heroine of romance.

. . .

Had the opportunity been seized in Dublin, the mere fact that so many young Irishmen had shown themselves ready to die for their country's cause would, according to Phil's belief, have aroused the whole nation as nothing else could do, would have thrilled the hearts and hopes of Irishmen all over the world, and perhaps have brought on that foreign intervention which seemed fairly among the possibilities of '48.[11] 'We have missed our grand opportunity', Phil said to himself. 'We have let the tide at its flood pass by us: we must now take to a policy of preparation and of caution. All that we can do for the present is to make ourselves ready. The right time will come when we are prepared to make use of it; and, unless or until we are thus prepared, it cannot come at all or it will come in vain.'

Philip was still enjoying the hospitality of Mr Conrad. Indeed, Mr Conrad had prevailed upon the young man to give him, for the present, some help in preparing his school work and in conducting his correspondence; and he had succeeded in convincing Philip that this co-operation was of great practical value to him. Philip was only too glad to be able to lend a hand in any way; and the undisturbed use of Mr Conrad's study during school hours and the constant use of Mr Conrad's

---

11   Some insurgents were hoping that the French might rally to their cause and send troops to Ireland. In fact, earlier in 1848, Young Ireland leaders William Smith O'Brien and Thomas Francis Meagher had visited Paris, where Meagher was presented with the green-white-orange tricolour that is now Ireland's national flag. Although the French sympathized with the Irish cause, they did not grant military support to the rising. See L.M. Geary, *Rebellion and Remembrance in Modern Ireland* (Dublin: Four Courts Press, 2001).

library were of great advantage to Philip's literary work, which he was pursuing with increased energy. Mr Conrad's advice was most helpful to him, both as regards his present work and his immediate prospects. The elder man and the younger both studied the situation coolly and composedly, not making too much of its dangers, not treating too lightly its difficulties. Philip is never likely to forget the benefit it was to him at that crisis in his career to have the counsel and the companionship of so sympathetic and so thoughtful a friend.

Philip had a small annual income secured for him by the investments which his uncle had made of such property as his father had left him. The young man expected soon to be called to the bar, where he thought he might fairly hope to make a position in time; and, in the mean while, during the long interval usually spent in writing for briefs, he hoped to be able to write for newspapers and magazines, and thus make some addition to his very modest means. Philip had even formed some great but rather vague ideas in his mind of attempting a novel which might picture Irish life as he thought it ought to be pictured, and convince the world 'that the comic Paddy of the stage was not the complete and all-sufficing representation of the Irish Celt'.[12] He had thoroughly taken to heart the encouraging lesson which Thackeray[13] had been teaching to all young literary people, – the lesson that the pursuit of literature requires no more capital to make a beginning than the possession of a quire of paper, an ink-bottle, and a pen. Even the amount to be invested in a typewriter, which might be considered as a necessary part of a young author's capital in our days, did not make part of the calculation then. Philip, therefore, had his quire of paper, his pens and his ink and his blotting pad; and he was steadily disciplining himself to be an author and to make money by literature. Meanwhile it need hardly be said that he was a frequent visitor at the cottage of the Desmonds; that he had evening walks with Mononia,[14] and consulted her about all her doings and his projects; that Maurice and

---

12 A reference to the then prevalent stereotyping of the Irish on the English stage. See D. Kiberd, *Inventing Ireland: The Literature of the Modern Nation* (Cambridge, MA: Harvard University Press, 1997), p. 533.

13 William Makepeace Thackeray (1811–63), a famous nineteenth-century novelist. Thackeray also published extensively on Ireland, for instance in *The Irish Sketch Book* (London: Chapman & Hall, 1843), which was based on his sojourn in Ireland, where he had spent five months in 1842.

14 Mononia Desmond, Maurice's sister.

he were close companions; and that these three enjoyed their walks and their talks none the less, indeed all the more, because they were in constant expectation of some great national crisis, which might scatter all the personal plans and projects to the political winds.

During those busy days of politics, literature, and love, Philip found time to throw off a string of verses, which he published anonymously in a Dublin newspaper. The sudden measures which were taken by the authorities of Dublin Castle for the seizure of arms all over the country, and the punishment of those who were found to have arms in their possession without a license, compelled most of the Confederates to stow their weapons carefully away in some safe hiding-place. The hiding-place often consisted of nothing more elaborate than a deep hole dug in some field, under cover of night, wherein the rifle was deposited, as carefully encased or wrapped up as might be, and over which the mould and the grass were replaced and trampled down. A piece of bog land was often thus converted into a temporary cemetery for the proscribed rifles, a portion of riverbank or seashore covered by every rising tide often did similar duty, and even a neighbouring churchyard was occasionally made the secret receptacle of occupants on whom the worms had little chance of feeding.

Philip and Maurice both knew well that it would not be of the slightest use for either of them to seek a magisterial license to carry arms; and, indeed, when the head of the house of Desmond himself had applied for such a license, he was promptly refused on the ground that many of his personal friends and associates were engaged in the work of propagating sedition, and that his own son was one of the recognised local champions of revolution.[15] So there was nothing for it but to commit the weapons, for the time at all events, to the sheltering care of mother earth; and Philip and Maurice buried them darkly at dead of night, carved not a line, raised not a stone, but left them alone with their yet unearned glory.

---

15   Maurice Desmond.

Louis J. Walsh (1880–1942)

Louis Joseph Walsh was born in 1880 in Maghera, Co. Derry. He was educated at Catholic schools in Derry and Dublin, and then studied at University College Dublin, where he was a contemporary of James Joyce, who satirized him in *Ulysses* (1922). A well-known Catholic solicitor and politician, he stood for Sinn Féin in the 1918 general election, though his bid was not successful. In 1920, because of his unremitting nationalist efforts, he was arrested on a charge of sedition and spent some time in prison and an internment camp. Soon after his release, he published an account of this experience, *'On My Keeping' and In Theirs* (1921), in which he inveighs against the British response to the increasingly intense struggle for an independent Ireland, claiming, for instance, that the police were wont to plant evidence when raiding the house of a suspected revolutionary.[1] After the establishment of the Irish Free State in 1921, he was made a district judge, and frequently made the newspapers with his statements on myriad issues, including religion and the status of the Irish language.[2] He died in 1942. Apart from *The Next Time* (1919), Walsh published plays, memoirs, sketches of legal life in early twentieth-century Ulster, and a biography of John Mitchel (1934).

The Next Time was described by a reviewer as 'a presentation of Irish national life and feeling during the period from the days of Catholic Emancipation to 1848'.[3] While it is for the most part set during the Great Famine, *The Next Time* can be read as an effort to legitimize the early twentieth-century Irish opposition to British rule, even though, as Melissa Fegan argues, it might be seen as self-consciously fatalistic. According to Fegan, the novel's depiction of several failed nationalist efforts – especially the Young Ireland movement – underscores 'the fatuity of such aspirations'.[4] Yet such a reading – although countenanced by the novel's historical context – seems to suggest that Walsh's relentless nationalist tone

---

1   L.J. Walsh, *'On My Keeping' and In Theirs: A Record of Experiences 'On the Run', in Derry Gaol, and in Ballykinlar Internment Camp* (Dublin: Talbot Press, 1921), p. 27.
2   This biographical sketch is based on P. Maume, 'Walsh, Louis Joseph (1880–1942), Irish nationalist', *Oxford Dictionary of National Biography*, Oxford University Press, 2004, online edn, 2008, http://www.oxforddnb.com/view/article/64477.
3   Review of *The Next Time*, *The Irish Monthly*, 47 (1919), p. 517.
4   M. Fegan, *Literature and the Irish Famine* (Oxford: Clarendon Press, 2002), p. 230.

– and his real-life exertions on behalf of the cause – are not entirely confident or even sincere. Nevertheless, the narrative tone is indeed mixed: at times, the book seems disenchanted with the limited results of nationalism, but, on the whole, the novel's indignant treatment of British colonial rule should be taken at face value.

Like other later-generation Famine authors, such as Mildred Darby, Walsh asserts that his depiction of the Famine is 'founded on the actual experiences of eye-witnesses'.[5] Walsh admits that his representation of the crisis follows earlier depictions and that he has 'stolen descriptions, phrases and observations with the most unblushing effrontery'.[6] The novel focuses on Art O'Donnell, whose life runs alongside major developments in Irish nationalism, including Daniel O'Connell's Catholic Emancipation and Repeal movements and the Young Ireland movement, which he joins. Many historical figures and publications are mentioned, including John Mitchel, whose writings were among Walsh's main sources for his novel.[7]

From *The Next Time: A Story of 'Forty-Eight*

(Dublin: M.H. Gill, 1919), pp. 164–8, 230–1.

'Damn their Economics!'[8] exclaimed the other.[9]
'I was reading in the *Freeman*[10] lately where a deputation from

---

5   L.J. Walsh, *The Next Time: A Story of 'Forty Eight* (Dublin: M.H. Gill, 1919), p. 6.
6   Ibid.
7   Fegan, *Literature and the Irish Famine*, p. 228.
8   Art is referring to the doctrine of Political Economy and the liberal theories of the Manchester school of economics. Political Economy was a peculiar mixture of economic theories and religious doctrine, justifying a highly objectifying market-driven approach to policy making by claiming that the British Empire had the divine imperative to modernize the world. See T.A. Boylan and T.P. Foley, *Political Economy and Colonial Ireland: The Propagation and Ideological Function of Economic Discourse in the Nineteenth Century* (London: Routledge, 1992).
9   Hugh O'Donnell, Art's brother.
10   *The Freeman's Journal*, established in 1763, was an important nationalist newspaper during the nineteenth century. More moderate than *The Nation* and *United Irishman*, it was nonetheless very influential, and in the 1880s became an important supporter of Charles Stewart Parnell and the Irish Parliamentary Party.

Achill waited on Sir R. Routh,[11] representing the total destruction of their potatoes there and asking for a supply of food from the Government stores for which they were ready to pay. And do you know what his answer was? He would do nothing of the kind, for, says he, "nothing is more essential to a country than strict adherence to free trade", and he begged to assure the reverend gentleman that if he had studied Burke,[12] "his illustrious fellow countryman", he would see the wisdom of his view! Did you ever hear such stupidity or malice?'

'It's terrible to be tied to such people', said Art.

'And, of course, the Relief Works were administered like all such Government undertakings. There were hordes of useless officials, and crowds of stupid Scotch and English overseers, drawing big salaries and knowing nothing about the country. They sometimes walked the unfortunate workers miles to their work, and then the poor creatures, too tired to handle pick or shovel, would faint at the cutting or lie down on the roadside and never rise again. It was maddening to see it; but what could a body do?'

'Wouldn't the greatest massacres in battle or even deaths at the stake have been pleasant compared with that slow torture!' Art exclaimed.

'It was certainly terrible to see the deaths that took place on those Relief Works', continued his brother. 'You remember poor Paddy Loan?'

'My God!', replied the younger brother, 'Is he dead?'

'Aye, and Susie, and every one of the little children. He got work on the new road and had to walk four miles to it every morning, and so instead of dying of hunger in December they all died of hardships and fever in March.'

'Heavens!' cried Art rising to his feet and pacing the room as if to quell the passion that burned in his heart. 'How long is Ireland going to stand all this?'

---

11 A colonial administrator who was knighted for his services to the Crown, Sir Randolph Routh was the Chairman of the Relief Commission, and was in that capacity responsible for famine relief in Ireland between 1845 and 1848. See J. Sweetman, 'Routh, Sir Randolph Isham (1782–1858)', *Oxford Dictionary of National Biography*, Oxford University Press, 2004, online edn, http://www.oxforddnb.com/view/article/24183.

12 Edmund Burke (1729–97), the famous Anglo-Irish philosopher, is considered one of the founders of liberal conservatism, an important strand of free-market thinking. A good analysis of Burke's impact on Irish society and politics is given by Luke Gibbons in *Edmund Burke and Ireland: Aesthetics, Politics, and the Colonial Sublime* (Cambridge: Cambridge University Press, 2003).

'What can you do?' asked Hugh quietly. 'They can crush us to atoms any time we seek to resist them. We must make the best of things, and get through as easily as we can.'

'It's heart-rending', said the younger brother, resuming his seat.

'Of course, everything else was managed as badly as the Relief Works', continued the elder brother. 'Lord John Russell[13] declared that it would be against his economic principles "to interfere with the regular operations of merchants", or "with the retail trade", and so you saw the way in which Indian meal that had been bought to relieve the distress, was allowed to go up to famine prices so that the "meal men" and the corn speculators might have their profit.'

'I have heard of wheat', said Art, 'that crossed the Irish Sea four times, because speculators were offering new bids in their delirium and rushing stuff from the English to the Irish markets and back again in their eagerness to score in big profits.' ...

'Their chief method of meeting all this horrible distress seems to have been to pass fresh Coercion Acts, Disarming Acts, and more police,[14] and transporting starving wretches for stealing a few vegetables at night, and nobody to be out of his house after dark, and all the rest of it!'

'And to think', said Art bitterly, 'that all this destruction and misery and ruin and death might have been avoided, if we had had a native government.'

---

13 Lord John Russell's staunch adherence to laissez-faire was shared by many commentators on Ireland's condition. C.H. Gaye, in *Irish Famine: A Special Occasion for Keeping Lent in England* (London: Francis & John Rivington, 1847), for example, argues that 'Ireland ought, ere now, to do more towards bearing her burthens. Great as the calamity is, perhaps, she ought not to have been so utterly paralyzed by it, and to have cast herself so helplessly upon the resources of the sister-country' (p. 21).

14 Throughout the nineteenth and the early twentieth century, British governments implemented more than 100 such penal acts, which legitimized various (draconian) measures to contain and suppress nationalist insurgency in Ireland. These included the periodic suspension of habeas corpus, which meant that a person could be arrested and put in jail without a trial. As can be read in John Mitchel's *The History of Ireland; From the Treaty of Limerick to the Present Time*, vol. 2 (Glasgow: Cameron & Ferguson, 1869), in 1848, when rumours began to grow and spread 'of a very general arming amongst the peasantry and the clubmen of the towns, and the police had but small success in their searches for arms', Parliament immediately suspended the Habeas Corpus Act in Ireland, so that 'any person or number of persons whom they might think dangerous' could be seized and thrown 'into prison without any charge' (p. 234). Instantly, warrants were issued to the police; and sudden arrests were made. The penal acts also included the extension of the powers of the Royal Irish Constabulary, and the restriction of political congregations and the right to possess arms. In *The History of Ireland*, Mitchel is fiercely critical of such measures (pp. 212–14).

'We could not have avoided it entirely', put in Hugh, 'for the potato crop had failed; but it could have been avoided very largely, I admit.'

'There was no famine in the country at all', protested Art. 'Doesn't everybody admit that, though the potatoes failed, there were ample supplies of grain and cattle and other stock to feed twice as many people as we had, only these things had to be sold to pay the absentee rents and taxes to England. A national Government would have at once closed all the ports till its own people were preserved from starvation.[15] In 1845 there was a similar blight on the potatoes in Canada, the United States, Holland, Germany, and several other countries; but there were no famines there. For the governments of the countries, which were seriously threatened by the blight, closed the ports and established national granaries as the *Nation* urged constantly should have been done in this country. How long, O Lord, how long!' And the young man clenched his hands, whilst an angry flush overspread his countenance.

'It's all terribly aggravating', said Hugh; 'but what's the remedy?'

'Better go down fighting against the Unholy Thing', cried the younger brother, 'even though it crush you to atoms. Anything would be preferable to this misery in the midst of which we are living.'

'Don't talk nonsense, Art', Hugh remonstrated. 'What's the use of sending an unarmed starving people out against the bayonets and big guns of England? Why, one of her big ships could almost blow our whole little island into smithereens. You may talk to me about anything else but not about fighting now.'

'If O'Connell had given the word at Tara or Mullaghmast or when the gauntlet was thrown down at Clontarf',[16] exclaimed Art, 'wouldn't it have

---

15 Even though the native population was starving, Ireland exported large amounts of food to England, including corn and pork. During the Famine, many writers expressed their disgust at this state of affairs; they resented the fact that Irish tenants and labourers worked the land only to pay their dues to landlords and provide produce for export. In her poem 'The Irish Mother's Lament' (1851), for instance, Elizabeth Willoughby Varian writes: 'Was there not plenty in the land? the earth gave forth her store – / The glad and fruitful mother earth, with riches brimming o'er. / Not for the slave who till'd the soil the garner'd wealth was won; / Our tyrant masters gorged their fill, and murder'd thee, my son!' In C. Morash, *The Hungry Voice: The Poetry of the Irish Famine* (Dublin: Irish Academic Press, 2009), p. 75.

16 Art is referring to famous monster meetings organized by O'Connell as part of his campaign for the repeal of the Union. In 1843, O'Connell spoke before 100,000 people at Mullaghmast, and at another meeting the same year addressed an audience of 750,000 at the Hill of Tara. See P.M. Geoghegan, *Liberator: The Life and Death of Daniel O'Connell, 1830–1847* (Dublin: Gill & Macmillan, 2010).

been better, even for the men who were slaughtered, to have died on the field, with a proud hope in their hearts and defiance in their faces, than as they have done since, dying like dogs on the ditch banks, with the hunger at their hearts, or sometimes in their delirium struggling with their wives and children, like wolves, for the last morsel of food in their cabins?'

. . .

One March evening in the year 1875, nearly thirty years after the death of Art O'Donnell, Mary O'Flanagan was praying in the chapel at Gortnasmol. Every evening, for the preceding week or so, she had come to pray about the same hour. It was the time of John Mitchel's election for Tipperary;[17] and her special intention had been, that the noble 'Felon', who had dared and suffered so much for his country, might be returned for the seat by an overwhelming majority, as another act of protest and defiance against British rule in Ireland. The election was over now, and though she had not heard the result she had no doubt what it was; and so her prayer that evening was one of thanksgiving for the victory and of supplication, that it migh eventuate in good for her down-trodden land.

Earnestly she prayed; but in her prayers there mingled very vivid memories of the events in Irish history and in her own life, with which the name of Mitchel was associated. Every incident in that crowded springtime and summer of 'Forty-Eight seemed poignantly present to her mind's eye – all the wild hopes of those months of exultation, when Mitchel was braving the tyrant with such superb courage in the glowing pages of the *United Irishman*;[18] that scene that will live for ever in Irish history, when he spoke his last proud message from the dock; the excitement of the succeeding weeks; Art's holiday in Gortnanan and all the bright dreams they dreamed together in those golden days of youth and promise; the last time their prayers mingled before that altar, and the words he spoke to her beneath the moon, as they lingered by the little

17 The Protestant John Mitchel (1815–75) was one of the most important Irish nationalist activists of the nineteenth century. He is particularly known for his involvement with the Young Ireland movement and nationalist publications such as *The Nation* and *United Irishman*, and for books such as *Jail Journal* (1854) and *The Last Conquest of Ireland (Perhaps)* (1861).
18 Founded by John Mitchel after he left the *Nation* in 1848, the fiercely nationalist *United Irishman* ran for only sixteen issues, as it was banned by the British government. Mitchel was subsequently arrested and exiled.

wooden bridge; the bitter news of his death, and the grief that overwhelmed her soul, when she heard the rattle of the sods on his coffin in the graveyard outside.

And as these scenes flashed upon her memory and she seemed to hear the music of *his* voice and the merry notes of *his* boyish laughter, she prayed all the more earnestly; and with a strange sense of pride she besought *her own saint* and *her own martyr* to carry her petitions before the great White Throne.

Maidens, Mothers and Old Crones

Julia O'Ryan (?–1887) and Edmund O'Ryan
(c. 1824–1903)

> Cleverly written, and showing intimate knowledge of
> Munster ways of speech and thought among the farming and
> lower classes. Good taste and strong faith in the people and
> in the people's faith are everywhere discernible.[1]

Thus reads Stephen Brown's judgement of Julia and Edmund O'Ryan's
novel *In re Garland* (1870) in *Ireland in Fiction*. The critic reviewing *In re
Garland* in the *Irish Monthly* also draws attention to the Ryans'
'naturalness' when dealing with local speech and the strength of the novel's
characters, stating that the actors 'interest us at once'.[2] Considering that
several of the stories authored by one of the O'Ryans are published as
written 'by one of the authors of "In re Garland"',[3] and that the critic of the
Irish Monthly only guesses at their identity, it appears that Julia and
Edmund O'Ryan at first did not claim authorship for their writing.
However, their anonymity did not last long, as in the *Irish Monthly* in 1874
Julia did sign her own name to the poem 'My Twa Luves' (My Two Loves).[4]

Very little biographical information concerning Julia and Edmund
O'Ryan, author siblings, is known. Edmund was born in 1824 or 1825 and
died in Youghal in 1903, at the age of 78. He was a doctor. Of Julia we only
know her date of death, 1887. Edmund wrote for *The Tablet, The Nation,
The Lamp* and other journals. Julia also contributed her (short) stories
and poetry to literary publications such as the *Irish Monthly*, the New York
journal *Catholic World*, and *Chamber's Journal*.[5] Julia seems to have made
extensive use of her 'intimate knowledge' of local speech, for she also wrote
poetry making use of other regional dialects. One such example is the
above mentioned 'My Twa Luves', written by 'an Irish heart overflowing in
Lowland Scotch'.[6]

---

1   S.J.M. Brown, *Ireland in Fiction* (Dublin: Maunsel & Company, 1919).
2   Review of *In re Garland, Irish Monthly*, 20, 1 (1873), p. 313.
3   See, for example, the two stories published in the first volume (1873) of *Irish Monthly*: 'Nancy
    Hutch and her Three Troubles' and 'The Uses of Hope, and the Pleasures of Adversity'. These
    stories are attributed to 'one of the writers of "In Re Garland"' (p. 220).
4   J.M. O'Ryan, 'My Twa Luves', *Irish Monthly*, 21, 2 (1874), pp. 520–1.
5   Brown, *Ireland in Fiction*, p. 249.
6   O'Ryan, 'My Twa Luves', p. 520.

In re Garland's first chapters are set during the Famine, and relate the story of Sally Landy. Sally has given birth to the illegitimate daughter of the son of Squire Garland, who fails to fulfil his promise to marry her. She flees to London to start a new life, leaving the child with farmer Connor Kennedy and his wife, who raise the child as their own. Sally is ominously never heard from again, which suggests a dire fate in diaspora. The child, Mary, grows up to become a strong and sensible woman. In the meantime her biological father, Richard Garland – 'the Squire' – is ruined by the Famine and his unwise lifestyle, and has a life of beggary ahead. Although Mary was never acknowledged by Garland, she offers to take him in, and the squire lives with Mary and her family until he dies. The novel thus presents an interesting narrative of female strength and compassion in the wake of the Famine, but despite this positivist message also carries an ambiguous undertone: Mary loses her position in her adoptive family after the death of her foster father Connor Kennedy. Squire Garland and Mary never truly connect and after his death nobody really mourns him. Like many post-Famine novels, *In re Garland* portrays 'a disjointed society, changed utterly'[7] in which lives can no longer be unambiguously happy and the future is obscure.

From *In re Garland: A Tale of a Transition Time*

(London: Thomas Richardson & Son, 1870), pp. 16–22, 169–71.

Aye, down with you indeed! thought the unfortunate Sally. She had come down to this; down to be an object of pity, half contemptuous pity to Billix Santry, on whom contemptuous pity (unmingled save by perhaps a little dread) was the feeling bestowed by every one of good repute she knew. Billix, the very Pariah of the parish! Sally's national

---

7   M. Fegan, *Literature and the Irish Famine 1845–1919* (Oxford: Clarendon Press, 2002), p. 230.

education had served to inform her what a Pariah is; though, unhappily, having imbued a character naturally vain, with undue conceit of a little learning, and so strengthened her false hopes of being made a lady of,[8] it had failed utterly to serve her as a stay against occasions of herself become such a one. She had often, most likely, read and written, that 'pride goes before a fall'; but only now did she realize the truth of this forecasting. And now, upon the sudden sharp contrast of what she was with what she had fancied she should be, hot tears burst from the eyes which a few minutes before looked as though no such things as tears belonged to them. And these tears, at once effect and cause of a mood more and more soft than that in which she had encountered Billix, led her to take sympathy to heart from even *him*. It was, perhaps, a relief to her to have her confidence thus taken by surprise; as it certainly was soothing to be spoken to by some one knowing her story, in whose tone contempt did not altogether overbear compassion.

'An' the ould man refused out an' out?' pursued Billix. 'Why, thin, as that's the case, wasn't it a pity you didn't stay longer down the counthry?'

'I – I couldn't', Sally replied, her tears swelling to sobs: 'a – a bachelor was coming to me aunt's to-night match-making for one of her girls;[9] and – '

'I see', considerately interrupted Billix. 'Shrof'[10] was an awkward time – out an' out is the way to say it so, egor! Well, well; an' where'll you take airth at all, at all?'

---

8   This plotline of a landowner seducing or even raping a girl from among the tenant class features more often in Famine fiction. Another example is Captain Mervyn, the otherwise sympathetic landlord in Louise Field's *Denis: A Study in Black and White* (London and New York: Macmillan, 1896) who ruins Denis Moriarty's fiancée.

9   In nineteenth-century Ireland the use of matchmakers, or *basadóiri*, who for a fee would arrange marriages, was an important tradition. The purpose was to match up contracting parties with similar social status and economic parity. Sir Henry Arthur Blake's *Pictures from Ireland* (London: Kegan Paul, 1888) describes the practice of matchmaking: 'This he declined, and after much pressure by the matchmaker, assisted by the girl's mother, Egan at length consented to the marriage, undertaking to give his daughter openly a fortune of fifty pounds and a second fifty secretly' (p. 115). Interestingly, later in Edmund and Julia O'Ryan's novel the marriage of protagonist Mary Kennedy is also arranged: 'The match was made. The fortune that Connor named for Mary would have constrained her in very gratitude to please him, had she even a substantial objection so to do. Preparations for the wedding, hurried by the shortness of the time between then and Shrovetide, filled both head and hands' (p. 89).

10 Shrovetide is Shrove Tuesday and the two days preceding it, when it was formerly customary to go for confession. Marking the beginning of Lent, it is the Irish and English equivalent of what is known elsewhere as Carnival.

'The earth I'd like to take is the earth I'd go to feet foremost', returned the girl, when she could speak connectedly.

'Hush, girl, hush!' Billix said. 'We must all wait God's time, the good and bad iv us. You'll go away, may be, to America, afther a while?'

'I'll go away somewhere, without any while before it, Billix, if I can. Somewhere, as my aunt says, where there'll be nobody to know me or mine.'

'Very fine', commented Billix. 'Well, then, I hope she put her hand in her pocket an' gev' you the mains o' goin'? She didn't?'

'If she'd give it to me I wouldn't have it from her. I had enough meself to pay the fare back in the night mail to the cross yonder. And little or much let it be that'll take me farther, I'll look for it from them that can't lay it on me as an obligation.'

'A body may guess where you're goin' to now, then?' said Billix, after a moment's thought, and in a manner expressive rather of having already guessed than of desiring to be told in plain words whither.

'Every body will soon enough know where I'm going to, an' where I came from', rejoined Sally, in a manner that fairly retorted upon that of Billix: one which made the words convey a jealously-put question rather than the simple assertion that its form would make the phrase.

'Be the law of arms! If they don't find out any other way, I promise you they 'ont be the wiser for your bein' overtaken be Billix to-day morning', responded the rabbit-catcher. 'Honour bright, no! I can tell you I come be sthranger secrets in me day, Sally – though you mightn't think me a very likely confidant; an' faithful I kep' 'em. I defy man or mortal to say I ever broke trust on the thing I undertuk to keep dark on!'

Sally drew a long breath of relief. 'I'm going, Billix, on a fool's errand, may be – where I went too often on a fool's errand before', she said, after a moment's pause.

'I'll tell you what, then', Billix said, 'may be 'twouldn't be a bad job for you if I went along 'ith you where you're goin', eh?'

'May be he wouldn't like it – though what do I care what he likes or dislikes, now!'

'I 'ouldn't if I was you – unless it was a thing you wor expectin' – '

'I'm expecting nothing but that he'll give me a trifle to get rid of me. An' I'll take it; that others that don't want me now any more than he does, may be rid of me, too.'

'He knows you're comin'?'

'I wrote to tell him I was coming; an' that if he didn't come to meet me I'd go up to the house to look for him.'

'Egor, that was the way to say it or not to say it at all', remarked Billix.

'That's what I wouldn't have the courage for', Sally said, 'though I said it.'

'An' he wrote back to you? He didn't put his name to it?'

'He needn't', said Sally, with a bitter sigh.

'I b'lieve you: you knew the hand.' 'An' (aside) so do you, too, Billix boy!' 'An' he wrote back to you to come?'

'If I was coming to come as usual.'

'An' as us'yal was airly in the morning?'

'Yes', Sally said, a deep flush restoring for the moment to her poor pale face the bloom of health and beauty which had caught the fickle fancy of her betrayer.

'How crabbit these magisthrates grow!' commented Billix, 'even when they're not bred lawyers. They know what black an' white can do agin a man. He was afeared he'd commit himself, as Curran[11] said to the judge long ago. "Walk a mile before you write a line",[12] I hear wan iv 'em say. So he expects you: but he doesn't expect me – this morning. But for all that I'll be to the fore, or my name is Antony.[13] There's great vartue in a witness. "Two to wan 'ould kill a poor man", they say. But, be the law of arms, two to wan 'ill sometimes defait a rich man! An' two to wan we'll be with the Squire yondher to-day morning!'

'I was sure iv it', continued Billix, to himself, as, on hazarding this last by no means random shot, he glanced at Sally Landy. 'Silence gives consent. He's the very man. An' all the bether; for he's no great cower to deal with on a pinch, or I'm much mistaken in me man.' After which conclusion, Billix walked on awhile in silence, but attentively shortening his customary strides, so as to suit Sally's languid and listless, though impatient steps.

---

11   John Philpot Curran (1750–1817) was an Irish politician, orator, poet, wit and very popular barrister.

12   A saying meaning that before you criticize someone, you should try to place yourself into his or her position.

13   This is a reference to Mark Antony (83–30 BCE), Roman general and politician and trusted friend of Julius Caesar. Billix, when telling Sally that he will stand up for her and her illegitimate child because he does not want to act as Antony, could be referring to the murder of Julius Caesar.

'Be the law of arms, I have it all now!' he cried at length. 'See here to me, Sally girl. First, I'll take me stand, meself an' Vix – you'll be mute as a mouse, old girl; 'ont you, Vixie?' to the dog which had been standing and walking, as they stood and walked, between the speakers, looking alternately, and as if understandingly, at each – 'where we'll see an' hear how he'll thrate you. An' if he 'ont do as he ought be you, we'll just dhrop in on him, (as we did on yourself 'ithout intending it while ago), an' I'll tell him I was hidin' in the same cover before an' hear him swear he'd marry you'.

'An' so you might if you were listening', eagerly put in Sally.

'An' may be I was', interrupted Billix.

'Many a time he said he'd marry me; that he didn't care for fine ladies to spend his money; that he knew I was a good housekeeper an' a decent father an' mother's child. More shame for me not to give more heed to that part of his soft talk!'

'Solomon[14] wasn't always sensible', said Billix, consolingly.

'I was never sensible, I see too late', returned Sally.

'May be he'd keep his word yet, now the ould lady is out of the way?'

'No', Sally said; 'I lost me only chance – if chance I had – in not going to her before she got too bad to speak to any one – an' before any one but our two selves knew of it. He offered me fifty pounds that morning to buy clothes, or whatever I liked to do with it, to wait an' not disturb her peace o' mind. I scorned it then.'

'More fool you not to take it, whatever come afther, money is always in saison', said Billix. 'I wish you had that same said fifty pounds in your pocket to-day morning, an' bid good bye to him for a bad bargain. The never a chance you had of anything else, take my word for it, my dear girl. I always hear the ould lady was very high in herself, humble as she'd spaik to poor people. She was a dail o' betther family than his father, high as the Garlands held their heads.'

---

14   Reference to the Jewish king of Israel, Solomon, who, according to biblical accounts, possessed
      great wisdom, but eventually strayed from the virtuous path and was punished by God for his
      sins. Solomon had a staggering number of wives and concubines, who came from many different
      places. His 'wives turned his heart after other gods', and Solomon built different temples for all
      of his wives' gods, evoking the anger of God (1 Kings 11). Billix's reference to Solomon shows
      Sally that even the wisest of men can make immoral decisions.

'I don't know', returned Sally; 'but I'm sorry I didn't try. He had his own reasons for preventing me when he made that offer – he that's so fond o' money.'

'Didn't he say he didn't like to disturb her mind?' Billix said. 'An', of coorse, she couldn't be the aisier o' knowing her son brought sorrow on an old neighbour's child. He was always very fond iv his mother an' respected her – her word was law with him; I see that meself: but marriage is a word he'd never hear from her in regard to Pether Landy's daughter, believe you me.'

'No matter now', Sally said, impatiently.

'Aye', resumed Billix, 'give every rogue his jue, whatever other faults Squire Garland has, he ever an' always was a good son: an' may be – what did you call it?' he asked, interrupting his speech, and glancing at the little burden now covered up again.

'Mary.'

. . .

On the day appointed for his mission, Connor set off at once loath and willing to go; needing, and yet not needing, the instances of the Colleen dhas;[15] for, as he told her, 'it was only his courage that gev' way; an' in them cases, there was nothing like a woman's tongue for bringing it round.' Making what he called 'a circumbendibus o' the house', he succeeded in attracting the notice of Nance Kettlewell without a formal application for admittance at the door; and so quietly made his way, following her, to his former landlord's former library. Everything in the mansion appeared altered and out of place, saving only the stag-hunt, in brown and white, which so long had held its course along the paper-hangings of the hall and stair-case, and which Connor, for the first time, followed up. It touched his heart to yet greater tenderness towards the poor old huntsman now himself at bay. Carefully wiping his shoes, on a mat not held good enough to take away, he entered, hat in hand.

'Well, Connor?' enquired Mr Garland.

Under other circumstances it would have been 'Kennedy'. Connor observed so much to himself.

---

15   Pretty girl.

'Well, your honour', he replied, 'I just tuk the liberty of coming over to inquire after you.'

'It is after me you'll be enquiring before long, if you continue to take that trouble', said the Squire, with a miserable laugh.

'I hope not, Sir; an' I thrust not', Connor said.

'I believe you are the only one here that cares, Connor.'

'Not the only wan, Sir; there are two more, if they might make so bold on you.'

Mr Garland's parti-coloured visage flashed full red, but he said nothing.

'That little girl an' her husband, Sir', pursued Connor.

'A girl I forgot when I could serve her?' said the Squire.

'Well, Sir, 'tis no business nor wish o' mine, nor indeed o' theirs, to bring that up to you, now. Better late than never. If you remember her now, she an' her husband 'll be proud to do their part towards you.'

The pride of the aristocrat caught at, and clung to what seemed the saving word. His notion had not been refined by the passage through his moneyed trials, and possibly never had been nice enough to suggest how poor a pride this would be in John Meany's case.[16]

'Mary was on'y waiting for your laive to come an' tell you herself what she felt at your – '

'Fall', supplied the Squire.

'Oh, many a man falls to rise again', Connor said, cheerily.

'Not so I, Connor.'

'Well, Sir, time enough to talk o' the future; time enough to bid *somebody* good morrow when you meet him. Your room is settled an' ready for you; an' Mary is like, I dun' know what', he continued, rejecting the comparison that had come to his lips – 'a hen with an egg' – 'about you; anxious to know if you'd come to her, the poor *colleen*.'[17]

---

16 John Meany is Mary's husband.
17 Girl.

'Ireland'

Virtually nothing is known about the anonymous female writer who used 'Ireland' as her pen name. Presumably, she wrote two texts about the Great Irish Famine: *A Tale of the Irish Famine in 1846 and 1847, Founded on Fact* (1847) and *Forlorn but not Forsaken* (1871). Though the author clearly feared that a 'familiarity with accounts of woe and want should at last have an indurating effect' upon the minds of her readers,[1] her first Famine narrative nevertheless fully exposes the dire suffering of the Famine-stricken. Honour McCarthy, an exemplary farmer's wife, has to endure the terrible blight and hunger of 1846 while her husband Dennis tries to make a living in a 'far-off country'.[2] Honour is the epitome of the sacrificing mother who 'grudged every morsel that she put into her own mouth' but cannot prevent seeing her children starve before her very eyes.[3] When father Dennis returns, he finds that all his children and his spouse are dead, except for one infant, Mike, who is 'so reduced by starvation, that he had lost the use of his eyes',[4] upon which both leave for America to build up a new existence.

A Tale of the Irish Famine in 1846 and 1847 is strongly rooted in Protestant ideology; for instance, a clergyman prevents the porter from carrying off the corpses of the children 'without coffin, cover or prayer'.[5] *Forlorn but not Forsaken* is also clearly embedded in this Protestant tradition, as one of its central characters, Mrs Gwynne, is an avid scripture reader who teaches her servants to read so they may study the New Testament by themselves. She and her husband are landowners who are themselves badly affected by the blight, adopting a sober lifestyle so they may help the poor: 'meat was always boiled, with a view to keeping up the supplies of broth, needful for the children and the poor.'[6]

---

1   'Ireland', *A Tale of the Irish Famine in 1846 and 1847, Founded on Fact* (Reigate: William Allingham, 1847), the Preface has no page numbers.
2   Ibid., p. 8.
3   Ibid., p.12.
4   Ibid., p. 18.
5   Ibid., p. 32.
6   'Ireland', *Forlorn but not Forsaken. A Story of the Famine of 1848, the 'Bad Times' in Ireland* (Dublin: G. Herbert, 1871), p. 10.

The extract below focuses on Biddy Lynch, a young girl who, after the death of her parents, has to fend for her little brothers and sisters, while making sure that the family home is not attached by the bailiff. Though this plan fails and her siblings are taken to the poorhouse, Biddy finds a position as a servant girl in the Gwynne household, where she is instructed in Protestant doctrine, until her aunt fetches her to try her luck in America.

From *Forlorn but not Forsaken. A Story of the Famine of 1848, the 'Bad Times' in Ireland*

(Dublin: G. Herbert, 1871), pp. 28–33.

One piercing shriek rang through the cabin. Biddy flung herself on the bed as she had seen her mother do in her paroxysm of grief. Then she got up and looked about her, stunned with sorrow, and faint from hunger. The children were crying in the cold chimney-corner. She got them a few mouthfuls of the stirabout, keeping the rest until the morning, intending to make it go far with the raw turnip they gnawed from time to time. The little ones nestled in to her, and asked, what ailed their mother, which roused Biddy to a fresh sense of despair. But now she remembered what her mother had told her, so she loosened Johnny's hold of her ragged frock, and went to try what she could do to carry out the directions she had received. Poor child! she had no strength to make any change. She laid the clean cap on the pillow, and turned again to the corner, where, crouching down with the little ones, on the cold stones, covered with an old shawl, she fell asleep.

Mr Power, the relieving officer of the district, came next day, and carried out his duties. He had seen so many cases like this, his sympathies were exhausted; but he advised Biddy to go to the poorhouse with her little brother and sister, and seeing she made no reply, he considered he had done all he could for her.

And now Biddy reflected on her mother's chief directions. The house was to be defended at all hazards, and not given up to the bailiff, who was coming to take possession. Yet the children must be provided for, and she must get food; so she set her wits to work. She locked the door; then she dragged over the table, and put it against it; on that she built a regular wall of turf sods, so thick, that she imagined it could never be shaken. Next she managed to take two loose boards out of the door underneath the table, and by patient perseverance, she taught Nelly, her little sister, to replace them if she went out, and roll the big pot, which she had brought over, against the boards. By this means she hoped to conceal the opening she had contrived. Then she strictly cautioned the children not to answer any one who knocked, nor to say their mammy was gone; and taking up her tin can, and squeezing her thin form through the hole under the table, just waiting to see that Nelly understood how to shut up the hole tightly, she sped away down the mountain path to Brookhill.[7]

'Biddy Lynch, ma'm', said Ellen,[8] taking in the well-known tin can.

'Ah! poor thing, she wants rice, I think; how is her husband, Ellen?'

''Tis a little girl is here to-day, ma'am.'

'Bring her in, Ellen', said Mrs Gwynne, finishing a letter which she held in her hand; for she always saved the intervals of precious time by diligently using her rapid pen in her large daily correspondence.

'Well, little girl, who are you?' she asked, when the gaunt, pale-faced child appeared.

'Biddy Lynch, your honour.'

'From Glounaheena?'

'Yes, yer honour', and Biddy fixed her eyes ravenously on a half loaf lying near Mrs Gwynne.

'Are you hungry, Biddy?'

'Yes, ma'am.'

'Take this, then.'

---

7   Brookhilll is the estate of the Gwynnes. The narrative states that all classes are affected by the blight, for 'poor people were dying of hunger, and rich people had become poor' (p. 10).
8   Ellen is the family's servant.

If Janie could have seen the wild look of delight with which the poor child tucked the loaf under her shawl, she could not, as her mother said, have refused her supper.[9]

'Why don't you eat it, Biddy?'

Biddy got red, but did not answer.

'And how is your father?' continued Mrs Gwynne.

Biddy got redder still, and still kept silence. She was full of the idea that if her sad story were told the cabin would be taken possession of, and this she had resolved to resist. On the other hand, she had never told a lie; and although in her ignorance she knew nothing of the sin, her natural honesty recoiled from the act of telling one. So she was placed in great difficulty, and she held her tongue obstinately, earnestly longing to escape with her treasure of food from the presence of the kind friend whom her necessity had driven her to seek.

She had to thank Ellen for speedy relief.

''Tis my opinion, ma'am', said she, fixing her eyes on Biddy, 'that the child isn't all right. She's innocent like – though indeed she looked crabbed enough when she got the bit of bread. Maybe she isn't used to talk to the likes of ye, the craythur; 'tis seldom she sees the quality, only when they'd throw her halfpence on the road. Maybe I'd better lave her go.'

This speech saved poor Biddy for this time, and soon she was back in her wretched home, dividing the food she had got between the two hungry little ones.

By much clever contrivance, Biddy managed to keep it a secret that she was now the only head of the little household. Time fails me to describe how she dragged on existence in the lonely cabin. But at last Mrs Gwynne found out why the little messenger always hid the piece of bread she gave her under the shawl, and why she never mentioned her mother, and always seemed longing to escape notice. She was greatly shocked at the tale she heard. She had taken a fancy to poor Biddy at first, and now Mr Gwynne agreed that by some means the child should be made to give up the cabin and ground, and allow the little ones to be taken to the poor-house, while she herself might come to Brookhill to help in the giving out of relief, and learn kitchen-maid's work.

---

9   At the beginning of the narrative we learn that Mrs Gwynne's daughter Janie refuses to eat 'stale bread'. She is told off by her mother for this behaviour, as 'multitudes are starving round us' (p. 8).

The terrible day came when the bailiff kicked down poor Biddy's frail barricade, and walked in to take possession. Mr Gwynne sent a horse and cart to convey the children away, and Biddy to Brookhill. She made a desperate resistance, poor child! nor could she be pacified until Mrs Gwynne persuaded her that if her parents had lived, they should have been compelled to give up the house too, and all go into the poor-house, but that it would please her mother if she could have known that her little girl was going to be servant at the big house; and Biddy's own sense told her the same, so she made up her mind to be a good girl, and please 'the mistress', though she did not yet know Whom, above all, to thank for her new home, and plenty to eat.[10]

---

10 This passage prefigures Biddy's later knowledge of the Bible: 'Those were precious lessons, for Biddy learned in that Testament about the Saviour who loved her and came to die for her' (p. 38).

Margaret Brew

'And I see now with the eyes of memory as clearly as I once did with those of the body the unfortunate man crouching behind the door of the study in that day that is so far back in the past.'[1] Thus the narrator of Margaret Brew's 'An Unknown Hero' (1891) sums up the impression made on her youthful mind by poor tenant Jack Hanyeen and the story of his 1828 eviction after he had voted against the wishes of his landlord in order to stay true to his creed. While the story betrays a fascination with the fate of the suffering, it is also written from the perspective of the child of landed gentry; as Tina O'Toole and others have argued, Brew likely came from a Catholic landowning background.[2] Brew wrote essays and poems for *The Irish Monthly* and other periodicals[3] and published two novels focusing on Irish life: *The Burtons of Dunroe* (1880) and *The Chronicles of Castle Cloyne; or, Pictures of the Munster People* (1885).

Although Brew herself stated that she had made no concessions to enliven her tale, as '[t]he story of the Irish Famine could not be told with a pen dipped in rose-water, even in a work of fiction,'[4] *The Chronicles of Castle Cloyne* was favourably received by many critics with varying political affiliations.[5] Brew's three-decker novel was discussed in *The Times, The Athenaeum, The Irish Monthly* and several other periodicals.[6] The latter stated that '[i]t is an excellent Irish tale, full of truth and sympathy, without any harsh caricaturing on the one hand, or any patronising sentimentality on the other'.[7]

The novel is set during the Famine, and meditates 'on famine's place in a developmental narrative of progress and modernisation'.[8] It represents

---

1   M. Brew, 'An Unknown Hero', *The Irish Monthly*, 19 (1891), p. 68.
2   T. O'Toole, *Dictionary of Munster Women Writers, 1800–2000* (Cork: Cork University Press, 2005), p. 26.
3   Ibid.
4   M. Brew, *The Chronicles of Castle Cloyne; or, Pictures of the Munster People*, vol. 1 (London: Chapman & Hall, 1885), p. viii.
5   M. Kelleher, 'Prose Writing and Drama in English, 1830–1890: From Catholic Emancipation to the Fall of Parnell', in M. Kelleher and P. O'Leary (eds), *The Cambridge History of Irish Literature*, vol. 1 (Cambridge: Cambridge University Press, 2006), p. 466; O'Toole, *Dictionary of Munster Women Writers*, p. 27.
6   O'Toole. *Dictionary of Munster Women Writers, 1800–2000*, p. 27.
7   'Notes on New Books', *The Irish Monthly*, 14 (1886), p. 456.
8   Kelleher, 'Prose Writing and Drama in English, 1830–1890', p. 466.

the Famine as all-pervasive: the Great Hunger has its effects on rich and poor alike, which is illustrated by Brew's choice of two parallel narratives of Famine-related hardships, one concerning the young peasant woman, Oonagh McDermott, and another centring on the young landlord's son, Hyacinth Dillon. However, the novel does not see the Famine as 'completely destructive of traditional hierarchies'.[9]

The excerpts printed below focus on Oonagh McDermott, who, during the Famine, turns into a veritable heroine, attempting to save her fellow Irishmen from starvation. Her self-sacrifice and charity culminate in the scenes displayed below, in which she first mourns over the dead body of her one true love, John – a superficial Anglo-Irish dandy who breaks off their engagement to marry her richer cousin – and later pledges to take care of his and her cousin Susie's child.

From *The Chronicles of Castle Cloyne; or, Pictures of the Munster People*

(London: Chapman & Hall, 1885), vol. 2, pp. 271–3, 286–92.

Oonagh never slackened her pace until she came to the nearest town, and then only for a few moments to buy tea, sugar, candles, and, lastly, a bottle of good port wine. The purchase of those absolute necessaries reduced one of her notes to a few shillings; but though her purse was lightened, it made her heart glad to know that she was bringing nourishment and comfort to her sick friends. Notwithstanding her intense anxiety to get forward on her journey, she was compelled after a little time to proceed more slowly, lest she should be knocked up by walking too fast in the extreme heat of the day. But in a couple of hours the sun began to decline, the heat got less trying, and she was able to push on again with increased speed. With feverish anxiety she counted all the mile-stones as

---

9   J.H. Murphy, *Irish Novelists and the Victorian Age* (Oxford: Oxford University Press, 2011), p. 32.

she sped along, and absorbed by one sole desire to get on, and animated by the hope of arriving in time to be of use to those she loved in their great extremity, she never thought of the length of the journey.

In asking Mrs Mulhall's leave to set out on her mission of charity,[10] she had spoken of her love for her cousin, and her desire to be of use to her, but though this was true, it was not all the truth. Much as she loved Susie, she loved Susie's husband a great deal more. He had been the lover of her youth, the only man, with the exception of her father, that she had ever loved. She had given him up silently; when her own self-respect and womanly pride had told her that it was the right thing to do. She could not have borne to interfere with Susie's happiness, or give a wound to the affectionate heart that had always loved her dearly. She had stolen away from them like a thief when they were rich and happy, and now in their poverty and desolation she was returning to them, with no thoughts in her heart but those of kindness and helpful sympathy, and a firm resolution to be a true and loving sister to them.

She never thought at all of the danger she incurred by attendance on persons smitten with malignant typhus fever, or of the fatigue and hardship she should inevitably endure in the course of her labour of love. The large heart of the girl had no place in it for such selfish considerations as these. She had health and strength and great love to bring to the performance of the task she had set herself and the issue of it she left in the hands of God.

. . .

Now remembering that in all human probability Susie's life depended on having a long undisturbed sleep, she controlled herself by a mighty effort, and stood silently with straining eyes and clasped hands, a veritable statue of horror.

The unfortunate man must have been dead for many hours, for his body was as cold and rigid as marble. He had died alone! There was no

---

10 Mrs Mulhall is Oonagh's mistress. At the beginning of the novel the Mulhalls are well-to-do farmers, but the Famine affects their fortunes. Later in the narrative, Mrs Mulhall dies, and her sons decide 'on selling the interest of their farm, and emigrating to America' (Brew, *Chronicles of Castle Cloyne*, vol. 3, pp. 1–2), Oonagh's long and faithful service comes to an end and she takes to the road.

kind hand near him at the last to close his eyes, for they were wide open, and their fixed and glassy stare was perfectly horrible to look on. The worn face was half covered by a stubbly black beard of a fortnight's growth, and was like nothing earthly but a yellow parchment mask, wrinkled, haggard, and careworn. The throat and chest, laid bare by having the quilt drawn down, were so thin that the bones were in a manner held together only by the skin, and could literally be counted. It was a shocking sight, the body of this poor wretch that had died of famine! He had worked as a labourer beside men who were healthy and tolerably well fed, and tried to keep up with them till sheer weakness and exhaustion had compelled him to fall out of the ranks. Will and determination are good things, but they cannot supply the place of food, or make up for the want of it. The contest between will and starvation was too unequal, and as a matter of course, the latter won, particularly when its natural and certain ally, typhus fever, came in to finish the battle. He was completely vanquished, like many another man in that unhappy time, and, throwing down the spade he was no longer able to lift, crept back to his wretched home, to die without sympathy or succour.

There was no bashfulness about Oonagh now, no proud reserve, or womanly shame. She knelt down beside the dead man, she twined her arms round his neck, she clasped the wasted body to her bosom, she rained down bitter, scalding tears on the cold, pallid face. He was her own now, at last – this false sweetheart, for whose sake she had rejected many a good man's proffered love – her very own! He had been loosed from the tie that bound him to another woman, death did them part, and he had passed away to that world where there is neither marrying nor giving in marriage. Who or what could prevent her now from showing her love – the love that had always been steady and true, that had never died? She had loved him when he was a handsome young man – the 'pleasant' John of the old times; she had loved him when he had cruelly flung her from him because of her poverty; but she never loved him so well as now when he lay dead between her arms – dead – on a heap of rotten straw in that foul and darksome den! And with this great undying love was blended an unutterable pity for the poor victim of famine, who had endured, in addition to his own suffering, the great agony of seeing his wife and child perishing of hunger, while he was powerless to relieve them.[11] It was a frightful thing to her to know that he had died alone! – died without the clasp of a friendly hand, or the sound of a tender voice to whisper words of human love or hope in God to the ear that was fast closing to all earthly sounds, and the feebly fluttering heart to which all earthly things would soon be nothing.

She rocked herself to and fro, as all her countrywomen do when in great affliction, and moaned over him with a low but very bitter cry.[12] She remembered no longer her slighted love, her wounded pride, her wasted youth, her joyless womanhood. Everything was forgotten, forgiven; and she could think only that he had suffered and sorrowed, and lay within her arms – starved to death!

'John, my best beloved, I am with you at last', she moaned in the beautiful and expressive language of her native country, than which none on the earth is so rich in terms of love, endearment, or sorrow. 'Though you can neither see or hear me, I am here. You are my own at last – at last you are my own, and no one can take you from me. You flung away my love as if it was only a worthless weed, and made a plaything of the poor heart that would have followed you all over the world, for no greater reward than one loving word at the end. But I came back to you, oh white spot of my soul! when everyone else had deserted you, and left you to die untended and alone. Oh sweet, ever in my ears was the sound of your voice! gentle and gracious were all your words and ways to me! It was not for nothing that you were called pleasant, for you won all hearts, and no one who knew you could help loving you. Where are they all now? – they who took delight in your handsome young face and pleasant ways, and there is no one but Oonagh – poor forsaken, desolate Oonagh! – to raise the *caoine* over the dead body of her beloved.' …

Oonagh quickly poured more wine into the cup and held it to Susie's lips, but it ran down again at the corners of the mouth. The dying girl had

---

11 While Famine narratives traditionally focus on suffering maternal figures unable to suckle their babies or feed their children as archetypal victims (M. Kelleher, *The Feminization of Famine: Expressions of the Inexpressible* [Cork: Cork University Press, 1997], p. 5), there are also texts which foreground the despair of a father and husband failing to provide for his family. For example, in *A Tale of the Irish Famine in 1846 and 1847; Founded on Fact* (Reigate: William Allingham, 1847), written by 'Ireland', one can read that father Dennis arrives too late from America to save his wife and children from starvation: 'I cannot dwell upon the bitter anguish, and deep disappointment of the poor husband' (p. 35).

12 An allusion to the *caoine* or keen.

lost the power of swallowing it, and then Oonagh knew that the end was indeed come. It was not a matter of hours but of moments.

'Did you see poor John?' she said very faintly, thinking in that supreme hour more of him than of herself.

'Yes, darlin', I seen him.'

'I wish that I could see him too, Oonagh. I can't put him out ov my mind night or day.'

'You will see him soon now, *a hudyeen thael!*[13] *very soon.*' It was evident that the dying girl understood what Oonagh meant, for though she spoke no word, she raised her eyes to heaven, and an expression that was half joy, and half resignation, passed over her face. But it soon faded away, and in its place came one of anxiety and care.

'Something is troublin' you, asthore.[14] Tell it now to your own Oonagh', and as she spake she drew he girl's head to rest on her bosom.

'The child, Oonagh! the weeny thing that is hardly two years old! 'Tis goin' between me an' God to think that he'll be rared in the workhouse.'

'*Acushla sthoreen,*[15] let not that thought go between your soul an' God! Your child an' John's child shall never be rared in the workhouse, nor ever ate a morsel of charity bread as long as I live. I promised that on my knees when I was inside there spakin' to him an' now I promise it over again to you. Don't let the child be throublin' you, for you have no call to do. For your sake, Shusy, and for his father's sake, I take that child, an' he'll be like my own to me.'[16]

---

13 'My share of the world you are' (translation given by Brew).
14 My darling.
15 Little treasure of my heart.
16 Oonagh clearly displays the 'heroic, self-sacrificing attributes' (Kelleher, *Feminization of Famine*, p. 74) characteristic for mother figures in Famine fiction.

Rosa Mulholland (1841–1921)

Rosa Mulholland, later known as Lady Gilbert, was born in Belfast in 1841 as the second daughter of Dr Joseph S. Mulholland. She was educated at home and later also studied art in South Kensington, London. While she aspired to a career as an artist, her pictures were rejected by *Punch*.[1] After her father passed away, Mulholland travelled to the remote mountainous parts of West Ireland, were she stayed for some years. This stay supposedly had a decisive influence on her literary talents and interests.[2] In 1891 Mulholland married the historian John T. Gilbert. The couple had one of the largest private libraries in Ireland. Rosa Mulholland died at Villa Nuova, Blackrock, Co. Dublin, in 1921.[3]

Mulholland wrote under her own name and the pseudonym Ruth Murray, and enjoyed considerable success with her poetry, short stories and novels, going back to when she 'had just left her teens behind her'.[4] She could count Charles Dickens among her supporters,[5] and he published two of her stories – 'Hester's History' and 'The Late Miss Hollingford' – in his *All Year Round*[6] – texts which were later republished as full-length novels, in 1869 and 1886 respectively.[7] She also contributed regularly to *The Irish Monthly*,[8] *Cornhill Magazine*, *The Lamp* and *Duffy's Hibernian Magazine*.[9] Mulholland's fiction is informed by proper knowledge of the peasantry – quite possibly because of her time in West Ireland. Nevertheless, it was sometimes regarded as 'overly romantic'.[10]

---

1   A.U. Colman, *Dictionary of Nineteenth-Century Irish Women Poets* (Galway: Kenny's Bookshop, 1996), p. 162.

2   C.A. and T. P. O'Connor (eds), *The Cabinet of Irish Literature*, vol. 4 (London: Blackie & Son, 1884), p. 270.

3   Colman, *Dictionary of Nineteenth-Century Irish Women Poets*, p. 162.

4   'The Literary Output of Three Irish Women', *The Irish Monthly*, 38 (1910), p. 200.

5   As can be read in the preface to Rosa Mulholland's novel *The Late Miss Hollingford* (London: Blackie & Son, 1869), 'Mr Dickens was so pleased with this tale, and some others by the same author, then a very young beginner, that he wrote asking her to contribute a serial story of considerable length to his journal' (p. ii).

6   Read and O'Connor (eds), *Cabinet of Irish Literature*, p. 270.

7   A.U. Colman, *Dictionary of Nineteenth-Century Irish Women Poets*, pp. 162–3.

8   M. Kelleher, 'Prose Writing and Drama in English, 1830–1890: From Catholic Emancipation to the Fall of Parnell', in M. Kelleher and P. O'Leary (eds), *The Cambridge History of Irish Literature*, vol. 1 (Cambridge: Cambridge University Press, 2006), p. 454.

9   Colman, *Dictionary of Nineteenth-Century Irish Women Poets*, p. 162.

10 Hogan et al. (eds), *Dictionary of Irish Literature*, p. 479.

In 1891, W.B. Yeats published his two-volume anthology *Representative Irish Tales,* which included 'The Hungry Death'.[11] The excerpt below is taken from Yeats's collection and narrates the life of Brigid Lavelle, a proud Irish woman from a well-to-do farming family who, after repeatedly rejecting her suitor Coll Prendergast's marriage proposals, is finally spurned by him and ends up a spinster. When hunger haunts her fellow islanders on Inishbofin, Brigid transforms into a heroine, providing aid and food, eventually giving her life to save that of her rival Moya Mailie, who has married Coll in her place. Although the story deals extensively with Famine-related hunger, and in so doing makes use of Gothic convent-ions,[12] '[i]ssues of political causation receive little attention' and 'hunger and starvation are presented as regular occurrences' in the narrative world.[13] Thus, in contrast with late-nineteenth-century nationalist discourse, the hunger in Mulholland's story does not seem to be related directly to the wider political sphere.[14]

From 'The Hungry Death', in W.B. Yeats (ed.), *Representative Irish Tales*

(London: Putnam, 1891), pp. 387–95.

Lavelle and his daughter were among the last to suffer from the hard times, and they shared what they had with their poor neighbours; but in course of time the father caught the fever which famine had brought in its train, and was quickly swept into his grave, while the girl was left alone in possession of their little property, with her stocking in the thatch and her small flock of 'beasts' in the field. Her first independent act was to despatch all the money she had left by a trusty hand to Galway to buy

11   S. Deane, A. Carpenter and J. Williams (eds), *The Field Day Anthology of Irish Writing, vol. 5: Irish Women's Writing and Traditions* (New York: New York University Press, 2002), p. 925.
12   C.A. Malcolm and D. Malcolm (eds), *A Companion to the British and Irish Short Story* (Oxford: Blackwell, 2008), p. 58.
13   Deane, Carpenter and Williams (eds), *Field Day Anthology, vol. 5,* p. 925.
14   Ibid.

meal, in one of those pauses in the bad weather which sometimes allowed a boat to put off from the island. The meal arrived after a long, unavoidable delay, and Brigid became a benefactor to numbers of her fellow-creatures. Late and early she trudged from village to village and from house to house, doling out her meal to make it go as far as possible, till her own face grew pale and her step slow, for she stinted her own food to have the more to give away. Her 'beasts' grew lean and dejected. Why should she feed them at the expense of human life? They were killed, and the meat given to her famishing friends. The little property of the few other well-to-do families in like manner melted away, and it seemed likely that 'rich' and poor would soon all be buried in one grave.

In the Widow Maillie's house the famine had been early at work. Five of Moya's little sisters and brothers had one by one sickened and dropped upon the cabin floor. The two elder boys still walked about looking like galvanized skeletons, and the mother crept from wall to wall of her house trying to pretend that she did not suffer, and to cook the mess of rank-looking sea-weed, which was all they could procure in the shape of food. Coll risked his life day after day trying to catch fish to relieve their hunger, but scant and few were the meals that all his efforts could procure from the sea. White and gaunt he followed little Moya's steps, as with the spirit of a giant she kept on toiling among the rocks for such weeds or shell-fish as could be supposed to be edible. When she fell Coll bore her up, but the once powerful man was not able to carry her now. Her lovely little face was hollow and pinched, the cheek-bones cutting through the skin. Her sweet blue eyes were sunken and dim, her pretty mouth purple and strained. Her beauty and his strength were alike gone.

Three of the boys died in one night, and it took Coll, wasted as he was, two days to dig a grave deep enough to bury them. Before that week was over all the children were dead of starvation, and the mother scarcely alive. One evening Coll made his way slowly across the island from the beach, carrying a small bag of meal which he had unexpectedly obtained. Now and again his limbs failed, and he had to lie down and rest upon the ground; but with long perseverance and unconquerable energy he reached the little fishing village at last. As he passed the first house, Brigid Lavelle, pallid and worn, the spectre of herself, came out of the door with an empty basket. Coll and she stared at each other in melancholy amazement. It was the first time they had met since the memorable scene on the rocks many months ago, for Coll's entire time had been devoted to the Maillies, and Brigid had persistently kept out of his way, striving, by charity to others, to quench the fire of angry despair in her heart. Coll would scarcely have recognized her in her present death-like guise, had it not been for the still living glory of her hair.

The sight of Coll's great frame, once so stalwart and erect, now stooping and attenuated, his lustreless eyes, and blue, cold lips, struck horror into Brigid's heart. She utttered a faint, sharp cry and disappeared. Coll scarcely noticed her, his thoughts were so filled with another; and a little further on he met Moya coming to meet him, walking with a slow, uneven step that told of the whirling of the exhausted brain. Halfblind with weakness she stretched her hands before her as she walked.

'The hungry death is on my mother at last. Oh, Coll, come in and see the last o' her!' ...

It was a long, hard task for Coll and Moya to bury her, and when this was done they sat on the heather clasping each other's wasted hands. The sky was dark; the storm was coming on again. As night approached a tempest was let loose upon the island, and many famishing hearts that had throbbed with little hope at the news of the relief that was on its way to them now groaned, sickened, and broke in despair. Louder howled the wind, and the sea raged around the dangerous rocks towards which no vessel could dare to approach. It was the doing of the Most High, said the perishing creatures. His scourge was in His hand. Might His ever blessed will be done!

That evening Moya became delirious, and Coll watched all night by her side. At morning light he fled out and went round the village, crying out desperately to God and man to send him a morsel of food to save the life of his young love. The suffering neighbours turned pitying eyes upon him.

'I'm 'feared it's all over with her when she can't taste the sayweed any more', said one.

'Why don't ye go to Brigid Lavelle?' said another. 'She hasn't much left, poor girl; but maybe she'd have a mouthful for you.'

Till this moment Coll had felt that he could not go begging of Brigid; but, now that Moya's precious life was slipping rapidly out of his hands, he would suffer the deepest humiliation she could heap upon him, if only she would give him so much food as would keep breath in Moya's body till such time as, by Heaven's mercy, the storm might abate, and the hooker with the relief-meal arrive.

Brigid was alone in her house. A little porridge for some poor creature simmered on a scanty fire, and the girl stood in the middle of the floor, her hands wrung together above her head, and her brain distracted with the remembrance of Coll as she had seen him stricken by the scourge. All these months she had told her jealous heart that the Maillies were safe enough since they had Coll to take care of them. So long as there was a fish in the sea he would not let them starve, neither need he be in any danger himself. And so she had never asked a question about him or them. Now the horror of his altered face haunted her. She had walked through the direst scenes with courageous calm, but this one unexpected sight of woe had nearly maddened her.

A knock came to the door which at first she could not hear for the howling of the wind; but when she heard and opened there was Coll standing betore her.

'Meal', he said faintly – 'a little meal, for the love of Christ! Moya is dying.'

A spasm of anguish and tenderness had crossed Brigid's face at the first words but at the mention of Moya her face darkened.

'Why should I give to you or Moya?' she said coldly. 'There's them that needs that help as much as ye.'

'But not more', pleaded Coll. 'Oh, Brigid, I'm not askin' for myself. I fear I vexed ye, though I did not mean it. But Moya niver did any one any harm. Will you give me a morsel to save her from the hungry death?'

'I said I niver would forgive either o' ye, an' I niver will', said Brigid, slowly. 'Ye broke my heart, an' why wouldn't I break yours?'

'Brigid, perhaps neither you nor me has much longer to live. Will ye go before yer Judge with sich black words on yer lips?'

'That's my affair', she answered in the same hard voice, and then suddenly turning from him, shut the door in his face.

She stood listening within, expecting to hear him returning to implore her, but no further sound was heard; and, when she found he was gone, she dropped upon the floor with a shriek, and racked herself in a frenzy of remorse for her wickedness.

'But I cannot help everyone', she moaned; 'I'm starving myself, an' there's nothin' but a han'ful o' male at the bottom o' the bag.'

After a while she got up, and carried the mess of porridge to the house for which she had intended it, and all that day went about, doing what charity she could, and not tasting any thing herself. Returning, she lay down on the heather, overcome with weakness, fell asleep, and had a terrible dream. She saw herself dead and judged; a black-winged angel put the mark of Cain on her forehead,[15] and at the same moment Coll and Moya went, glorified and happy, hand in hand into heaven before her eyes. 'Depart from me, you accursed', thundered in her ears; and she started wide awake to hear the winds and waves unabated round her head.

Wet and shivering she struggled to regain her feet, and stood irresolute where to go. Dreading to return to her desolate home she mechanically set her face towards the little church on the cliff above the beach. On her way to it she passed prostrate forms, dying or dead, on the heather, on the roadside, and against the cabin walk A few weakly creatures, digging graves, begged from her as she went past, but she took no notice of anything, living or dead, making straight for the church. No one was there, and the storm howled dismally through the empty, barn-like building. Four bare, whitewashed walls, and a rude wooden altar, with a painted tabernacle and cross – this was the church. On one long wall was hung a large crucifix, a white, thorn-crowned figure upon stakes of black-painted wood which had been placed there in memory of a 'mission' lately preached on the island and on this Brigid's burning eyes fixed themselves with an agony of meaning. Slowly approaching it she knelt and stretched out her arms, uttering no prayer, but swaying herself monotonously to and fro. After a while the frenzied pain of remorse was dulled by physical exhaustion, and a stupor was stealing over her senses when a step entering the church startled her back into consciousness. Looking round she saw that the priest of the island had come in, and was wearily dragging himself towards the altar.

Father John was suffering and dying with his people. He had just now returned from a round of visits among the sick, during which he had sped some departing souls on their journey, and given the last consolation of religion to the dying. His own gaunt face and form bore witness to the

---

15   As Timothy Morton has pointed out, according to Malthusian discourse 'hunger and the suppressed revenge of hunger' tended to stamp 'the ferocity of want like the mark of Cain' on the foreheads of the starving. See *Shelley and the Revolution in Taste: The Body and the Natural World* (Cambridge: Cambridge University Press, 1994), p. 215. Interestingly, in *The Great Famine, by a Friend of Ireland* (Cheltenham: Wright & Bailey, 1847), the Famine is seen as a retribution by God for the heavy bloodshed in the country, while Ireland is compared to Cain: 'the blood of the slain, like the blood of Abel, has called *long and loudly* for vengeance' (p. 2).

unselfishness which had made all his little worldly goods the common property of the famishing.[16] Before he had reached the rails of the altar Brigid had thrown herself on her face at his feet.

'Save me, father, save me!' she wailed. 'The sin of murther is on my soul!'

'Nonsense, child! No such thing. It is too much that you have been doing, my poor Brigid! I fear the fever has crazed your brain.'

'Listen to me, father. Moya is dying, an' there is still a couple o' han'fuls o' male in the bag. Coll came an' asked me for her, an' I hated her because he left me, and I would not give it to him, an' maybe she is dead.'

'You refused her because you hated her?' said the priest. 'God help you, my poor Brigid. 'Tis true you can't save every life but you must try and save this one.'

Brigid gazed up at him, brightly at first, as if an angel had spoken, and then the dark shadow fell again into her eyes.

The priest saw it.

'Look there, my poor soul', he said, extending a thin hand towards the figure on the cross. 'Did He forgive His enemies, or did He not?'

Brigid turned her fascinated gaze to the crucifix, fixed them on the thorn-crowned face, and, uttering a wild cry, got up and tottered out of the church.

Spurred by terror lest her amend should come too late, and Moya be dead before she could reach her, she toiled across the heather once more, over the dreary bags, and through the howling storm. Dews of suffering and exhaustion were on her brow as she carefully emptied all the meal that was left of her store into a vessel, and stood for a moment looking at it in her hand.

'There isn't enough for all of us', she said, 'an' some of us be to die. It was always her or me, her or me; an' now it'll be me. May Christ receive me,

---

16   This idea of the charitable priest who is self-effacing to relieve his congregation is prevalent in Famine fiction. For example, in Richard Baptist O'Brien's *Ailey Moore, A Tale of the Times* (London and Baltimore, MD: Charles Dolman, J. Murphy & Co., 1856), when the Famine sets in and the parishioners look haggard and worn, Father Mick economizes on food to help his parishioners. Restricting his diet to 'the Indian meal', he is said to go 'the road of his parishioners' (p. 261), starving away himself. This comment bears upon the reality that many priests fell victim to the Famine and its related diseases: in 1847 at least 36 priests died in Ireland as a result of sickness and starvation. See M. Costello, *The Famine in Kerry* (Tralee: Kerry Archaeological and Historical Society, 1997), p. 28.

Moya, as I forgive you.' And then she kissed the vessel and put it under her cloak.

Leaving the house, she was careless to close the door behind her, feeling certain that she should never cross the threshold again, and straining all her remaining strength to the task, she urged her lagging feet by the shortest way to the Middle Quarter Village. Dire were the sights she had to pass upon her way. Many a skeleton hand was outstretched for the food she carried; but Brigid was now deaf and blind to all appeals. She saw only Coll's accusing face, and Moya's glazing eyes staring terribly at her out of the rain-clouds. Reaching the Maillies' cabin, she found the door fastened against the storm.

Coll was kneeling in despair by Moya, when a knocking at the door aroused him. The poor fellow had prayed so passionately, and was in so exalted a state, that he almost expected to see an angel of light upon the threshold bring the food he had so urgently asked for. The priest had been there and was gone, the neighbours were sunk in their own misery; why should anyone come knocking like that, unless it were an angel bringing help?

'Am I in time?' gasped she, as she put the vessel of food in his hand.

'Aye', said Coll, seizing it. In his transport of delight he would have gone on his knees and kissed her feet; but before he could speak, she was gone.

Whither should she go now? was Brigid's thought. No use returning to the desolate and lonesome home where neither food nor fire was any longer to be found. She dreaded dying on her own hearthstone alone, and faint as she was she knew what was now before her. Gaining the path to the beach, she made a last pull on her energies to reach the whitewashed walls, above which her fading eyes just dimly discerned the cross. The only face she now wanted to look upon again was that thorn-crowned face which was waiting for her in the loneliness of the empty and wind-swept church.[17] Falling, fainting, dragging herself on again, she crept within the shelter of the walls. A little more effort, and she would be at His feet. The struggle was made, blindly, slowly, desperately, with a last rally of all the passion of a most impassioned nature; and at last she lay her length on

---

17   A reference to Christ. See Matthew 27:29: 'twisting together a crown of thorns, they put it on his head and put a reed in his right hand. And kneeling before him, they mocked him, saying, "Hail, King of the Jews!"'

the earthen floor under the cross. Darkness, silence, peace, settled down upon her. The storm raved around, the night came on, and when the morning broke, Brigid was dead.

Mildly and serenely that day had dawned, a pitiful sky looked down on the calamities of Bofin, and the vessel with the relief-meal sailed into the harbour. For many even then alive, the food came all too late, but to numbers it brought assuagement and salvation. The charity of the world was at work, and though much had yet to be suffered, yet the hungry death had been mercifully stayed! Thanks to the timely help, Moya lived for better times, and when her health was somewhat restored, she emigrated with Coll to America. Every night in their distant backwoods hut they pray together for the soul of Brigid Lavelle, who, when in this world, had loved one o' them too well, and died to save the life of the other.

Section 7

Emigration and Exile

'DESTITUTION IN IRELAND, – FAILURE OF THE POTATO CROP.'
Pictorial Times, 22 August 1846, p. 121.

Miss Mason

While there is much Famine fiction that explores the Irish diaspora in North America, there are considerably fewer texts which represent the experiences of Irish immigrants belonging to the poorest classes, who could often not afford the passage to America and settled in English cities such as Liverpool, Manchester and London instead.[1] One exception is the novel *Kate Gearey; or, Irish Life in London*, which was serialized in *The Rambler* from February till October 1852.[2]

Scholars have speculated about the identity of the novel's writer, Miss Mason, suggesting that she could be Emily Virginia Mason (1815–1909), niece of Senator Mason of Virginia, whose father was 'appointed secretary of the territory of Michigan' in 1830, and who attended Miss Willard's school for young girls in Troy, New York.[3] However, this seems unlikely, as the novel's depiction of the Buildings, a district of tenement houses in London, was at the time generally believed to be portrayed 'with … vivacity, and … deep interest',[4] and the preface claims that '[m]ost scenes were witnessed by the Authoress herself'.[5]

Upon publication, the novel was praised for drawing attention to the miserable circumstances of the poor in the city slums, to which many contemporaries turned a blind eye. According to *The Dublin Review*, the novel shows the alienation sensed by immigrants in their crowded housing which the narrative brings 'before the public with sickening distinctness': 'they become more and more huddled together, and so closely packed, that at last all notion of a home is lost'.[6] *Kate Gearey* indeed pictures the Irish immigrants as living together in overcrowded, squalid apartment blocks where the desire to build up a homely life cannot be fulfilled. The male migrants in particular, such as Pat Sheehan, often fail to find employment, neglect their wives and children, and even get involved in

---

1   See R. Swift (ed.), *Irish Migrants in Britain, 1815–1914: A Documentary History* (Cork: Cork University Press, 2002), pp. 6–7; and L. Hollen Lees, *Exiles of Erin: Irish Migrants in Victorian London* (Manchester: Manchester University Press, 1979), p. 39.

2   *The Rambler* was a London-based Catholic journal.

3   Miss E.V. Mason, 'Chapters from the Autobiography of an Octogenarian, 1830–1850', *Michigan Pioneer and Historical Collections*, 35 (1907), pp. 248–50.

4   'Notices of Books', *The Dublin Review*, 35 (1853), p. 522.

5   Miss Mason, 'Preface', *Kate Gearey; or, Irish Life in London* (London: Charles Dolman, 1853).

6   'Notices of Books', p. 522.

criminal affairs, while the temptation of the bottle is too much to withstand.

Reviews of the time also emphasized the strongly Catholic morality of Miss Mason's narrative. *The Metropolitan Catholic Almanac and Laity's Directory for the year of Our Lord 1854*, for example, recommends the novel to Catholic readers and 'Catholic libraries', because '[t]he moral of the tale is excellent'.[7] Catholicism is central to the plot, which shows the threats to which the religious Irish immigrants are exposed in a hostile climate where 'the grossest calumnies were propagated' against Catholic priests and Protestants persistently seek to convert the Irish.[8] Many of the Irish characters in the novel ignore their faith, particularly the heroine Kate Gearey, who is pressured by her Irish immigrant husband Florry Daly to marry him without a priest and who subsequently neglects her prayers and stays away from Mass. Her unsanctified marriage to a frequently drunk husband in the end proves her downfall, for Florry is persuaded by the Englishman Ned Pratt to steal and pawn their belongings, and causes Kate's arrest by leaving some stolen goods behind in their apartment. Kate is found innocent, but discovers that her marriage is unlawful, as Florry's presumably deceased first wife, left behind in Ireland, proves to be alive and comes to reclaim him. It is only by returning to her native creed and through her association with other women that Kate manages to restore her ruined reputation and get her life back on track. The passage below, set in the spring of 1849, depicts Kate's arrival in London. Having escaped from a Famine-stricken Ireland, as the extract suggests, innocent and unspoilt Kate is exposed to the brutalities of her new habitat in London.

---

7   *The Metropolitan Catholic Almanac and Laity's Directory for the Year of Our Lord 1854* (Baltimore, MD: Fielding Lucas, 1854), p. 16.
8   Mason, *Kate Gearey*, p. 47.

From *Kate Gearey; or, Irish Life in London: A Tale of 1849*

(London: Charles Dolman, 1853), pp. 8–10, 38–9.

An exclamation of surprise and pity burst from the lips of Mrs Casey; the first a tribute to the girl's beauty, the second was drawn forth by her forlorn situation. Norry was too old a stager to mistake the young stranger's position in society; she knew her at a glance for one of the 'Gracians'[9] just arrived; and as she gazed at the timid modest countenance, she wished the child had stayed with her people, and not come to lose herself intirely with the riff-raffs of the Buildings.[10] Great, indeed, was the mistake which caused Kate Gearey to stand a houseless wanderer at the corner of – Street; but it is a mistake into which the majority of her countrywomen fall. Of course I speak of those who bear a good character from home; for those who have lost both name and prospects, London does as well as any other place: they pick up a precarious livelihood by fair means or foul, disgrace their country, rendering it a byword of scorn in the mouths of strangers; evade the watchfulness of their priests, neglect their religion, dupe and laugh at those who would reclaim or save them, and alas! die! – but of that thereafter.[11]

---

9   A term referring to a newly arrived, inexperienced immigrant. It can be compared to the term 'greenhorn', which was used in the United States.

10   The Buildings are an archetypal example of the tenement house blocks which accommodated newly arrived immigrants and which were notorious for bad hygiene, squalor and overcrowding. In Henry Mayhew's seminal work on the London lower classes, *London Labour and the London Poor: The London Street-Folk* (London: Griffin, Bohn & Co., 1861), one can read that in lodging-houses populated by Irish one often 'found ten human beings living together in a small room' (p. 111) in deprived circumstances. Moreover, as Mayhew pointed out, these tenement districts in London often contained segregated 'nests of Irish … rarely visiting or mingling with the English costers' (p. 109).

11   The novel suggests that immigrant girls are most likely to be led astray by the temptations of the host country. In this respect, *Kate Gearey* is similar to many Irish-American novels of the Famine generation, which direct themselves specifically to the female immigrant whose faith and virtue are under threat in the New World. For example, the preface of Peter McCorry's *The Lost Rosary* (Boston, MA: Patrick Donahoe, 1870) addresses a female readership and underlines the urgency for immigrant girls to preserve 'Faith, and … those rare virtues which were their distinguishing traits in Ireland' (p. v).

This was not, however, the case with Kate Gearey. True, her childhood had been passed in a mud-cabin; but that cabin stood on the fair banks of the Awbeg,[12] amidst the fertile valleys of Castletown Roche, beneath the time-worn parapets of the Lords of Fermoy,[13] just where the rock-hewn path with its hundred steps leads to the river below – that river whose wooded banks and fertile corn-fields glow with a thousand hues in the golden sunlight.[14] True, her parents were poor; but the blue sky of Ireland was above her, its soft green turf beneath her feet, its pure air around her; and Kattie flourished as the wild flowers in her path. And she was happy too, – happy, good, and beautiful. Who that had seen her kneeling in a quiet corner of the little chapel, telling her beads, and offering her fervent petitions to the dear Mother of her God;[15] or watched her when, wending her homeward way, she paused near the margin of the river, beneath the shadow of the castle walls, and bending with feelings of purest devotion, quaffed in her little palm the clear water of the holy well; – who, I say, would then have deemed that sin and poverty (the poverty of London) could have aught in common with a being as spotless as Kattie? In her fifteenth year, the child grew old in the world's cares; the pig died first, then the cow, then her gentle pious mother.[16] The father moped, took to drinking, and became good for nothing; kept company with those who would only lead him to ruin; talked of leaving the little cabin, and taking Kattie with him. To avoid this, the poor girl determined to join a party

---

12 *An Abhainn Bheag* means 'the small river'. The Awbeg runs through the Southern part of Ireland and flows into a larger river in Co. Cork.

13 Edmond Burke Roche (1815–74), first Baron of Fermoy, held a seat in the House of Commons for Co. Cork from 1837 to 1855.

14 Interestingly, a pastoral image is evoked, which contrasts greatly with the allusions to the Famine in the subsequent paragraph.

15 The image of the immigrant girl praying to the Virgin Mary is also prominent in much Irish-American fiction on the Famine. For example, in Mary Anne Sadlier's Irish-American novel *Bessy Conway; or the Irish Girl in America* (New York: D. & J. Sadlier, 1861), the eponymous heroine fervently prays to the Virgin Mary, the 'Star of the Sea' (p. 44), during the tempestuous crossing from Ireland to America. In this novel, it is Bessy's persistent faith which appears to settle the storm, and which will also prove her stronghold in the 'great Babylons of the West' (p. 3).

16 The passage appears to refer to the calamity of the Famine, during which cattle and people died in almost equal numbers. Compare, for example, this passage from *Bessy Conway*, in which the Famine horrors are also represented indirectly by allusions to the loss of cattle: 'the stock could not live without eating, and one after another every hoof was taken to the fair and sold' (Sadlier, *Bessy Conway*, p. 263).

from the next post-town about to embark for Liverpool,[17] and seek her fortune at a distance. It was in vain the good priest of Castletown, who had known her from her infancy, shook his head. He it was who had poured the regenerating waters on her infant brow, received her first confession, stood by her mother's death-bed until the spirit passed away; no wonder, then, his heart bled for the worse than orphan.

But Kate, with many virtues, shared the faults of most of her country-women, and was obstinate in an eminent degree, careless, improvident. Why should she not make a fortune in London? She was young, strong, and, alas, good-looking; what more could the English want? She would get a good service, and be a lady after all. Kate forgot, or probably did not know, that the ways of her father's cabin and those of a town mansion are totally different. London gentlemen do not usually milk cows, fatten their pigs, or bake oaten cakes on turf-ashes. The English have also another peculiarity, an unpleasant one to be sure; they require a character with their domestics, and even when they have one, are not predisposed in favour of the 'dirty and untidy' habits of those from the Emerald Isle. The venerable priest had a vague idea of all this; but it was of no use arguing, the girl was obstinately bent on taking her own way, therefore he gave her his blessing, with the better half of the contents of his slenderly-stocked purse; and Kate left her mother's grave and her birth-place, to starve and suffer in a foreign land.

...

This menace, which was backed by Mrs Carty's threatening to lock up, produced the desired effect. The picture of sullen ill humour, Nelly proceeded towards the 'small room', already occupied by the Sheehans, followed in silence by the weary and spiritless Kattie. Sheehan had thrown himself down under the dirty rug, without undressing, and was already snoring audibly; Mary, having previously placed the sleeping child by his side, pushed a large box against the door. There was no knowing, if the

---

17   Liverpool was the city where most Irish emigrants disembarked, either to travel on to North America or to destinations in Britain. *The Illustrated London News* of 6 July 1850 called Liverpool 'the great port of intercourse with the United States', and wrote that in 1849, the year in which *Kate Gearey* is set, 'out of the total number of 299,498 emigrants, more than one-half, or 153,902 left from the port of Liverpool'.

min were dhrunk, what 'ud be the upshot.'[18] She then merely removed her gown, to save time in the morning, and speedily followed her husband's example. Kate paused a moment. This was indeed the bitterest trial of her life; her eyes filled with tears as memory led her back to the small but neat chamber of her humble home. Every feeling of modesty revolted at the thought of passing the night in the same room with one of the opposite sex, even though protected by the presence of his wife; and then there were the lawless revellers, from whom she was only separated by a crazy plan, and whom even Mary, initiated as she was, seemed to fear. Was this London, the El Dorado of her thoughts,[19] the golden city of her day-dreams? She glanced at the crazy bedstead, worm-eaten and dirty; the bundle of filthy rags spread for her accommodation, which gave fair promise of being tenanted by a busy race, who had for years flourished unmolested; but all this was literally nothing to the bold, bad girl who was to share the couch of the pious, unsophisticated Kattie, and for whom she felt an invincible repugnance, – a feeling returned with interest by Miss Sullivan, who took no pains to conceal her dislike. There was, however, no help for it now; so, turning her back on her disagreeable companion, whose eyes she felt were still upon her, the girl knelt down, and, drawing from her bosom a string of beads which had belonged to her dead mother, she fervently and humbly entreated 'Mary, the comforter of the afflicted', to intercede for her who had no earthly stay, no human friend. She thought of the stable of Bethlehem,[20] of Mary's poverty, and was consoled; she thought of Mary's happiness, and hope once more reanimated her bosom; again, as she had done from childhood, she resolved to imitate Mary's favourite virtues, and by humility and purity to merit the protection of her beloved patroness, and the favour of her divine Son. Alas, Kate, why were you not ever thus? Does not the mountain violet best

18   In the novel the male immigrant characters are notorious for alcohol abuse. An example is Pat Sheehan who is 'a good-for-nothin' lazy husband, who parts all for the dhrink' (p. 23). In this respect, the novel underscores the bias many English held against Irish immigrants. 'The Report on the State of the Irish Poor in Great Britain', *Parliamentary Papers*, 34 (1836), for instance, states that the Irish are more 'prone to violence' when 'excited by spirits' (p. xx) and that Irish immigrants are often engaged in 'drunken broils' (p. xxi).

19   Spanish word meaning 'the golden one'. El Dorado is a mythical city of gold, allegedly in Latin America.

20   See Luke 2:15–16. 'When the angels went away from them into heaven, the shepherds said to one another, "Let us go over to Bethlehem and see this thing that has happened, which the Lord has made known to us." And they went with haste and found Mary and Joseph, and the baby lying in a manger.'

flourish in its obscurity, delighting by its simple loveliness, and invigorating odour, easily distinguishable from the enervating perfume of more brilliant flowers? Yet tear it from its native shade, transplant it to a richer soil, it either withers and dies beneath the first fervid rays of an unclouded sun, or if it survives the change, loses in intrinsic worth what it acquires in lustre and beauty. Such was the type of the poor Irish girl; vanity and self-reliance were the flaws of her mind's jewel. No marvel, then, it was utterly destroyed when exposed in the trebly-heated furnace of temptation.

Reginald Tierney (Thomas O'Neill Russell)
(1828–1908)

The extract included here describes how Dick's friend, the peasant Tom
Nolan, undertakes the transatlantic passage, together with his lover Norah
and her mother, Mrs Conroy. The widow has been rendered homeless by
her cruel landlord, who would not forgive her husband Michael for having
once voted against him. The passage illustrates the dire conditions on
coffin ships and presents an ambivalent picture of Irish life in America,
which is not the longed-for promised land yet nonetheless offers opportunities for material success. In an interesting passage towards the end of
the novel the omniscient narrator addresses writer Harriet Beecher Stowe,
suggesting provocative parallels between the suffering of her Uncle Tom
and the miserable conditions of helpless Irish immigrants.

From *The Struggles of Dick Massey; or, The Battles of a Boy*

(Dublin: James Duffy, 1860), pp.162–3, 226–7, 373–5.

The ship was advertised to sail in three days from the day Tom agreed
with the agent for the berths;[1] but it was nearly three weeks before she
left the docks. The time spent in waiting did not hang very heavily on Tom,
for he amused himself by wandering up and down the spacious quays,
and looking at the many strange creatures wearing the human face, that
composed the crews of ships from almost every part of the world. Tom
had been for a long time anxious to see a 'black', especially since Dan Carty
had told him of some of them being so rich, and how the female part of
them had such a wish for white husbands. He was not long before an

---

1   Although the prices for the passage to America had been lowered, many destitute emigrants
     could not afford the fares. They therefore came as indentured servants or had their passage paid
     for by their landlords or family members who had already settled in the US. See K. Kenny, *The
     American Irish: A History* (New York: Longman, 2000), p. 101.

opportunity offered for gratifying his curiosity, for as he was walking along
the docks one evening, he happened to see a brig that had just arrived
from Sierra Leone,[2] the greater part of the crew of which was composed
of Negroes; and as luck would have it, there was a fair sprinkling of
Negresses also. Tom eyed them with the most intense eagerness as they
bustled about the deck; but it is but fair to say that the ladies came in for
the greater part of his attention. He was, evidently, not much taken with
either their colour, face, or figure; and as he wandered slowly away, he
might be heard saying to himself: –

'Why, thin, bad scran to ye, Dan Carty! Shure the devil a one o' them
black girls I'd marry if she was hung wid diamonds, and had a guinea agen
every star in the sky. Sugh! Sugh!'[3]

...

At length the day of sailing arrived. The enormous ship appeared
swarming with human beings, as she was hauled by the steam-tug down
the river. The agent told Tom that the ship would only have five hundred
passengers aboard; but any one at all used to the emigrant trade would
have seen at once that there were nearer eight hundred than five hundred
souls crowded on the deck like a great swarm of bees.

Nine-tenths of them were Irish; there were two hundred and fifty off one
estate in Connaught, of whom none, save half-a-dozen old men, could speak

---

2   Interestingly, the black women Tom sees in the harbour are from a country traditionally
associated with slave trade, which was introduced in the fifteenth century by European colonists
who came to Sierra Leone.

3   Tom's opinion about the African women is interesting, since Irish immigrants to America were
often seen as not racially white. H.S. Constable's drawing *Ireland from One or Two Neglected Points
of View*, published in *Harper's Weekly* in 1899, illustrates this by portraying an Irishman who
resembles an African-American rather than the superior Anglo-Saxon, an image which is
underlined by the caption, which states that the Iberians, originally an African race, 'came to Ireland
and mixed with the natives of the South and West, who themselves are supposed to have been of
low type and descendants of savages of the Stone Age' who in turn made way 'according to the
laws of nature, for superior races.' Printed in G. Bornstein, *Material Modernism: The Politics of the
Page* (Cambridge: Cambridge University Press, 2004), pp 145–6. As David Roediger points out,
the Irish were considered 'low-browed, savage, groveling, bestial, lazy, wild, simian, and sensual'
– terms almost identical to those used to describe blacks. *The Wages of Whiteness: Race and the
Making of the American Working Class*, rev. edn (London: Verso, 1999), p. 133. In fact, immigrants
from Ireland were often ranked lower than African-Americans because of their willingness to
undertake undesirable work for very low wages. As Noel Ignatiev argues, the Irish ultimately became
accepted as white by displaying 'the highest degree of race consciousness' (*How the Irish Became
White* [New York: Routledge, 1996], p. 137), which is precisely what Tom does in this scene.

a word of English. They had given up their little spots of land: once in America, they would be engaged at wages so enormous that they would have to work only a few years and then retire and 'live fair an' aisy' for the rest of their lives. They seemed to be nearly, if not entirely, depending on the small allowance of victuals doled out by the ship once a week; and as for clothing or bedding, they had absolutely none, except the few rags that covered them scantily by day. All the money they received from their landlord and whatever little they scraped together themselves went to pay for their passage. They were nearly all either very old, very young, or very feeble: Tom Nolan could see only four or five able-bodied men amongst them. Queer kind of people to face the horrors of a voyage, and then hard work, burning sun and ague! It was like driving a lot of sheep into a butcher's yard to be slaughtered: the deaths were just as certain and nearly close at hand.

. . .

'I'm glad to see, Tom', said Dick, 'that your travelling has done you some good. You surely are much wiser now than when you set out for America, six months ago.'

'I am, Misther Dick: but somehow or an other, I think I'll never have the same heart again. I often dhraam at night of what passed aboord that cursed ship – an' think I see the brutish faces ov the captain an' mates, an' hear their shouts an' oaths. It was too much for my poor aunt, anyhow; the terrors ov that voyage broke her heart claan; an' shure it was no wondher.'

'I suppose there are nearly as many Irishmen in America now, as there are in Ireland', said Dick, wishing to turn the conversation from the awful topic of the voyage, which he plainly saw affected poor Tom so much; and which sent deep pangs through his own bosom also.

'Faix', replied Tom, 'if you wor in part of New York, you'd a'most imagine you wor in Stonybathther, by raason ov all the people you'd hear talkin' wid the *brogue*.'[4]

---

4   The passage underlines that Irish immigrants usually settled in particular urban neighbourhoods, such as the Lower East Side, where they still found themselves subject to poverty, horrible conditions, disease and death. The Irish in America also founded schools, churches and hospitals of their own in order to protect a typical Irish-American identity first and foremost grounded in Irish Catholicism. See M.F. Jacobson, *Special Sorrows: The Diasporic Imagination of Irish, Polish, and Jewish Immigrants in the United States* (Berkeley, CA: University of California Press, 2002), p. 97.

'Don't you think, Tom, that many of those that have emigrated could do as well had they remained at home?' asked Dick.

'I do, Sir, provided they could only get a little spot ov land; but you know it's one thing to be workin' for eight-pence a day, an' another thing to be workin' for five shillings a day.'

'True', replied Dick. 'At all events our countrymen have one good quality, which, I'm sure, in the eyes of a sensible people like the Americans, covers a multitude of sins, – they are good workers.'

'Misther Dick', cried Tom, starting up from his chair and upsetting the glass of whisky Emily Massey had poured out for him, – 'that's the only thing I was raal proud ov. I'll never forget what an American man said to me one day as I was ramblin' about the quays in New York. I noticed him eyin' me very purticular for a long time, an' he half laughin' as he looked down at my knee breeches an' brogues. "You come from the ould counthry", says he to me. "Oh! bedad I do", says I, "I can't deny that at all." "Your counthry people", says he, speakin' through his nose in a way I never could imitate, – "your counthry folk beat all creation for workin': an' if they'd only let this darned whisky alone,[5] they'd soon be at the top of the wheel." "In throth I b'leeve you're right", says I; "they are a thrifle too fond ov it." "Now", says he, "you may think it a lie what I'm goin' to tell you; but it's not; it's a rall fact." "What is it?" says I. "Why", says he "your counthrymen have carried New York on their backs." I couldn't tell what he meant, at first; but afther awhile as I looked around me at a thrimendous big house they wor buildin', an' there, shure enough, wor a whole lot ov Irishmen cantherin' up long laddhers, wid hods on their backs, bricklayers. Well, Misther Dick, I'll tell you no lie, I felt prouder out ov what that Yankee man said, than ever I felt afore, knowin' that wherever the hardest work was to be done, there was no man to be found so willin' to do it as an Irishman.

...

---

5   While many Irish immigrants indeed tried to cope with their homesickness and miserable conditions by taking to the bottle, the idea of the Irish-American drunkard was primarily a negative stereotype that reinforced discrimination. For example, Thomas Nast's caricature, 'The usual Irish way of doing things', published in *Harper's Weekly* on 2 September 1871, pictures the Irishman as a drunken troublemaker who threatens to overthrow the social order, holding a fuse to a barrel of gunpowder.

[F]or where is the rustic family to be found in Ireland now, that has not some relative in the Great Land beyond the Atlantic? You should have been amongst us when we were rooted by chains as strong as adamant to the old soil;⁶ when the words America and Australia were terrible words, suggesting nothing but strange faces and strange toil; but it is not so now; our hold is all but broken; millions of our kindred have crossed the sea, and leaving Ireland is only going to them – a sorrow that is half a joy. But, Mrs Stowe, if you want matter for another book as heart-rending as Uncle Tom's Cabin,⁷ come and we will supply you, and not draw much on the past either. Are you in want of materials for Simon Legrees?⁸ Come, we'll supply you; but they won't be exactly of the same species as your prototype. They may be equally cruel, equally selfish, and more proud; but their characters will not be so readily scanned – their actions may not appear so flagrant, for they will lack the bullying boldness and devil-may-care straightforwardness of the ruffian of the Red River.⁹ Do you want to depict the haughtiest tyranny on the one hand, and the most bowed down, hopeless sorrow on the other; such a sorrow as only those know, who have to leave for ever the spot of earth where they first saw light, where all their hopes and joys were centered; and go out amongst strangers, forlorn, desolate, ruined, maddened, shamed! Do you want such materials? Come, and we will give you plenty.

We can draw on the past, also, when things were even worse than at present; for, God be thanked! Light is breaking upon all the dark places of

---

6   The person addressed by the omniscient narrator is Harriet Beecher Stowe (1811–96), the American abolitionist and author. She and her husband, theologian Calvin Stowe, supported the Underground Railroad, which sought to assist runaway slaves.

7   The bestselling anti-slavery novel by Stowe, initially serialized in *National Era*, an abolitionist periodical, and published in book form in 1852. *Uncle Tom's Cabin* focuses on a middle-aged Christian slave, Tom, who, after years of faithful service, is separated from his family and sold by his owner, Arthur Shelby. It was written in response to the 1850 Fugitive Slave Act, which made it mandatory to return runaway slaves to their owners, even from states where slavery had been abolished.

8   In Stowe's novel Simon Legree epitomizes the cruel and greedy slave owner who derives pleasure from his power. He sexually exploits his female slave Cassy and has Tom whipped to death for his unbreakable faith in God.

9   Also called the Red River of the South, it is a major tributary of the Mississippi and Atchafalaya. In Stowe's novel the Red River symbolizes the sufferings of slaves: 'On the lower part of a small, mean boat, on the Red river, Tom sat, – chains on his wrists, chains on his feet, and a weight heavier than chains lay on his heart.' *Uncle Tom's Cabin; Or Life Among the Lowly* (Boston, MA: J.P. Jewett, 1852), p. 347. Russell draws an analogy between the transatlantic passage of the Irish and the Middle Passage in this scene, comparing the Irish experience of exile with that of transported slaves.

the earth, even upon Ireland; and show you, as in a hateful vision, gaunt forms shivering under poles and sheets in a ditch;[10] not in the gentle summer time when Dick Massey saw them, but in the depth of the rude winter; what was their warm hearth only a day before ploughed up, obliterated, in order that grass may grow more plentifully, to give food to the 'beasts that perish'. Look at that young mother, how she presses her week-old babe against her own cold bosom, and asks, half blasphemously, if there is a God in heaven! See, in yonder dark corner, in the most sheltered spot, is the old woman of 'four-score and upwards'; death is fast glazing her hollow eye; and she, though she suffered all her life long, never doubted that there was a God, and that He was good; for like Uncle Tom, her faith and hope, although she was lowly, were strong; but now dark doubts begin to beset her, and as she feels the cold winds piercing her vitals, and thinks of her once warm hearth, she fancies, with horror, that perhaps all trust in God's mercy was a miserable delusion! what wrong had she ever done that she should be left to die under a hedge, in the bleak winter?

Here is another picture; look at this, Mrs Stowe; quail not; you will not, I am certain, because you are good and gentle, and therefore marvellously strong. You need all your heroism now, for this is a scene upon which devils would rather not gaze. Lo, where are we! Down in file steerage of a plague-stricken ship, that is tossed like a nut-shell on the angry billows. Dead and dying men, women, and, alas! little children, are wallowing around in filth and wretchedness. Some pray, some weep, some swear; some shriek out in frenzied agony, believing they are already in hell, and curse themselves and their birth-day, and God! Anon, splash! splash! splash! as the warm corses are flung overboard, the sea swallows them down, and the country of their birth is not even at the expense of their burial.

One picture more. It is on land this time, but not on Ireland. What people are these that stare about so wildly, and stagger as if they were intoxicated? They are the remnant of a band of emigrants, whom cholera and dysentery have spared. They are in a strange land, and strange people

---

10 This description points to the homelessness of many Irish during the Famine: evicted from their cottages, many families were forced to sleep by the roadside. In *Ireland* (London: T. Fisher Unwin, 1891), Emily Lawless records memories of some who witnessed the 'people crawling along the road' or 'lying dead under the walls or up the grass at the roadside' (p. 397).

gaze and wonder at them but there is pity in their gaze, although thousands of miles of deep sea rolled between their birth-places. It is winter; snow around; frost, keen as a razor, in the air without, in the air within, on the ground, in the sky, everywhere. They are brought into wooden sheds, temporary poorhouses, erected in haste through fear of contagion; there is no warmth in them, for the keen frost pierces the frail boards as it would a curtain of gauze. Hot drinks are given to the famishing creatures, and plenty of victuals are put before them; but it is too late. Flesh and blood could not outlive the hardships they underwent; and the terrible cold soon puts out the last little flickering spark of vitality that rested in them. They die without knowing where they are. Their very names are unknown to the men who bury their bodies in the frozen glebe.

Charles Joseph Kickham (1828–82)

On 5 January 1866 Charles Joseph Kickham (1828–82) was sentenced to fourteen years' penal servitude. A year earlier Kickham had been appointed by Fenian leader James Stephens as supreme executive of the Irish republic and editor of the Fenian newspaper *The Irish People*.[1] On 15 September 1865 the Dublin Police, suspecting that the paper's editors were involved in plans for an uprising, raided *The Irish People*'s headquarters. John O'Leary, Thomas Clarke Luby and Jeremiah O'Donovan Rossa were arrested immediately, while Kickham was caught after having been on the run for a month.[2]

It was during his imprisonment at Woking Prison that Kickham wrote his first novel, *Sally Cavanagh*. As Kickham claims in the preface, written after he had been released, *Sally Cavanagh* has 'the merit of being *true*', as it is rooted in his lived memories of the Famine years: 'the scenes of suffering I have endeavoured to describe have occurred under my own eyes'.[3] As his friend and fellow Fenian John O'Leary claimed, Kickham 'knew the Irish people thoroughly, but especially the middle and so-called lower classes, and from thoroughness of knowledge came thoroughness of sympathy'.[4]

This sympathy for the plight of the peasant class is central to *Sally Cavanagh*, which focuses on the eponymous heroine's adherence to her moral principles in the face of starvation. When her husband Connor is pressured into excessive payment of the bailiff fee by landlord Oliver Grindem and leaves his native Tipperary to make a living in America, Sally and her infants are left to struggle with poverty and hunger on their own. Sally majestically withstands the attempts of Lord Grindem to seduce her and chooses rather to let herself and her children starve than to give in to him. After the death of her four children, Sally's mind becomes deranged, and she starts hovering about what she supposes are their graves. When Connor returns at last, a bitter welcome awaits him: Sally is suffering from the final stages of 'brain fever'.[5]

1   R. Hogan et al. (eds), *Dictionary of Irish Literature*, vol. 2 (London: Aldwych, 1996), p. 664.
2   C. Campbell, *Fenian Fire: The British Government Plot to Assassinate Queen Victoria* (London: Harper Collins, 2003), pp. 38–9.
3   C.J. Kickham, *Sally Cavanagh* (Dublin: W.B. Kelly, 1869), pp. xvi–xvii.
4   J. O'Leary, *Recollections of Fenians and Fenianism*, vol. 2 (London: Downey & Co., 1896), p. 265.
5   Kickham, *Sally Cavanagh*, p. 161.

Kickham believed that the national question was bound up with the land question:[6] the preface to the novel elaborately goes into the agrarian outrages and evokes the memory of formative nationalist episodes in Irish history, such as the 'Young Ireland' rebellion in which Kickham also took part.[7] The following extract is concerned with another central theme: the pain concomitant with emigration. The novel contains a romantic plot centring on the village schoolmaster, who harbours a secret passion for his 17-year-old pupil Rose Mulvany but dares not propose to her because of his humble station.[8] Rose is invited by a relative to come to America, but, as the schoolmaster learns, soon strays from the path of virtue. He subsequently travels to America to rescue her from her sinful life. The storyline, partly recounted in the form of an embedded tale the character Brian Purcell has written down in his scrapbook, and partly in the form of letters he receives from the schoolmaster, represents America as a den of vice and temptation that brings the Irish female immigrant to ruin.

From *Sally Cavanagh; or, The Untenanted Graves. A Tale of Tipperary*

(Dublin: W.B. Kelly, 1869), pp. 106–11.

'First of all, I found out the person through whom I had learned Rose Mulvany's fate. He accompanied me to the house where she had lived. With what mingled feelings of rage, and grief, and loathing I passed the threshold! It was one of those places where vice is decked

---

6   R.V. Comerford, *Charles J. Kickham: A Study in Irish Nationalism and Literature* (Dublin: Wolfhound, 1979), p. 255.

7   Hogan et al. (eds), *Dictionary of Irish Literature*, p. 664.

8   Most village schoolmasters were of low standing, being employed in teaching the poor, ignorant children of the peasant classes. As Asenath Nicholson writes in *Annals of the Famine in Ireland, in 1847, 1848 and 1849* (New York: E. French, 1851), schoolmasters worked in 'dreadful pauper schools where ninety children received a piece of black bread once a day' and were dressed in 'a state of rags, barefooted, and squatted on the floor waiting for a few ounces of bread' (p. 219). As her account reveals, schoolmasters aimed to uphold an aura of respectability, which was difficult because families were often unable to pay for their children's education.

out in tawdry finery.[9] But I shall not disgust you with a description of it. The poor lost creature whom I sought had left the place in ill health some months before. A dissipated looking woman remarked with a laugh, that the pace was too fast for the young 'greeny', and she broke down. This account excited my pity for the lost one, against whom I was beginning to feel something like resentment as I looked round on her brazen companions in shame. I was informed that Rose had gone to a city in the far west, and thither I started in search of her on the following day.

'I got employment in the great western city. My days were devoted to work, and from midnight till dawn I spent amid scenes the remembrance of which makes me shudder. Well, I found her at last – found Rose Mulvany in one of the very lowest haunts of crime and debauchery. The scene has left but a confused impression on my mind; music and dancing, the fumes of alcohol and tobacco, oaths and laughter and shrill screams of anger. And in the midst of this pandemonium I saw the once innocent Irish maiden with –

'I was quite calm. Do you not wonder that I was so? I even felt a sort of satisfaction, not at having found her, but at seeing her degradation with my own eyes. I felt as if the spell were broken, and my sufferings at an end. The thought that she was what I now saw her had made me miserable for years; yet I felt for a moment an impulse to laugh outright at my folly. I saw before me a creature too low for contempt, too debased for pity, too loathsome to be hated. Turning away, not with disgust, but with utter indifference, I was hurrying out of the polluted atmosphere into the open air, when a thought struck me that made me pause.

'"Is it not my duty", I asked myself – "am I not bound as a Christian to make an effort to save her?"

---

9   This representation of New York as a hotbed of sin is very similar to the images of American urban life that we find in Irish-American novels from the same period. For instance, in John McElgun's *Annie Reilly* (New York: J.A. McGee, 1873) immigrant James O'Rourke is 'disgusted' (p. 152) by the dirt and 'drunken curses' he observes around him. In Peter McCorry's *The Lost Rosary* (Boston, MA: Patrick Donahoe, 1870), the narrator suggests that urban New York is full of the 'allurements of the devil' (p. 129), a moral degradation that will shock Irish women's 'virgin modesty' (p. 102) and tempt them to abandon their Catholic faith as well as their maidenly honour.

'My conscience whispered, that not to make the effort would be a crime. I had a message sent to her that a person wished to see her in an adjoining room. The door opened, and, with a smirk on her face, Rose Mulvany approached me. For a moment she looked surprised, but this was only because her reception was different from what she expected. She soon, however, began to retreat slowly backwards, while her eyes were fixed on me with a wild stare. In this way she had reached the door, and was turning the handle behind her back, when I stepped forward and placed my hand against the door.

"'I believe", said I, "you remember me."

'She moved away from me again, and asked me in a low hoarse tone to let her out.

"'Not until I have first spoken to you, Rose", I replied.

"'Don't speak to me", said she.

"'I wish to speak to you for your good."

"'Do you not see what I am?" she asked.

"'I do", said I, "and that is the reason I have sent for you."

"'Am I not lost?"

"'But, Rose, you may be saved – your soul may he saved."

'She covered her face with her hands, and the bright auburn hair fell down, as I so often saw it fall in the old schoolhouse.

"'Rose", said I, in a softened voice, "I do not want to reproach you."

"'Reproach me!" she exclaimed, looking up quickly; "what right have you to reproach me?"

'The question took me by surprise, for I certainly thought I had the best right in the world.

'She put her hand to her throat as if she were choking, and said: "If it were not for you, I should not be what I am."

"'Good God!" I exclaimed, "what do you mean?"

"'I mean", said she, "that when I was young and innocent – but why should I talk of that now?"

'I was confounded; for I thought she meant to accuse me of having led her from the path of virtue in some way.

"'Yes", she continued, after a pause, "you won my young, innocent heart, before I knew I had a heart. And after winning it you despised it. You let me go, just as if I was a worthless weed. I did not care what would become of me. I joined in every folly I was asked to join in. Poor Mary was gone, and I had no one to warn me. Oh! if I knew the world was so bad, I might be able to take care of myself!"

'You can have no idea of the shock her words gave me. For the first time, the thought occurred to me that in some degree I might be accountable for this poor girl's fall. I was so moved I could not help saying:

'O Rose! I never despised you. On the contrary, I loved you better than my life.'

'Her whole face lighted up. I gazed at her with wonder. There was something startling in the transfiguration I beheld. Everything about her – her eyes, her lips, her blushes, her attitude – everything about her was "pure womanly".

'"And I have come here", I continued, "for no other purpose but to save you."

'These words reminded her of what she really was, and the poor girl turned deadly pale. I thought she was fainting, and hastened to prevent her from falling.

'"Don't touch me", she cried, holding out her arms to keep me off, "oh! do not touch a thing like me."

'There was something appalling in the change that had come over her. She appeared to have withered in an instant. I actually saw the wrinkles creeping over her face and forehead. She sank into a chair which I had placed near her. After considering for a moment, I decided upon the course I should pursue.

'"Rose", said I, "here is my address. You know now you have a friend. And may God give you strength to turn back before it is too late." I laid my card on a table near her, and withdrew.

'It was a moonlight night, and I spent an hour or two looking out on the waters of the great lake. I thought of Ireland, and of the sufferings of her children; and in my desolation I thanked God that there was still something left me – that my heart could yet thrill with mingled love and pride and grief for that dear old land. Then I thought of the peaceful valley and my own home. That same moon looked mildly down upon them! I flung myself down by the shore of the great lake, far, far away, and for the first time since my great sorrow fell upon me, I burst into tears. Since that moment I have been an altered man. Life is no longer a burden to me. There is, to be sure, a shadow upon my path; but it is not the black one that rested on it so long. I dislike crowds, and hence I have exchanged the busy city for the lonesome prairie.[10] But since Connor Shea's arrival I begin to think that I could enjoy the society of my old friends;[11] and I am already longing to see my hermitage lighted up by poor Sally Cavanagh's bright looks. Connor and I are in deep plans for the future.

'But before I come to the end of my paper, let me tell you the result of my interview with Rose Mulvany. I got a note from her, which I shall copy here:

'"Never ask to see me again. I am not worthy. I could not bear it. But send some one else to take me away from this place. May God for ever bless you. Something tells me *that I am saved.*"

'I hastened to a good Irish priest, and told him the whole story. The result is, that poor Rose Mulvany has been for the last twelve months an inmate of an industrial institution under the superintendence of the Sisters of Charity.[12] I am slow to believe in complete reformation in cases of this kind; but my reverend friend assures me that it would be harder now to tempt Rose Mulvany from the path of virtue than if she had never left it.

---

10   Most poor Catholic Irish of the Famine generation initially settled in urban areas on the Atlantic seaboard. The better-off immigrants left the cities and moved westwards, where they were better able to advance economically, politically and socially than their peers in the east. See M. Campbell, 'Ireland's Furthest Shores: Irish Immigrant Settlement in Nineteenth-Century California and Eastern Australia', *The Pacific Historical Review*, 71, 1 (2002), p. 89. Here the schoolmaster's choice to dwell in the lonesome western prairies appears to be an attempt to recover an innocent, rural life by distancing himself from the vice and temptation that the city symbolizes.
11   Connor Shea, the schoolmaster's friend and Sally Cavanagh's husband.
12   The Order of the Sisters of Charity of New York was established in 1846. Their main duties included providing relief to the poor, religious education, and helping unmarried mothers.

Margaret Brew

Below are two more excerpts from Margaret Brew's *Chronicles of Castle Cloyne*. The fragments focus on the emigration and return of landlord's son Hyacinth Dillon and his servant Pat. Hyacinth is a benevolent character who, after his family experiences financial ruin because of the Famine,[1] leaves for California, taking his father's servant Pat with him. As the first excerpt shows, after much hard work and hardship, Hyacinth and Pat are rewarded: they find an abundance of gold, which allows them to return to their beloved native country and live in affluence there. Although Hyacinth embraces the American ideals of democracy and class equality, traditional Irish hierarchies do not disappear in Brew's novel.[2] Interestingly, however, these class distinctions are internalized by the servant Pat rather than imposed on him by Hyacinth, as Pat, against Hyacinth's explicit wishes, keeps referring to himself as his 'boy'. The second excerpt focuses on Hyacinth's return to post-Famine Ireland, which has changed beyond recognition and proves a disillusionment.

From *The Chronicles of Castle Cloyne; or, Pictures of the Munster People*

(London: Chapman & Hall, 1885), vol. 3, pp. 161–4, 191–5.

But the time came at last – truly it had been long in coming – when the golden dream became a palpable and positive reality. They arose one morning, poor in all but health and hope, and when the night fell, they found themselves rich beyond all that their wildest imaginations had ever pictured. They had come upon the gold at last, not in dust, nor in the little

---

1   Melissa Fegan categorizes the novel as belonging to a category of fiction in which 'the fate of the estate is symptomatic of the state in Ireland'. See 'The Great Famine in Literature, 1846–1896', in J.M. Wright (ed.), *A Companion to Irish Literature*, vol. 1 (Malden, MA: Blackwell, 2010), p. 455.
2   J.H. Murphy, *Irish Novelists and the Victorian Age* (Oxford: Oxford University Press, 2011), p. 32.

bits scarcely larger than the grains of dust, but in a great solid lump, or rather lumps, for before they could scoop it out of the earth in which it lay imbedded, it was unavoidably broken in several places, the very smallest fragment forming in itself a very respectable nugget.[3] Long as they had hoped for this good fortune, and hard as they had worked for it, they were perfectly bewildered by its magnitude. Neither spoke to the other, when, after a long day of incessant labour, they had disinterred the mass of glittering metal, but they gazed on it lying at their feet, as if they were in a dream from which they feared to awake, lest they should find their treasure gone. Pat was the first to find his tongue.

'Hurroo! Ould Ireland for ever!' he cried, or rather shouted, throwing down the spade on which he had leaned, in the first moment of his great amazement. 'Oh yarra! to the divil I pitch California an' all the hard work I ever done in it. Blast the spade I'll ever take in my hand agin, till I git home to Castle Cloyne!'

Hyacinth extended his hand, hard and sore from incessant toil, and as he grasped that of Pat, said in a voice overflowing with cordiality and happiness: 'Neither in Castle Cloyne, nor in any other place shall you ever handle a spade again, Pat Flanagan, unless indeed it may be for your own amusement and pleasure.'

'I hope, sir, that you're not goin' to part wid me now that you're so rich', said Pat in dismay. 'I'd feel it very quare intirely to be obleeged to look out now for another situation.'

'You shall never again be servant to any one, Pat, but you will be my friend and true comrade, as you have been for many a long and weary day.'

'Eyeh, Masther Hyacinth! sure 'tis your own goodness, sir, that makes you say so.'

'Half this gold is yours', continued Dillon, 'well and fairly earned by your own hard toil. When we go home to Ireland, you can purchase a fine property, and live in clover[4] for the rest of your life.'

'By your lave, sir, 'tis nothing ov the kind. 'Tis all ov it your own, for sure I'm only your boy, the same as when we wor at home in Castle Cloyne. I

---

3   Hyacinth and Pat appear to belong to what Megan O'Hara describes as a group of 'ambitious Irish immigrants' who 'moved west'. As she writes in *Irish Immigrants, 1840–1920* (Mankato, MN: Capstone Press, 2001), '[m]any joined the Gold Rush of 1849 after miners discovered gold in the hills of California' (p. 21).

4   To live a life of luxury.

hired wid you on boord the ship, if you recollect, an' you agreed to give food an' wages for my service, the same as I had from the poor ould masther at home. But as for sharin' the goold, or settin' up for bein' an estated gintleman on the strength ov it, I'd have no call to that sort ov thing at all. I'm a dacent honest boy, sir, an' won't lay claim to what's not my own, though it is a thing that you're good enough to say that I have a share ov it. But when I said that I'd pitch hard work to the ould *dhunnus*[5] for evermore, I meant that I'd go home wid you to the ould ground, the same as when we came out ov it, and be your servant boy all through. Oyeh! what else? Maybe you'd give me a good farm on the estate when you buy it back agin, as in coorse you will, plase God. That's what would shuit me, an' not an estate, that's not fit for me, nor the likes ov me, but for born an' rared gintlemin like yourself.'

. . .

As the mail car – a very primitive, battered-looking old vehicle, drawn by a pair of poor lean horses that appeared as if a feed of oats was a rare treat to them – went lumbering slowly along, Hyacinth had full opportunity of seeing the great change that had taken place in the country during the two years of his absence. The teeming population that had once made the air resound with the sounds of life and labour, was all gone. Mile after mile was passed over in the glad light of that summer morning, without a human creature becoming visible, for the Famine had done its appointed work with a resolute and masterful hand. For want of labourers, there was hardly any tillage to be seen, and the whole country seemed to have become one vast grazing-field, wholly given up to the use of cattle.[6] Where Dillon had once known snug farm-houses, and little hamlets of a few houses grouped together, he saw nothing now but heaps of stones and rubbish, tumbled about in unsightly, lonely ruin. The country had been in

---

5   Lords.
6   The Famine brought about major changes in the agrarian class structure, causing the virtual disappearance of the poorest layer of society. The Famine also changed Irish agriculture, which became strongly commercialized. This change had already begun prior to the Famine, but the Famine greatly sped up the process. Deserted smallholdings were merged into large tracts of grassland where graziers pastured their cattle. The emphasis within Irish agriculture shifted from raising crops to keeping livestock, which in the 1870s already counted for as much as 75 per cent of the total output of Irish agriculture. See M.E. Daly, *Social and Economic History of Ireland since 1800* (Dublin: Educational Company of Ireland, 1981), p. 27.

a bad way when he left it two years ago, and his sister's letters had not prepared him for finding any material improvement on his return, but what he now saw as he drove along, was very much worse than he had expected, and gave him a truer idea of the fiery ordeal through which the country had passed, than any verbal description could have conveyed.

When the car stopped at the little village of Castle Cloyne to deliver the mails, Hyacinth, having given the driver so large a 'tip' as to make the poor half-starved, half-clad creature almost speechless with joyful surprise, walked to Father O'Rafferty's house, which was about a mile farther on. As he proceeded, he saw many persons were going in the same direction, and concluded that they were bound for some fair or market in the neighbourhood. None of them recognised him in the least, which was hardly a matter of surprise, for he was indeed greatly changed. The tall, slender youth had become a stately, well-developed man, whose proportions were all enlarged by constant exercise and labour. The upper part of his face was browned almost to swarthiness by the fierce action of the American sun, and the lower part was quite concealed by a full tawny beard. He was another manner of man now from the stripling that had left Castle Cloyne, but the change in his appearance had come on so gradually and imperceptibly that he did not know how great it was until now.[7]

When he came to the little avenue leading up to the priest's house, he noticed with surprise that everyone halted on arriving there, and as he came in sight of the hall-door he saw a good many persons lounging outside, as if waiting there for something, or some one.

'What is it has brought those people here, may I ask?' he said to a decent-looking old countryman. 'Are they waiting for anyone?'

---

7   The great change in physique is common to various Irish and Irish diaspora narratives of migration and return. For example, in Irish-Canadian writer Dillon O'Brien's novel *The Dalys of Dalystown* (St Paul, MN: Pioneer Printing, 1866), protagonist Henry Daly comes back to Ireland to regain his father's estate with the fortune he has made in the Canadian backwoods. Upon his return to Ireland, Henry Daly's friend and lawyer Mr Carroll advises him to not let it 'be known that you are here to bid for it [Dalystown estate], or O'Roarke's creditors would put it up to a high figure. You must remain incog. until after the sale' (p. 509). Thus, Henry's plan only succeeds because no one, including the land grabber O'Roarke who has taken his family estate, recognizes him until he reveals his identity. In O'Brien's and similar narratives, the great outer change reflects the character's inner transformation. They have been influenced by the ethos of hard work and the American or Canadian ideals of democracy and equality among classes, as is the case with Hyacinth Dillon. See also L. Janssen, 'The Impossibility of Transporting Irishness: The Representation of Diasporic Irishness in Works of Fiction by Mary Anne Sadlier, Dillon O'Brien and James W. Sullivan', forthcoming in the MESEA 2010 conference proceedings, 2012.

'For the funeral they're waiting, your honour. I see that the hearse isn't come yet; but it must be here soon now', was the answer.

'Whose funeral is it?'

'Why, thin, Miss Grania's.[8] Maybe, sir, you didn't happen to know her? Miss Grace Dillon, I mane. 'Tis a great pity, for she was very good and charitable, and, moreover, was a rale lady, every inch ov her, an' come ov the ould stock ov the country. All the land hereabout was the estate ov her family; fine, sperrited people they wor, an' 'twas aisy to live undher 'em. They had the full hand an' the warm heart for the poor an' the dissolute, ever an' always; ay, had they! an' 'twas a loss to the whole country when they wor broke, horse an' fut. Och mavrone![9] 'tis a new story, an' a quare wan, too, to have a hotel-keeper from London owning the estate of the ould Dillons ov Castle Cloyne!'

The old peasant, with the garrulity of age, would have rambled on in this strain much longer, but that he saw his auditor become deadly pale, and lean as if for support against one of the piers of the gate.

'I'm in dhread, sir, that you're not well?' he said kindly. 'I'm sorry I told you about poor Miss Grania so sudden like. Maybe, you're a frind ov the family.'

'It is nothing', replied Hyacinth, trying to recover himself. 'I have been travelling all night, and am much tired.'

'That would tire you, sir, surely. An' then if you knew the family, it would be no admiration in life that you'd feel a thrifle downhearted. They are all gone now, *foreer*! the Dillons, I mane. Miss Grania an' her brother wor the last ov' em. He wint away to foreign parts, a good while back, poor boy! an' maybe 'tis dead *he* is this way, an' *she's* to be brought to-day to her long home!'

They had now arrived at the hall-door. The old man joined the people waiting outside, and Hyacinth, who felt as if his heart was turned to stone, entered the hall where Father O'Rafferty was giving some directions about the funeral. When he saw a strange gentleman, bronzed and bearded, come in, he came forward, saying courteously: 'Can I do anything for you, sir?'

---

8   Hyacinth's sister Grace. She is referred to here as 'Grania', a name which suggests a link between the Dillon family and a royal family of Irish mythology, marking the Dillons as rightful landlords or rulers in line with ancient tradition. According to mythology, Grania was the daughter of the High King of Ireland, Cormac mac Art, and the betrothed of the Irish mythical hero Fionn mac Cumhaill (Finn McCool).

9   An expression of sorrow, meaning 'alas!'

'Oh, Father John! don't you know me?' burst from the heart of the poor young fellow. Though his outer man was so changed, his voice was still the same, and the priest recognised him the moment that he spoke.

'Oh, Hyacinth, my boy! My dear boy!' he exclaimed, extending both his hands, while his voice trembled with powerful emotion, 'don't speak a word, but come in here out of this crowd', and he drew him gently into the little parlour, closing the door after them.

The unhappy young man sat down in silence, and resting his head on the arm of the sofa, burst into such a passion of sorrow, that it shook with the violence of his sobs. And as if to have nothing wanting to complete his misery, the wild, melancholy notes of the *keen* arose from the next room, shrill and piercing. The women were crying the death-chant for the last time, before the coffin should be borne from the house.

And this was Hyacinth Dillon's welcome home!

References

Primary and Contemporary Texts

'A Barrister'. *What Have the Whigs Done for Ireland? Or The English Whigs and the Irish Tenants* (Dublin: E.J Milliken, 1851).

Alison, W.P. *Observations on the Famine of 1846–47* (Edinburgh and London: William Blackwood, 1847).

'An Irish Landlord'. *Ireland: Her Landlords, Her People, and Their Homes* (Dublin: George Herbert, 1860).

'An Irishman'. *Poor Paddy's Cabin; or, Slavery in Ireland*, 2nd edn (London: Wertheim & Macintosh, 1854).

'An Irishman'. *The Irish Widow; or A Picture from Life of Erin and her Children* (London: Wertheim & Macintosh, 1855).

'An Irishman'. *The Fenian Brotherhood. A few Useful Hints to Irishmen, and Some Valuable Information for Americans, Concerning Ireland* (Boston, MA: Dakin, Davis, and Metcalf, 1864).

Barry, W.F. *The Wizard's Knot* (London: T. Fisher Unwin, 1901).

Beaumont, G. *L'Irlande Sociale, Politique et Religieuse*, vol. 1 (Brussels: Hauman & Co., 1839).

Berens, Mrs E.M. *Steadfast unto Death; a Tale of the Irish Famine of Today* (London: Remington, 1880).

Bowles, E. *Irish Diamonds; or, A Chronicle of Peterstown* (London: Thomas Richardson & Son, 1864).

Brew, M. *The Chronicles of Castle Cloyne; or, Pictures of the Munster People*, 3 vols (London: Chapman & Hall, 1885).

Brew, M. 'An Unknown Hero', *Irish Monthly*, 19 (1891), p. 68.

A Brief Account of the Famine in Ireland (London: J.H. Jackson, 1847).

Burritt, E. *A Journal of a Visit of Three Days to Skibbereen and its Neighbourhood* (London: Charles Gilpin, 1847).

Butt, I. *A Voice for Ireland; A Famine in the Land* (Dublin: James M'Glashan, 1847).

Campbell, T. 'The Exiles of Erin', in *The Poetical Works of Thomas Campbell* (London: Routledge, 2005), p. 125.

Carleton, W. *The Black Prophet: A Tale Of Irish Famine* (London: Simms & M'Intyre, 1847).

Carleton, W. *The Squanders of Castle Squander* (London: Illustrated London Library, 1852).

Carleton, W. 'Owen M'Carthy; or the Landlord and Tenant', in *Alley Sheridan and Other Stories* (Dublin: P. Dixon Hardy & Sons, 1858), pp. 113–66.

'Carleton's *Squanders of Castle Squander*', *Spectator*, 25, 1253 (1852), p. 638.

Cassell's Illustrated History of England, vol. 7 (London: Cassell, Petter & Gilpon, 1863).

Christmas 1846 and the New Year 1847 in Ireland (Durham: G. Andrews, 1847).

Clington, A.H. (D.P. Conyngham) *Frank O'Donnell* (Dublin: James Duffy, 1861).

Cobbett, W. *Rural Rides* (London: A. Cobbett, 1853).

Congreve, R. *Ireland* (London: E. Truelove, 1868).

Constable, H.S. 'Ireland from One or Two Neglected Points of View', *Harper's Weekly*, 1899.

Conyngham, D.P. *The Irish Brigade: Its Campaigns* (Glasgow: Cameron & Ferguson, 1866).

The Cork Examiner, 14 September 1846.

The Cork Examiner, 23 September 1846.

The Cork Examiner, 29 December 1846.

The Cork Examiner, 6 January 1847.

The Cork Examiner, 2 April 1847.

The Cork Examiner, 19 July 1847.

The Cork Examiner, 20 September 1847.

The Cork Examiner, 29 December 1847.

Corrigan, D.J. *On Famine and Fever As Cause and Effect in Ireland* (Dublin: J. Fannin & Co., 1846).

Dickens, C. *Oliver Twist; or, The Parish Boy's Progress* (London: Richard Bentley, 1838).

Doran, J. *Zanthon: A Novel* (San Francisco, CA: Bancroft, 1891).

Driscoll, C. *The Duty of Showing Mercy to the Afflicted* (London: Hatchard & Sons, 1847).

Dufferin, Lord and Boyle, G.G. *Narrative of a Journey from Oxford to Skibbereen during the Year of the Irish Famine* (Oxford: John Henry Parker, 1847).

Elizabeth, C. *The Rockite. An Irish Story* (London: James Nisbet, 1836).

'Employment for Women', *The Dublin Review*, 52 (1862–63), pp. 15–19.

L'Estrange, A.G.K. (ed.) *The Friendships of Mary Russell Mitford* (London: Hurst & Blackett, 1882).

The Farmer of Inniscreen; A Tale of the Irish Famine (London: Jarrold & Sons, 1863).

The Feast of Famine; An Irish Banquet with Other Poems (London: Chapman & Hall, 1870).

Field, Mrs E.M. *Ethne, Being a Truthful Historie of the Great and Final Settlement of Ireland by Oliver Cromwell* (London: Wells, Gardner, 1887).

Field, Mrs E.M. *Denis: A Study in Black and White* (London: Macmillan, 1896).

A Fisherman's Daughter (Dublin: John Robertson, 1852).

Fitzpatrick, W.J. *The Life of Charles Lever* (London: Ward, Lock & Co., 1884).

Gaye, C.H. *Irish Famine; A Special Occasion for Keeping Lent in England, A Sermon,* 2nd edn (London: Francis & John Rivington, 1847).

The Great Famine; By A Friend of Ireland (Cheltenham: Wright & Bailey, 1847).

Hare, J.C. *Charges to the Clergy of the Archdeaconry of Lewes,* vol. 2 (Cambridge: Macmillan, 1856).

Heuser, H.J. *Canon Sheehan of Doneraile* (New York: Longmans, Green & Co., 1917).

Hoare, Mrs. 'The Black Potatoes' in *Shamrock Leaves; or, Tales and Sketches of Ireland* (Dublin: J. McGlashan, 1851), pp. 32–49.

Hoare, Mrs. 'An Irish Peculiarity', *Household Words,* 3 (1851), p. 364.

Hoare, Mrs. *Shamrock Leaves; or, Tales and Sketches of Ireland* (Dublin and London: J. M'Glashan, Patrick & Oakey, 1851).

The Illustrated London News, 18 October 1845.

The Illustrated London News, 7 November 1846.

The Illustrated London News, 16 December 1848.

The Illustrated London News, 6 July 1850.

The Illustrated London News, 10 May 1851.

'Ireland and the Informers of 1798', *The Catholic World*, 3 (1866), p. 123.

'Ireland'. *A Tale of the Irish Famine in 1846 and 1847, Founded on Fact* (Reigate: William Allingham, 1847).

'Ireland'. *Forlorn but not Forsaken. A Story of the Famine of 1848, the 'Bad Times' in Ireland* (Dublin: G. Herbert, 1871).

Jones, T.M. *Old Trinity: A Story of Real Life*, 3 vols (London: Richard Bentley, 1867).

Keary, A. *Castle Daly: The Story of an Irish Home Thirty Years Ago*, 3 vols (London: Macmillan & Co., 1875).

Keary, E. *Memoir of Annie Keary, By her Sister* (London: Macmillan, 1882).

Keegan, J. 'The Dying Mother's Lament', in *Legends and Poems* (Dublin: Sealy, Bryers & Walker, 1907), p. 507.

Kickham, C.J. *Sally Cavanagh; or, The Untenanted Graves. A Tale of Tipperary* (Dublin: W.B. Kelly, 1869).

Lawless, E. *Ireland* (London: T. Fisher Unwin, 1885).

Lawless, E. *Hurrish: A Study*, 2 vols (Edinburgh: William Blackwood, 1886).

Lawless, E. 'After the Famine', in *Traits and Confidences* (London: Methuen, 1898), pp. 163–218.

Lawless, E. 'Famine Roads and Famine Memories', in *Traits and Confidences* (London: Methuen, 1898), pp. 141–62.

Lawless, E. 'Looking Eastward; Written in 1885', in *With the Wild Geese* (London: Isbister & Co., 1902), pp. 48–9.

Lecky, W.E.H. *A History of Ireland in the Eighteenth Century*, vol. 3 (London: Longmans, Green & Co., 1892).

Lever, C. *The Martins of Cro' Martin* (New York: Harper & Brothers, 1856).

'The Literary Output of Three Irish Women', *Irish Monthly*, 38 (1910), p. 200.

Lloyd, M.A. *Susanna Meredith: A Record of a Vigorous Life* (London: Hodder & Stoughton, 1903).

Lyons, R.T. *A Treatise on Relapsing or Famine Fever* (London: Henry S. King, 1872).

Mason, E.V. 'Chapters from the Autobiography of an Octogenarian, 1830–1850', *Michigan Pioneer and Historical Collections*, 35 (1907), pp. 248–50.

Mason, Miss. *Kate Gearey; or, A Tale of Irish Life in London. A Tale of 1849* (London: Charles Dolman, 1853).

Mayhew, H. *London Labour and the London Poor: The London Street-Folk* (London: G. Woodfall, 1851).

McCarthy, J. *Mononia: A Love Story of 'Forty-Eight* (Boston, MA: Small, Maynard & Co., 1901).

McCarthy, J. *Ireland and Her Story* (London: Chatto & Windus, 1903).

McCarthy, J. *The Story of an Irishman* (London: Chatto & Windus, 1904).

McCorry, P. *The Lost Rosary* (Boston: Patrick Donahoe, 1870).

McDowell, L. *The Earl of Effingham* (London: Tinsley, 1877).

McElgun, J. *Annie Reilly; Or, The Fortunes Of An Irish Girl In New York* (New York: J.A. McGee, 1873).

McNeile, H. *The Famine a Rod of God: Its Provoking Cause – Its Merciful Design* (London: Burnside & Seeley, 1847).

Meredith, S. 'Ellen Harrington', in *The Lacemakers* (London: Jackson, Walford & Hodder, 1865), pp. 56–64.

Meredith, S. *The Sixth Work; or, The Charity of Moral Effort* (London: Jackson, Walford & Hodder, 1866).

Merry, A. (M. Darby) *The Hunger: Being Realities of the Famine Years in Ireland, 1845–48* (London: Andrew Melrose, 1910).

The Metropolitan Catholic Almanac and Laity's Directory for the Year of Our Lord 1854 (Baltimore: Fielding Lucas, 1854).

'Missionary Records', *The Church of England Magazine*, 25 (1848), p. 366.

Mitchel, J. *The History of Ireland; From the Treaty of Limerick to the Present Time* (Glasgow: Cameron & Ferguson, 1869).

Mulholland, R. *The Late Miss Hollingford* (London: Blackie & Son, 1869).

Mulholland, R. 'The Hungry Death', in W.B. Yeats (ed.), *Representative Irish Tales* (London: Putnam, 1891), pp. 369–97.

Mulholland, R. *The Return of Mary O'Murrough* (Edinburgh and London: Sands & Co., 1908.

Murray, P. 'Traits of the Irish Peasantry', *Edinburgh Review*, 69, 196 (1852), pp. 384–90.

'Nancy Hutch and Her Three Troubles', *Irish Monthly*, 20, 1 (1873), pp. 223–32.

Nast, T. 'The Usual Irish Way of Doing Things', *Harper's Weekly*, 2 September 1871.

Nicholson, A. *Ireland's Welcome to the Stranger; or, an Excursion through Ireland in 1844 and 1845* (New York: Baker & Scribner, 1847).

Nicholson, A. *Annals of the Famine in Ireland, in 1847, 1848 and 1849* (New York: E. French, 1851).

Niles' National Register, 74 (July 1848–January 1849).

'Notes on New Books', *Irish Monthly*, 14 (1886), p. 456.

'Notices of Books'. *The Church-Warder and Domestic Magazine*, 8 (1854), p. 222.

'Notices of Books'. *The Dublin Review*, 35 (1853), p. 522.

O'Brien, D. *The Dalys of Dalystown* (St Paul, MN: Pioneer Printing, 1866).

O'Brien, L. *Ireland; The Late Famine and the Poor Laws* (London: Hatchard & Son, 1848).

O'Brien, R.B. *Ailey Moore, A Tale of the Times* (London: Charles Dolman, 1856).

O'Brien, R.B. *The D'Altons of Crag: A Story of '48 and '49* (Dublin: James Duffy, 1882).

O'Brien, W.S. *Principles of Government; or Meditations in Exile* (Boston, MA: Patrick Donahoe, 1856).

'O'Connell's Warning', in *The Repealer Repulsed!* (Belfast: William M' Comb, 1841), pp. 145–6.

O'Leary, J. *Recollections of Fenians and Fenianism*, vol. 2 (London: Downey & Co., 1896).

O'Meara, K. *The Battle of Connemara* (London: R. Washbourne, 1878).

O'Rourke, J. *The History of the Great Irish Famine of 1847, with Notices of Earlier Famines* (Dublin: M'Glashan & Gill, 1875).

O'Ryan, J. and E. *In re Garland: A Tale of a Transition Time* (London and Dublin: Thomas Richardson & Son, 1870).

O'Ryan, J.M. 'My Twa Luves', *Irish Monthly*, 21, 2 (1874), pp. 520–21.

Parliamentary Debates, 3rd series, vol. 4 (London: T.C. Hansard, 1845).

Percival, M. *Rosa, The Work-Girl; A Tale* (Dublin: Simpkin, Marshall & Co., 1847).

Percival, M. *The Irish Dove; or, Faults on Both Sides* (Dublin: John Robertson, 1849).

Pusey, E.B. *Chastiments Neglected, Forerunners of Greater*, 3rd edn (Oxford: John Henry & James Parker, 1859).

Rawlins, C.A. *The Famine in Ireland* (London: Joseph Masters, 1847).

Read, C.A. and O'Connor, T.P. (eds). *The Cabinet of Irish Literature; Selections from the Works of the Chief Poets, Orators, and Prose Writers of Ireland*, vol. 4 (London and Edinburgh: Blackie, 1880).

Read, C.A. and Hinkson, K.T. (eds). *The Cabinet of Irish Literature; Selections from the Works of the Chief Poets, Orators, and Prose Writers of Ireland*, vol. 4 (London: Blackie, 1903).

Reeves, J. *History of the English Law*, vol. 4 (London: n.p., 1814).

Reigh, J.D. 'Ireland Wrestles with Famine While Mr Balfour Plays Golf', *United Ireland*, 23 August, 1890.

Report of the Donoghmore Refuge for Famine Made Orphans in the South of Ireland for the Year Ending March 31, 1850 (Cork: George Nash, 1850).

'The Report on the State of the Irish Poor in Great Britain', *Parliamentary Papers*, 34 (1836), appendix 1.

Revell, S. 'Sorrow's Benison', in *Verses that Would Come; or the Five Worlds of Enjoyment* (Sudbury: Henry S. Pratt, 1873), pp. 105–6.

'Review of *Ailey Moore*', *Bronson's Quarterly Review*, 2 (1857), p. 232.

'Review of *Ailey Moore*', *The Rambler*, 5 (1856), p. 156.

'Review of A. Keary, *Castle Daly*', *Irish Monthly*, 14 (1886), pp. 455–6.

'Review of *In re Garland*', *Irish Monthly*, 20, 1 (1873), p. 313.

'Review of Kathleen O'Meara's *The Battle of Connemara*', *Irish Monthly*, 5 (1877), pp. 767–8.

'Review of New Publications', *The Christian Lady's Magazine*, 10 (1855), p. 120.

'Review of *Rosa, The Work-Girl; A Tale*', *The Christian Lady's Magazine*, 37 (1847), p. 468.

'Review of *Rosa, The Work-Girl; A Tale*', *Publishers' Circular and Booksellers' Record*, 10 (1847), p. 128.

'Review of *The Earl of Effingham*', *The Academy*, 9 March 1878, p. 208.

'Review of *The Earl of Effingham*', *The Spectator*, 9 February 1878, p. 192.

'Review of *The Next Time*', *Irish Monthly*, 47 (1919), p. 517.

'Review of T. Mason Jones, *Old Trinity*', *Christian Spectator*, 8, 3 (March 1867), p. 192.

'Review of W.F. Barry, *The Wizard's Knot*', *The Athenaeum*, 83 (1901), p. 84.

'Review of W.F. Barry, *The Wizard's Knot*', *The Living Age*, 229 (1901), p. 400.

Robinson, J.T. *A Sermon Preached in St. Leonard's Chapel, Newton Abbot, Devonshire* (Feignmouth: E. & G.H. Croydon, 1847).

Rossa, J.O. *Rossa's Recollections, 1838–1898* (New York: Mariner's Harbor, 1898).

Russell, T.O. *Is Ireland a Dying Nation?* (Dublin: M.H. Gill, 1906).

Sadlier, M.A. *New Lights; or Life in Galway* (Montreal: D. & J. Sadlier, 1853).

Sadlier, M.A. *Bessy Conway; or the Irish Girl in America* (New York: D. & J. Sadlier & Co., 1861).

Shakespeare, W. *Hamlet; Prince of Denmark*, Electronic Text Center, University of Virginia Library, 2007, http://etext.virginia.edu/toc/modeng/public/MobHaml.html.

Shakespeare, W. *The Merchant of Venice*, Electronic Text Center, University of Virginia Library, 2007, http://etext.virginia.edu/toc/modeng/public/MobMerc.html.

Sheehan, P. *Glenanaar: A Story of Irish Life* (London: Longmans, Green & Co., 1905).

Sigerson, H. 'Under the Snow', in R. Varian (ed.), *The Harp of Erin: A Book of Ballad Poetry and of Native Song* (Dublin: M'Glashan & Gill, 1869), pp. 106–7.

Sigerson, H. *A Ruined Race; or, the Last MacManus of Drumroosk* (London: Ward & Downey, 1889).

'Slieve Foy'. 'Attie and His Father', in *Stories of Irish Life, Past and Present* (London: Lynwood & Co., 1912), pp. 43–56.

Smith, W.H. *A Twelve Month's Residence in Ireland during the Famine and the Public Works, 1846 and 1847* (London: Longman, Brown, Green and Longmans, 1848).

Society of Friends. *Transactions of the Central Relief Committee of the Society of Friends During the Famine in 1846 and 1847* (Dublin: Hodges & Smith, 1852).

The Spectator, 5 August 1848.

'Speranza' (J.F. Elgee), 'The Stricken Land', in *Poems by Speranza* (Glasgow: Cameron & Ferguson, 1871), pp. 10–12.

Stowe, H.B. *Uncle Tom's Cabin; Or Life Among the Lowly* (Boston, MA: J.P. Jewett, 1852).

Sullivan, A.M. *New Ireland: Political Sketches and Personal Reminiscences of Thirty Years of Irish Public Life* (Glasgow: Cameron & Ferguson, 1877).

Sullivan, A.M. and Sullivan, D.B. *'Guilty or not Guilty? Speeches from the Dock, or Protests of Irish Patriotism* (Dublin: Lower Abbey Street, 1867).

Tenniel, J. 'The Irish Frankenstein', *Punch*, 20 May 1882.

Tennyson, A. 'The Palace of Art', in *The Poetical Works of Alfred Tennyson*, vol. 1 (Boston, MA: Ticknor & Fields, 1864), p. 68–78.

Thackeray, W.M. *The Irish Sketch Book of 1842* (New York: Charles Scribner's Sons, 1911). First published 1842.

Tierney, R. (T.O. Russell), *The Struggles of Dick Massey; or, The Battles of a Boy* (Dublin: James Duffy, 1860).

The Times, 17 September 1847.

Trevelyan, C. 'The Irish Crisis', *Edinburgh Review*, 87, 175 (1848), pp. 229–320.

Trollope, A. 'The Real State of Ireland', *The Examiner*, 30 March 1850, p. 201.

Trollope, A. *Castle Richmond*, 3 vols (London: Chapman and Hall, 1860).

Tynan, K. 'Dora Sigerson, a Tribute and Some Memories, by Katharine Tynan', in D. Sigerson Shorter, *The Sad Years* (London: Constable and Co., 1921), pp. vii–xii.

United Ireland, 23 August 1890.

Upton, W.C. *Uncle Pat's Cabin; or, Life Among the Agricultural Labourers of Ireland* (Dublin: M.H. Gill & Son, 1882).

'The Uses of Hope, and the Pleasures of Adversity', *Irish Monthly*, 20, 1 (1873), pp. 286–90.

Varian, E.W. 'Proselytizing', in *Poems. By Finola* (Belfast: John Henderson, 1851), p. 41.

Varian, E.W. 'The Irish Mother's Lament', in C. Morash, *The Hungry Voice: The Poetry of the Irish Famine* (Dublin: Irish Academic Press, 2009), p. 75.

Virchow, R. *On Famine Fever; and Some of the Other Cognate Forms of Typhus* (London: Williams & Norgate, 1868).

Walsh, L.J. *The Next Time: A Story of 'Forty-Eight* (Dublin: M.H. Gill, 1919).

Walsh, L.J. *'On My Keeping' and In Theirs: A Record of Experiences 'On the Run', in Derry Gaol, and in Ballykinlar Internment Camp* (Dublin: Talbot Press, 1921).

'The Wearing of the Green', http://www.ireland-information.com/irishmusic/thewearingofthegreen.shtml (2011).

Williams, R.D. 'Song of the Irish-American Regiments', in *The Poems of Richard Dalton Williams* (Dublin: T.D. Sullivan, 1883), p. 50.

Wills, F. *Life of W.G. Wills* (London: Longmans, Green & Co., 1898).

Wills, W.G. *Life's Foreshadowings; a Novel*, vol. 2 (London: Hurst & Blackett, 1859).

Wills, W.G. *The Love That Kills. A Novel*, 3 vols (London: Tinsley Brothers, 1867).

Winter, W. *Shadows of the Stage: Third Series* (New York and London: Macmillan & Co., 1895).

Yeats, W.B. 'Popular Ballad Poetry of Ireland', *The Leisure Hour*, 38, 11 (1889), pp. 93–108.

Secondary Sources

Alexander, J.C. 'Toward a Theory of Cultural Trauma', in J.C. Alexander et al., *Cultural Trauma and Collective Identity* (Berkeley, CA: University of California Press, 2004), pp. 1–30.

Anderson, B. *Imagined Communities: Reflections on the Origin and Spread of Nationalism* (London: Verso, 1987).

Assmann, J. 'Collective Memory and Cultural Identity', *New German Critique*, 65 (1995), pp. 125–33.

Bal, M. 'Introduction', in M. Bal et al. (eds), *Acts of Memory: Cultural Recall in the Present* (Hanover, NH: University Press of New England, 1999), pp. vii–xv.

Bell, A.D. 'Administration and Finance of the Reform League, 1865–1867', *International Review of Social History*, 10 (1965), pp. 385–409.

Bornstein, G. *Material Modernism: The Politics of the Page* (Cambridge: Cambridge University Press, 2004).

Boylan, T.A. and Foley, T.P. *Political Economy and Colonial Ireland: The Propagation and Ideological Function of Economic Discourse in the Nineteenth Century* (London: Routledge, 1992).

Brady, A.M. and Cleeve, B. (eds), *A Biographical Dictionary of Irish Writers* (Mullingar: Lilliput Press, 1985).

Brettell, C. *Anthropology and Migration: Essays on Transnationalism, Ethnicity, and Identity* (Walnut Creek, CA: AltaMira Press, 2003).

Brown, S.J.M. *Ireland in Fiction* (Dublin: Maunsel & Co., 1919).

Brown, T. *Ireland's Literature: Selected Essays* (Mullingar: Lilliput Press, 1988).

Byrne, J.P., Coleman, P. and King, J.F. *Ireland and the Americas: Culture, Politics, and History*, vol. 2 (Santa Barbara, CA: ABC-CLIO, 2008).

Byrne, M. 'Mrs Mildred Darby', *The Contribution of Offaly Writers to Irish Literature*, Offaly Historical and Archaeological Society, 2007, http://www.offalyhistory.com/articles/252/1/The-Contribution-of-Offaly-Writers-to-Irish-Literature/Page1.html.

Campbell, C. *Fenian Fire: The British Government Plot to Assassinate Queen Victoria* (London: Harper Collins, 2003).

Campbell, M. 'Ireland's Furthest Shores: Irish Immigrant Settlement in Nineteenth-Century California and Eastern Australia', *Pacific Historical Review*, 71, 1 (2002), pp. 59–90.

Caruth, C. 'Recapturing the Past: Introduction', in C. Caruth (ed.), *Trauma: Explorations in Memory* (Baltimore, MD: Johns Hopkins University Press, 1995), pp. 151–7.

Colman, A.U. *Dictionary of Nineteenth-Century Irish Women Poets* (Galway: Kenny's Bookshop, 1996).

Comerford, R.V. *Charles J. Kickham: A Study in Irish Nationalism and Literature* (Dublin: Wolfhound, 1979).

Corporaal, M.C.M. 'From Golden Hills to Sycamore Trees: Pastoral Homelands and Ethnic Identity in Irish Immigrant Fiction, 1860–85', *Irish Studies Review*, 18, 3 (2010), pp. 331–46.

Corporaal, M.C.M. 'Memories of the Great Famine and Ethnic Identity in Novels by Victorian Irish Women Writers', *English Studies*, 90, 2 (2009), pp. 142–56.

Corporaal, M.C.M. and Cusack, C.T. 'Rites of Passage: The Coffin Ship as Site of Immigrants' Identity Formation in Irish and Irish-American Fiction, 1855–1885', *Atlantic Studies*, 8, 3 (2011), pp. 343–59.

Costello, M. *The Famine in Kerry* (Kerry: Kerry Archaeological and Historical Society, 1997).

Cronin, M. *A History of Ireland* (Basingstoke: Palgrave, 2001).

Daly, M.E. *Social and Economic History of Ireland since 1800* (Dublin: Educational Company of Ireland, 1981).

Daly, M. *The Famine in Ireland* (Dublin: Dublin Historical Association, 1986).

Davis, M. and Davis, W. *The Rebel in his Family: Selected Papers of William Smith O'Brien* (Cork: Cork University Press, 1998).

Deane, S. *Strange Country: Modernity and Nationhood in Irish Writing Since 1790* (Oxford: Clarendon Press, 1997).

Deane, S., Carpenter, A. and Williams, J. (eds). *The Field Day Anthology of Irish Writing, vol. 5: Irish Women's Writing and Traditions* (New York: New York University Press, 2002).

Donnelly, J.S. *The Great Irish Potato Famine* (Stroud: Sutton, 2003).

Eagleton, T. *Heathcliff and the Great Hunger: Studies in Irish Culture* (London: Verso, 1995).

Edwards, O.D. 'Anthony Trollope, the Irish Writer', *Nineteenth-Century Fiction*, 38, 1 (1983), pp. 1–42.

English Standard Version Bible, online edn, http://www.esvbible.org.

Fairweather, C. 'Inclusive and Exclusive Pastoral: Towards an Anatomy of Pastoral Modes', *Studies in Philology*, 97, 3 (2000), pp. 276–307.

Fegan, M. *Literature and the Irish Famine 1845–1919* (Oxford: Clarendon Press, 2002).

Fegan, M. 'The Great Famine in Literature, 1846–1896', in J.M. Wright (ed.), *A Companion to Irish Literature*, vol. 1 (Malden, MA: Blackwell, 2010), pp. 444–60.

Flaxman, R. *A Woman Styled Bold: The Life of Cornelia Connelly, 1809–1879* (London: Darton, Longman & Todd, 1991).

Foucault, M. 'Of Other Spaces', *Diacritics*, 16 (1986), pp. 22–7.

Frawley, O. *Irish Pastoral: Nostalgia and Twentieth-Century Irish Literature* (Dublin: Irish Academic Press, 2005).

Frawley, O. 'Toward a Theory of Cultural Memory in an Irish Postcolonial Context', in O. Frawley (ed.), *Memory Ireland. Volume 1: History and Modernity* (Syracuse, NY: Syracuse University Press, 2011), pp. 18–34.

Freeman, T.W. *Pre-Famine Ireland: A Study in Historical Demography* (Manchester: Manchester University Press, 1957).

Garvin, T. 'Defenders, Ribbonmen and Others: Underground Political Networks in Pre-Famine Ireland', *Past and Present*, 96 (1982), pp. 133–55.

Geary, L.M. *Rebellion and Remembrance in Modern Ireland* (Dublin: Four Courts Press, 2001).

Geoghegan, P.M. *King Dan: The Rise of Daniel O'Connell 1775–1829* (Dublin: Gill & Macmillan, 2008).

Geoghegan, P.M. *Liberator: The Life and Death of Daniel O'Connell, 1830–1847* (Dublin: Gill & Macmillan, 2010).

Gibbons, L. *Edmund Burke and Ireland: Aesthetics, Politics, and the Colonial Sublime* (Cambridge: Cambridge University Press, 2003).

Gilley, S. 'Father William Barry: Priest and Novelist', *Recusant History*, 24 (1998–99), pp. 523–51.

Glendinning, V. *Trollope* (London: Hutchinson, 1992).

Gray, P. 'Ideology and the Famine', in C. Póirtéir (ed.), *The Great Irish Famine* (Dublin: Mercier Press, 1995), pp. 86–103.

Guerin, N. 'Darbys of Leap', *Irish Midlands Ancestry*, 2007, http://www.irish midlandsancestry.com/content/family_history/families/darbys.htm.

Gwynn, S.L. 'McCarthy, Justin (1830–1912)', rev. Alan O'Day, *Oxford Dictionary of National Biography*, Oxford University Press, 2004, online edn, 2009, http://www.oxforddnb.com/view/article/34681.

Hall, N.J. 'Trollope, Anthony (1815–1882)', *Oxford Dictionary of National Biography*, Oxford University Press, 2004, online edn, 2006, www.oxford dnb.com/view/article/27748.

Hansson, H. *Emily Lawless 1845–1913: Writing the Interspace* (Cork: Cork University Press, 2007).

Hartley, C. and Leckey, S. (eds). *A Historical Dictionary of British Women* (London: Routledge, 2003).

Hipple, Jr, W.J. *The Beautiful, the Sublime, and the Picturesque in Eighteenth-Century British Aesthetic Theory* (Carbondale, IL: Southern Illinois University Press, 1957).

Hirsch, M. *Family Frames: Photography, Narrative and Postmemory* (Cambridge, MA: Harvard University Press, 1997).

Hodgkin, K., and Radstone, S. 'Introduction: Contested Pasts', in K. Hodgkin and S. Radstone (eds), *Memory, History, Nation: Contested Pasts* (New Brunswick, NJ: Transaction, 2006), pp. 1–23.

Hogan, R. et al. (eds), *Dictionary of Irish Literature: Revised and Expanded Edition* (London: Aldwyck Press, 1996).

Hopkins, L. *Writing Renaissance Queens: Texts by and about Elizabeth I and Mary, Queen of Scots* (Danvers, MA: Rosemont, 2002).

Ignatiev, N. *How the Irish Became White* (New York: Routledge, 1996).

Innes, C.L. *Woman and Nation in Irish Literature and Society, 1880–1935* (Athens, GA: University of Georgia Press, 1993).

Jacobson, M.F. *Special Sorrows: The Diasporic Imagination of Irish, Polish, and Jewish Immigrants in the United States* (Berkeley, CA: University of California Press, 2002).

Janssen, L. 'The Impossibility of Transporting Irishness: The Representation of Diasporic Irishness in Works of Fiction by Mary Anne Sadlier, Dillon O'Brien and James W. Sullivan', forthcoming in MESEA 2010 conference proceedings, 2012.

Kelleher, M. 'Anthony Trollope's *Castle Richmond*: Famine Narrative and "Horrid Novel"?', *Irish University Review*, 25, 2 (1995), pp. 242–62.

Kelleher, M. *The Feminization of Famine: Expressions of the Inexpressible?* (Cork: Cork University Press, 1997).

Kelleher, M. 'Prose Writing and Drama in English, 1830–1890: From Catholic Emancipation to the Fall of Parnell', in M. Kelleher and P. O'Leary (eds), *The Cambridge History of Irish Literature*, vol. 1 (Cambridge: Cambridge University Press, 2006), pp. 449–99.

Kelly, J. 'Carleton, William (1794–1869)', *Oxford Dictionary of National Biography*, Oxford University Press, 2004, online edn, 2007, http://www.oxforddnb.com/view/article/4679.

Kenny, K. *The American Irish: A History* (New York: Longman, 2000).

Kerr, D. *The Catholic Church and the Famine* (Blackrock: Columba Press, 1996).

Kiberd, D. *Inventing Ireland: The Literature of the Modern Nation* (Cambridge, MA: Harvard University Press, 1997).

Kinealy, C. *A Death-Dealing Famine: The Great Hunger in Ireland* (London: Pluto Press, 1997).

Kinealy, C. *This Great Calamity: The Irish Famine 1845–52* (Dublin: Gill & Macmillan, 2006).

Kohl, L.F. 'Introduction', in D.P. Conyngham, *The Irish Brigade and its Campaigns* (New York: Fordham University Press, 1994), pp. ix–xxx.

Kreilkamp, V. *The Anglo-Irish Novel and the Big House* (Syracuse, NY: Syracuse University Press, 1998).

LaCapra, D. *Writing History, Writing Trauma* (Baltimore, MD: Johns Hopkins University Press, 2001).

Landsberg, A. *Prosthetic Memory: The Transformation of American Remembrance in the Age of Mass Culture* (New York: Columbia University Press, 2004).

Larkin, E. 'The Devotional Revolution in Ireland, 1850–75', *American Historical Review*, 77, 3 (1972), pp. 625–52.

Larkin, E. *The Consolidation of the Roman Catholic Church in Ireland, 1860–1870* (Dublin: Gill & Macmillan, 1987).

Lees, L.H. *Exiles of Erin: Irish Migrants in Victorian London* (Manchester: Manchester University Press, 1979).

Lengel, E. *The Irish Through British Eyes: Perceptions of Ireland in the Famine Era* (Westport, CT: Praeger, 2002).

Levy, D. 'Changing Temporalities and the Internationalization of Memory Cultures', in Y. Gutman et al. (eds), *Memory and the Future: Transnational Politics, Ethics and Society* (Basingstoke: Palgrave Macmillan, 2010), pp. 15–31.

Linehan, M.P. *Canon Sheehan of Doneraile: Priest, Novelist, Man of Letters* (Dublin: Talbot Press, 1952).

Lloyd, D. 'The Indigent Sublime: Specters of Irish Hunger', *Representations*, 92 (2005), pp. 152–85.

Luddy, M. *Women and Philanthropy in Nineteenth-Century Ireland* (Cambridge: Cambridge University Press, 1995).

MacKay, D. *Flight from Famine: The Coming of the Irish to Canada* (Toronto, ON: National Heritage Books, 1990).

Malcolm, C.A. and Malcolm, D. (eds). *A Companion to the British and Irish Short Story* (Oxford: Blackwell, 2008).

Marmion, J.A. 'Another Voice: The History of England for Catholic Children of 1850', *Paradigm: Journal of the Textbook Colloquium*, 24 (1997), http://faculty.ed.uiuc.edu/westbury/Paradigm/Marmion2.html.

Maume, P. *The Long Gestation: Irish Nationalist Life 1891–1918* (New York: St Martin's Press, 1999).

Maume, P. 'Walsh, Louis Joseph (1880–1942), Irish Nationalist', *Oxford Dictionary of National Biography*, Oxford University Press, 2004, online edn, 2008, http://www.oxforddnb.com/view/article/64477.

McCaffrey, L.J. *Textures of Irish America* (Syracuse, NY: Syracuse University Press, 1992).

McLean, S. *The Event and Its Terrors: Ireland, Famine, Modernity* (Stanford, CA: Stanford University Press, 2004).

Miller, K.A. *Emigrants and Exiles: Ireland and the Irish Exodus to North America* (Oxford: Oxford University Press, 1985).

Misztal, B.A. 'Memory and History', in O. Frawley (ed.), *Memory Ireland. Volume 1: History and Modernity* (Syracuse, NY: Syracuse University Press, 2011), pp. 3–18.

Moffitt, M. *Soupers & Jumpers: The Protestant Missions in Connemara 1848–1937* (Dublin: Nonsuch Press, 2008).

Mokyr, J. and Ó Gráda, C. 'What Do People Die of During Famines: The Great Famine in Comparative Perspective', *European Review of Economic History*, 6 (2002), pp. 339–63.

Morash, C. *Writing the Irish Famine* (Oxford: Clarendon Press, 1995).

Morash, C. *The Hungry Voice: The Poetry of the Irish Famine*, 2nd edn (Dublin: Irish Academic Press, 2009).

Morton, T. *Shelley and the Revolution in Taste: The Body and the Natural World* (Cambridge: Cambridge University Press, 1994).

Mulkerns, V. 'Introduction', in E. Lawless, *Hurrish: A Study* (Belfast: Appletree Press, 1992), pp. i–xii.

Murphy, J.H. *Catholic Fiction and Social Reality in Ireland, 1873–1922* (Westport, CT: Greenwood Press, 1997).

Murphy, J.H. *Irish Novelists and the Victorian Age* (Oxford: Oxford University Press, 2011).

Neumann, B. 'The Literary Representation of Memory', in A. Erll and A. Nünning (eds), *Cultural Memory Studies: An International and Interdisciplinary Handbook* (Berlin and New York: De Gruyter, 2008), pp. 333–45.

Nilsen, K.E. 'The Irish Language in New York, 1850–1900', in R.H. Bayor and T.J. Meagher (eds), *The New York Irish* (Baltimore, MD: Johns Hopkins University Press, 1996), pp. 252–74.

Nora, P. 'Between Memory and History: Les Lieux de Mémoire', *Representations*, 26 (1989), pp. 7–25.

O'Farrell, F. *Catholic Emancipation: Daniel O'Connell and the Birth of Irish Democracy, 1820–1830* (Dublin: Gill & Macmillan, 1985).

Ó Gráda, C. *The Great Irish Famine* (Cambridge: Cambridge University Press, 1989).

Ó Gráda, C. *Ireland Before and After the Famine: Explorations in Economic History* (Manchester: Manchester University Press, 1993).

O'Hara, B. *Davitt: Irish Patriot and Father of the Land League* (Temple, PA: Tudor Gate Press, 2009).

O'Hara, M. *Irish Immigrants, 1840–1920* (Mankato, MN: Capstone Press, 2001).

Orser, C.E. *A Historical Archeology of the Modern World* (New York: Plenum Press, 1996).

Ó Saothraí, S. 'Russell, Thomas O'Neill (1828–1908)', *Oxford Dictionary of National Biography*, online edn, 2004, http://www.oxforddnb.com/index/35/101035885.

O'Toole, T. *Dictionary of Munster Women Writers, 1800–2000* (Cork: Cork University Press, 2005).

Oxford English Dictionary, online edn, 2010, http://oed.com.

Pearce, M. and Stewart, G. *British Political History 1867–2001: Democracy and Decline*, 3rd edn (London and New York: Routledge, 2002).

Pine, E. *The Politics of Irish Memory: Performing Remembrance in Contemporary Irish Culture* (Basingstoke: Palgrave Macmillan, 2011).

Poggioli, R. 'Pastorals of Innocence and Happiness', in B. Loughrey (ed.), *The Pastoral Mode* (London: Macmillan, 1984), pp. 98–110.

Rhodes, R.M. *Women and the Family in Post-Famine Ireland* (New York: Garland, 1992).

Richards, J. *Sir Henry Irving: A Victorian Actor and His World* (Basingstoke: Palgrave Macmillan, 2005).

Rigney, A. 'Portable Monuments: Literature, Cultural Memory, and the Case of Jeanie Deans', *Poetics Today*, 25, 2 (2004), pp. 361–96.

Rigney, A. 'Plenitude, Scarcity and the Circulation of Cultural Memory', *Journal of European Studies*, 35, 1 (2005), pp. 11–28.

Rigney, A. 'Divided Pasts: A Premature Memorial and the Dynamics of Collective Remembrance', *Memory Studies*, 1, 1 (2008), pp. 89–98.

Roediger, D. *The Wages of Whiteness: Race and the Making of the American Working Class*, rev. edn (London: Verso, 1999).

Rothberg, M. *Multidirectional Memory: Remembering the Holocaust in the Age of Decolonization* (Stanford, CA: Stanford University Press, 2009).

Schama, S. *Landscape and Memory* (New York: Vintage, 1995).

Short, E. *Newman and His Contemporaries* (London: Continuum, 2011).

Sloan, R. *William Smith O'Brien and the Young Ireland Rebellion of 1848* (Dublin: Four Courts Press, 2000).

Sturken, M. 'Memory, Consumerism and Media: Reflections on the Emergence of the Field', *Memory Studies*, 1, 1 (2008), pp. 231–49.

Sutherland, J. *The Longman Companion to Victorian Fiction* (London: Longman, 1988).

Swift, R. (ed.). *Irish Migrants in Britain, 1815–1914: A Documentary History* (Cork: Cork University Press, 2002).

Tierney, A. 'The Gothic and the Gaelic: Exploring the Place of Castles in Ireland's Celtic Revival', *International Journal of Historical Archaeology*, 8, 3 (September 2004), pp. 185–98.

Trigg, D. *The Aesthetics of Decay: Nothingness, Nostalgia, and the Absence of Reason* (New York: Peter Lang, 2006).

Ward, P. *Exile, Emigration and Irish Writing* (Dublin: Irish Academic Press, 2002).

Welch, R. and Stewart, B. *The Oxford Companion to Irish Literature* (Oxford: Clarendon, 1996).

Wertsch, J.V. *Voices of Collective Remembering* (New York: Cambridge University Press, 2002).

Whelan, K. 'Reading the Ruins: The Presence of Absence in the Irish Landscape', in H.B. Clarke et al. (eds), *Surveying Ireland's Past: Multidisciplinary Essays in Honour of Anngret Simms* (Dublin: Geography Publications, 2004), www.ricorso.net/rx/azdata/authors/w/Whelan_K/xtra.htm.

Whelan, K. 'The Cultural Effects of the Famine', in J. Cleary and C. Connolly (eds), *The Cambridge Companion to Modern Irish Culture* (Cambridge: Cambridge University Press, 2005), pp. 139–54.

Wiley, P.R. *The Irish General: Thomas Francis Meagher* (Norman, OK: University of Oklahoma Press, 2007).

Woodham-Smith, C. *The Great Hunger: Ireland 1845–1849* (New York: Signet, 1991).

Zerubavel, E. *Time Maps: Collective Memory and the Social Shape of the Past* (Chicago, IL: University of Chicago Press, 2003).

Index

INDEX